THE ARABIC FREUD

The Arabic Freud

PSYCHOANALYSIS AND ISLAM IN MODERN EGYPT

Omnia El Shakry

PRINCETON UNIVERSITY PRESS

PRINCETON & OXFORD

Copyright © 2017 by Princeton University Press

Published by Princeton University Press,
41 William Street, Princeton, New Jersey 08540
In the United Kingdom: Princeton University Press,
6 Oxford Street, Woodstock, Oxfordshire OX20 1TR

press.princeton.edu

Cover art: *Ibn El Arabi* by Rachid Koraïchi (Algeria), 2009.
Lithograph (Set of 8), 60 × 40 cm (1 of 8)/Artists Rights
Society (ARS), New York

All Rights Reserved

First paperback printing, 2020
Paperback ISBN 978-0-691-20310-2
Cloth ISBN 978-0-691-17479-2
Library of Congress Control Number 2017940319

British Library Cataloging-in-Publication Data is available

This book has been composed in Miller

In Memoriam Michael T. Dreyfus

CONTENTS

ACKNOWLEDGMENTS

AS FREUD REMARKS, every finding is a refinding. This book constitutes, for me, a refinding of an object, the topic of the psyche with which I have remained concerned on and off for a little over a quarter of a century. It thus represents an intellectual odyssey and a (partial) recovery of an earlier self that I thought I had lost. It has returned me to the ephemera of conversations, long forgotten, but still imprinted. It has allowed me to revisit my undergraduate years, which were marked by a concern for schizophrenia and language, concerns that have never left me, but that find only the barest of subtle inlets into this text.

The writing of this book would not have been possible without the generous support of the ACLS Ryskamp fellowship, a Davis Humanities Institute fellowship, and numerous UC Davis research grants, all of which afforded me the opportunity to read far more widely and expansively than I might have otherwise. For allotting time and resources that enabled my work in the first place, I thank former dean George Mangun and department chairs Ted Margadant, David Biale, and Kathryn Olmsted. Suad Joseph and Sally McKee have continued to mentor me, even after I had long aged out.

While in Cairo, Muhammad 'Ali was a most convivial intellectual interlocutor and tracked down tomes and tomes of books on psychology, psychoanalysis, and the self, virtually all of the primary source material upon which this book is based. Halfway into this project I made the acquaintance of Samir Mourad, who was kind and generous enough to share with me recollections on the life of his father, Youssef Mourad, and facilitate access to primary source materials. I thank him not only for the pleasure of his friendship and conversation, but also for his forbearance in seeing his father's name transliterated in this text as Yusuf Murad.

Numerous scholars have sharpened my thinking and shaped the writing of this book, largely through sustained commentary at invited talks and seminars. I would especially like to thank the organizers and individual participants at a variety of venues, including the Middle East History colloquium and Anthropology Department at UC Berkeley; the Cultural Studies program, the Anthropology Department, and the Multidisciplinary Psychoanalytic research cluster at UC Davis; the History of Science colloquium, Center for European and Russian Studies, Department of Comparative Literature, and Near Eastern Languages and Cultures at UCLA; the Middle East Studies Center at the University of Pennsylvania; the Middle East and Middle Eastern American Center at the Graduate Center of the City University of New York; the Wissenschaftskolleg zu Berlin; the Women's Studies Program at Duke

University; the Center for Middle Eastern Studies at the University of Texas at Austin; the Women and Gender Studies program at Northern Arizona University; and the Institute for Humanities Research at UC Santa Cruz.

Conversations with participants in my 2008 "Theorizing the Self" Cultural Studies seminar helped me delineate the principal theoretical debates I wished to intervene in. Early presentations given at Beshara Doumani's Middle East History colloquium at Berkeley and at Caren Kaplan's Cultural Studies colloquium at UC Davis were especially formative for outlining the parameters of this project. Ranjana Khanna, and participants in her "Psychoanalysis in an International Frame" seminar at Duke, challenged me to think through a variety of theoretical knots in my work. Presentations given at conferences centered on Middle East, Islamic, or comparative studies at Princeton University, Amherst College, Stanford University, and the University of Chicago were crucial in nourishing a community of scholars with shared interests. The working group on psychoanalysis, hosted by the Psychoanalytic Institute of Northern California and the Townsend Center of the Humanities at Berkeley, offered much-needed inspiration during the final stages of writing.

The larger project upon which this book is based owes a deep intellectual debt to Stefania Pandolfo. Through a formidable body of work, she has explored the nature of subjectivity in the aftermath of colonialism and the interactions between the Islamic discursive tradition and psychoanalysis. A profound and continuous dialogical engagement with her, through conversations, e-mails, and a mutual reading of our work, has indelibly shaped my thinking and the writing of this book.

For providing feedback at a variety of stages of this project, I thank Rifaʿat Abou-El-Haj, Michael Allan, Paul Amar, Anjali Arondekar, Fadi Bardawil, Beth Baron, Orit Bashkin, Abigail Boggs, Joan Cadden, Patricia Clough, Diana Davis, Yoav Di-Capua, Hoda El Shakry, Marwa Elshakry, Khaled Fahmy, Leah Feldman, Jeff Fort, Kathleen Frederickson, Israel Gershoni, Peter Gran, Samira Haj, Alma Heckman, Naomi Janowitz, Suad Joseph, Ranjana Khanna, Hanan Kholoussy, Aishwary Kumar, Benjamin Lawrance, Philippa Levine, Ellen McLarney, Ali Altaf Mian, Susan Miller, Durba Mitra, Samuel Moyn, Afsaneh Najmabadi, Eve Troutt Powell, Sara Pursley, Michael Saler, Alan Tansman, Robert Tignor, Soraya Tlatli, and Li Zhang.

I want to especially thank Rajbir Judge and Stefania Pandolfo for reading the entire manuscript and providing exacting and constructive criticism. Likewise, reviewers for Princeton University Press provided meticulous comments, encouraging me to knit the manuscript more closely together. I am incredibly fortunate to work with an outstanding group of graduate students at Davis who have sustained me through intellectual conversations and shared political commitments. I am greatly indebted to Rajbir Judge, Stephen Cox, Caroline McKusick, and Laura Tavolacci for their assistance with secondary source material; the final stages of editing; and for the glossary, the bibliography, and the index.

Fred Appel of Princeton University Press was a most gracious editor, soliciting the book and offering sage advice on everything from its title to the substantive concerns of the text. I am appreciative of the care and attention he has devoted to the project. Thalia Leaf and Brigitte Pelner extended invaluable editorial assistance, and I am especially beholden to Dawn Hall for copyediting. I thank Leila El Shakry for introducing me to the work of Rachid Koraïchi, whose artwork graces this cover.

Jessica Thayer, Matt Salata, Benjamin Lawrance, Michael Gasper, Nesa Azimi, Elizabeth Merchant, Tamara Griggs, Emily Wittman, and Susette Min gave much-needed support, and I thank them for always being there, despite my tendency to disappear. The music of Shaykh Yasin al-Tuhami has accompanied me for decades, and throughout the writing of this book he has deepened my understanding of Ibn 'Arabi and Ibn al-Farid, but more importantly, provided tranquility in the saddest and most trying of times.

To my family, both nuclear and extended, I owe my deepest gratitude for their enduring support and forbearance of long absences—above all to my parents, Aida and Sayed, who always made themselves available for quick translation checks and twentieth-century recollections. Marwa, Hoda, Leila, Mark, Selma, Jed, Samira, and Joe have provided the warmth and comfort of family. Most of all I am so grateful for the presence of Nadeem in my life, for our love and laughter, and for his help in moderating the deathliness of my drive. My life would be so impoverished without you.

The joy of writing this book has been punctuated by profound losses and tragedies. As I continue to mourn 'Abd al-'Aziz al-'Assar, Driss, Barbara Abou-El-Haj, Assia Habash, Phillipe Hippolyte, and Michael T. Dreyfus, I recollect Freud's insights on the work of mourning and melancholia and the desire to recreate life worlds out of loss. This book is dedicated to the memory of Michael T. Dreyfus, buried on Hart Island. You were loved and you have not been forgotten.

{⸺⸻⸺}

© 2011 by Cambridge University Press. Reprinted by permission of Cambridge University Press.

Brief quotation from "Five Years of Psychoanalysis in Cairo" by Moustapha Safouan, translated by Juliet Flower MacCannell in *Umbr(a): A Journal of the Unconscious*. Islam (2009). Copyright © 2009 by *Umbr(a)*. Reprinted by permission of the author, translator, and *Umbr(a)*.

Brief quotations from *THE SEMINAR OF JACQUES LACAN: Book VII: The Ethics of Psychoanalysis 1959–1960* by Jacques Lacan, translated by Dennis Porter. Copyright © 1986 by Les Editions du Seuil. English translation copyright © 1992 by W.W. Norton & Company, Inc. Used by permission of W.W. Norton & Company, Inc. and Routledge/Taylor & Francis Group.

Brief quotation from *The Bezels of Wisdom* by Ibn al-ʿArabi, translated by R.W.J. Austin. English translation copyright © 1980 by Paulist Press. Reprinted by permission of Paulist Press.

Excerpt from *On Disciplining the Soul, Kitāb riyāḍat al-nafs, and on Breaking the Two Desires, Kitāb kasr al-shahwatayn, Books XXII and XXIII of the Revival of the Religious Sciences, Iḥyā ʿulūm al-dīn* by Al-Ghazālī, translated by T. J. Winter. English translation copyright © 1995 by Islamic Texts Society. Reprinted by permission of the Islamic Texts Society, Cambridge, UK.

Brief quotation from the *Complete Psychological Works of Sigmund Freud, Volume 14* by Sigmund Freud, translated from the German under the General Editorship of James Strachey, in collaboration with Anna Freud, assisted by Alix Strachey and Alan Tyson. First published in Great Britain by the Hogarth Press. Copyright © 1957 by the Institute of Psycho-Analysis. Reprinted by permission of The Random House Group Limited and by permission of The Marsh Agency Limited on behalf of Sigmund Freud Copyrights. Published in the United States as the *Collected Papers, Volume 4* by Sigmund Freud, copyright © 1959. Reprinted by permission of Basic Books, an imprint of Perseus Books, LLC, a subsidiary of Hachette Book Group, Inc.

Brief quotation from *Speech or Death?: Language as Social Order: A Psychoanalytic Study* by Moustapha Safouan, translated by Martin Thom. Copyright © 1993 by Les Editions du Seuil. English translation copyright © 2003 by Palgrave Macmillan. Reprinted by permission of the author.

ARABIC WORDS AND NAMES have been transliterated into the Latin alphabet according to a simplified system based on the *International Journal of Middle East Studies* (*IJMES*), with the exception of certain commonly accepted transliterations, such as Gamal Abdel Nasser and Naguib Mahfouz. To facilitate reading for the nonspecialist, all diacritical marks have been omitted except for the 'ayn (') and hamza ('). Arabic names of authors whose writings are predominantly in French or English have not been changed (e.g., Fethi Benslama, Moustapha Safouan). For authors who published predominantly in Arabic, but who also published in French and/or English, Arabic transliteration is used in the text, but alternate spellings of their names may be found in the notes and bibliography depending on the language of publication (e.g., Yusuf Murad and Youssef Mourad, Mustafa Ziywar and Mostapha Ziwer). In the text, I use the shortened form for Ibn 'Arabi, instead of the more formal Ibn al-'Arabī. Following the *IJMES* system, English capitalization rules have been applied to transliterated Arabic titles and the definite article *al-* is not capitalized unless it begins a sentence or endnote. All translations from Arabic and French are my own, unless otherwise noted.

THE ARABIC FREUD

Psychoanalysis and Islam

*In truth, we find treatises on the soul in Arabic works that evoke the
Freudian division among the parts of the personality: id, ego, and
superego.*

—MOUSTAPHA SAFOUAN

IN 1945 PSYCHOLOGIST Yusuf Murad introduced the Arabic term *al-la-
shuʿur*, a term borrowed from the medieval Sufi philosopher Ibn ʿArabi and
redolent with mystical overtones, as "the unconscious" in the newly founded
Egyptian *Majallat ʿIlm al-Nafs* (Journal of Psychology).[1] Only two years prior,
in 1943, Murad had published *Shifaʾ al-Nafs* (Healing the Psyche) as part of
the popular *Iqraʾ* (Read) series, a text that introduced its audience to the basic
theories and concepts of psychology and its schools of thought. In 1946, lawyer Muhammad Fathi Bey published a full-length treatise titled *The Problem
of Psychoanalysis in Egypt*.[2] Responding to allegations that Freudianism had
little to teach us about crime, he argued that, quite the contrary, psychoanalysis and criminology were entirely analogous disciplines. A decade later, in
1958, the Egyptian Lacanian analyst Moustapha Safouan translated Sigmund
Freud's *Interpretation of Dreams* into Arabic for an eager audience.[3]

The *Arabic Freud* explores how Freud traveled in postwar Egypt, invoking
Freudianism not as a pure form, "the source of an unchanging truth that was
the model, mold and dress code to be imposed on all our experience," but
rather as a multivalent tradition and metonym for broader Arabic debates
surrounding the status of the unconscious in psychic life.[4] An understanding
of the body of work developed on psychoanalysis in Egypt and of the intersec-
tions between Islamic thought and psychoanalysis enables us to reconsider
that quintessential question of modernity, the question of the self, in a non-
European context.[5] Indeed, the story of the elaboration of modern languages
of the self in twentieth-century Egypt moves us away from models of selfhood

as either modern or traditional, Western or non-Western, autonomous or heteronomous, and unsettles the assumption of an alleged incommensurability between psychoanalysis and Islam.

Significantly, the new science of the self that emerged drew both from Freudianism and other psychoanalytic traditions, as well as from key classical Islamic thinkers, such as Avicenna (d. 1037), Abu Hamid al-Ghazali (d. 1111), Fakhr al-Din al-Razi (d. 1209), and most extensively, Ibn 'Arabi (d. 1240). This contemporaneity of classical Islamic texts, coexisting and intermingling with psychoanalytic models, allows us to trace the epistemological resonances of discursive traditions as they come into contact.[6] Translating and blending key concepts from psychoanalysis with classical Islamic concepts, Egyptian thinkers explored the resonances between psychoanalytic and pre-psychoanalytic traditions in order to produce a theory of the self that was at once in concert with and heterogeneous to European analytic thought. According to novelist and playwright Tawfiq al-Hakim the impulse to blend traditions went as far back as Abu Nasr al-Farabi's neoclassical contemplation of Plato's *Republic*, one in which Greek ideas were poured into the mold of Islamic philosophy and Arabic thought and the intermarriage of literatures, epistemologies, and ontologies transpired.[7]

Tracing the lineaments of the unconscious, *The Arabic Freud* maps out the topography of modern selfhood and its ethical and epistemological contours in postwar Egypt. What does it mean, I ask, to think through psychoanalysis and Islam together, not as a "problem" but as a creative encounter of ethical engagement? Rather than view Islamic discourses as hermetically sealed, or traffic in dichotomous juxtapositions between East and West, this book focuses on the points of intersection, articulation, and commensurability between Islamic discourses and modern social scientific thought, and between religious and secular ethics. The hybridization of psychoanalytic thought with pre-psychoanalytic Islamic discursive formations illustrates that *The Arabic Freud* emerged not as something developed in Europe only to be diffused at its point of application elsewhere, but rather as something elaborated, like psychoanalysis itself, across the space of human difference.

A Copernican Revolution

Notions of the unconscious had seeped into Arabic writings in Egypt since at least as far back as the 1920s and through a myriad of sources, including for example Pierre Janet, Sigmund Freud, Carl Jung, and Alfred Adler.[8] Salama Musa, an avowed Fabian and public intellectual, published multiple books, beginning in the late 1920s, that touched on Freudian and psychoanalytic themes for a lay audience.[9] Musa had referred to the unconscious by the somewhat awkward compound phrase al-'aql al-batin (the inner mind), which he had to define extensively for his audience, in a 1928 text.[10] Yet the imprint of

Freudian psychology was becoming increasingly visible in the 1930s and 1940s in the focus on unconscious drives, as synopses and translations of Freud began to appear. For example, a 1938 article in *al-Hilal* noted that a generational shift had taken place and that Egyptian youth were avidly reading Freud and were familiar with his ideas on psychoanalysis, the unconscious, the interpretation of dreams, and the sexual drive.[11] A 1941 article in *al-Thaqafa* by intellectual and writer ʿAli Adham discussed Freud's attitude toward war, translating and summarizing portions of "Thoughts for the Times of War and Death" and *Beyond the Pleasure Principle*, while outlining the sexual or life drive and explicating the increased significance of the death drive for Freud in the aftermath of the Great War.[12] By the mid-1940s a burgeoning lay literature on psychology was so well developed that scholars felt compelled to critique the unscientific literature "drowning the marketplace"— a testament to the increased salience of psychology to popular public discourse.[13] And by 1951 Kamal al-Din ʿAbd al-Hamid Nayal, a secondary school philosophy teacher, proposed prenuptial psychological exams in order to prevent unhappy marriages due to unresolved Oedipus complexes.[14]

Indeed, no knowledge of Freud could be complete without an understanding of the Oedipus complex, which Arabic readers would have been familiar with through the two adaptations of Sophocles's *Oedipus Rex* that appeared in 1949 by playwrights Tawfiq al-Hakim and Ali Ahmad Bakathir, as well as the first scholarly Arabic translation in 1939 by Egyptian belle lettrist Taha Husayn.[15] Egyptian dramatist al-Hakim's version is noteworthy for its innovative interpretation that places the central conflict of the play not between man and fate, but rather between fact and (hidden) truth, a decidedly Freudian reading.[16] But it was above all in Naguib Mahfouz's masterful 1948 literary rendition that the Oedipus complex was brought to life for its Arabic readers. In *al-Sarab* (*The Mirage*) the highly introverted protagonist Kamil Ruʾba Laz immerses himself in a daily dreamscape to escape a stifling reality and a pathological attachment to his mother, characterized by "an unwholesome affection which had exceeded its proper limits ... a kind of affection that destroys."[17]

Understandings of Freud abounded in literary criticism as well. In 1947, the renowned Islamist thinker and writer Sayyid Qutb discussed the heuristic value of a psychological and specifically a psychoanalytic approach to literary criticism—itself defined as the attempt to understand literature as "the expression of a sensory experience in an inspired image."[18] Qutb demonstrated a psychoanalytical approach through a detailed consideration of Freud's study of Leonardo da Vinci.[19] Qutb's familiarity with Freud was gleaned directly from the pages of *Majallat ʿIlm al-Nafs*, as evidenced by his reference to the unconscious as *al-la-shuʿur*, as well as his use of the term *al-jinsiyya al-mithliyya* to refer to homosexuality, both terms of art put forth by the journal.[20] In 1953, two psychoanalytically oriented studies of the ʿAbbasid poet

Abu Nuwas, widely known for his homoerotic poetry, were published in Egypt. Both studies, one by literary critic Muhammad al-Nuwayhi and the other by poet and writer ʿAbbas Mahmud al-ʿAqqad, were greatly concerned with Abu Nuwas's psychosexual makeup.[21] In 1954, outside of Egypt, Iraqi sociologist ʿAli al-Wardi wrote on the importance of Freud and "unconscious drives rooted in psychological and social conditions."[22] The ardent interest in Freud was the purview of academics and novelists, prevalent in lay and scholarly literature alike, as well as an object of interest to both secular and religious thinkers. Freud, it would seem, was nothing short of ubiquitous in postwar Egypt and the Arab world.

Psychoanalysis and the Religious Subject

In his *Sources of the Self*, philosopher Charles Taylor discusses the shift that occurred in the moral topography of modern selfhood in the early modern West.[23] In particular, he locates the emergence of a space of moral interiority characterized by a language of inwardness, and separated from the divine, with the thought of Descartes. Post-Cartesian thought, he argues, located the sources of the self within humans, rather than in relation to a path toward the divine. Revisiting the Western European archive of selfhood, Jerrold Seigel departs from Taylor's account, which, he argues, overemphasizes the punctual and disengaged nature of selfhood as a "rejection of moral sources exterior to human existence (the original sin of modernity in Taylor's story)."[24] Rather than speak of modern selfhood in the singular, Seigel's more capacious conception allows for variation and vicissitude, to include those, for instance, who were animated by a "desire to preserve a connection with the very premodern conceptions of a transcendent universe able to guarantee the harmony between self and world whose decline Taylor laments."[25] Moreover, Seigel departs from views that "regard the notion of an individual and subjectively grounded selfhood as peculiarly Western and modern."[26]

This more nuanced and expansive understanding of the history of modern selfhood helps us unsettle assumptions regarding the singularity of Western selfhood, as well as the secular nature of modern selfhood, assumptions that have been usefully undone by a growing body of literature on the globalization of the unconscious that has placed European and non-European formations within a single analytic lens. Ranjana Khanna has introduced the notion of "worlding" psychoanalysis, arguing that "understanding psychoanalysis ethnographically involves analyzing its use, both by Europeans and by the colonized," thereby "provincializing a language that presented itself as universal."[27] Shruti Kapila has investigated "Freud and his Indian friends," demonstrating how psychoanalytic knowledge was challenged and reappropriated in the context of colonial India, particularly with respect to religion, which was placed within a normative rather than pathological domain.[28] Similarly, Christiane Hartnack has detailed Girindrasekhar Bose and the Indian Psychoanalytic Society's integration of classical Hindu texts and popular cultural traditions into their psychoanalytic theory, while Mariano Ben Plotkin has traced the emergence of a psychoanalytic culture in Argentina and its institutional dissemination throughout the twentieth century, and Rubén Gallo has excavated the "terra incognita that is Freud's Mexico."[29] Such reformulations of the global modern subject have refused to see the emphasis on the divine, for example, within non-European models of selfhood as atavistic remnants to be worn away by modernity and secularization. They have thus belied the implicit, albeit unsayable of European psychoanalysis, "the impossible achievement of selfhood for the colonized, who remain primitive and concealed."[30]

Despite this, the assumption that modern selfhood, and by extension psychoanalysis, are normatively secular, remains a tenacious one. Many scholars have assumed "the non-religious, radically atheistic, anti-metaphysical foundations of psychoanalysis," based on Freud's readings of monotheism in *Moses and Monotheism* and his statements in "Obsessive Actions and Religious Practices," *The Future of an Illusion, Civilization and Its Discontents*, and elsewhere in his writings.[31] Admittedly, there were early analysts who believed that religion "was an expression of the infantile in mental life," and that religious ideas were "illusory wish fulfillments." Religious practices were compared to obsessional neuroses, religious experience to infantile regression and desire for union, or a misinterpretation of sexual feelings and even to catatonia and schizophrenia. However, there were analysts who tried to bridge the gap between analysis and religion, such as Eric Fromm and Karen Horney.[32] Bruno Bettelheim, for example, argued that in the original German, Freud's language was full of references to the soul, going so far as to refer to analysts as "a profession of secular ministers of the soul."[33]

To be sure, Freud himself has been subject to a wide variety of interpretations, ranging from those who see him as singularly atheistic to those who argue for his positive affirmation of Judaism.[34] In a most controversial interpretation, psychoanalysis has even been seen as a secularized version of Jewish mysticism.[35] At the center of these analyses often lay Sigmund Freud himself who, many have claimed, demonstrated an ambivalence toward religion in general, and Judaism in particular. Edward Said's *Freud and the Non-European* addresses the question of Freud's complex and troubled relationship to his Jewish identity primarily through the prism of its implications for political and national identity. Said deftly reads *Moses and Monotheism*, and its assertion that Moses was an Egyptian, as indicative of an antinomian thinking and an "opening out of Jewish identity towards its non-Jewish background."[36] Said sees the strength of this Freudian insight regarding the non-unitary nature of identity as "attending to it as a troubling, disabling, destabilizing, secular wound—the essence of the cosmopolitan, from which there can be no recovery," once again connecting the cosmopolitanism of psychoanalysis to its secularity.[37] Other scholars have focused less on Freud as a historical personage or on *Moses and Monotheism* as indexical of Jewish identity, and more on psychoanalysis as a heteroglossic tradition that exceeds "the scope of Freud's explicit postulates and arguments," thereby revealing "an *other Freud*," or what is "in Freud more than Freud."[38] Such an attentiveness to the productive tensions and ambivalences in Freud's work have enabled the staging of a dialogue between psychoanalysis and theology.[39] In a reevaluation of the Freudian tradition, Eric Santner takes seriously the therapeutic elements of monotheism, while elaborating the psychotheological contours of everyday life (revelation as enabling accountability and openness to the Other), to borrow his turn of phrase.[40]

Moving away from the literality of determining "what Freud really meant" has led to an emphasis on understanding the relationship between psychoanalysis and religion through the prism of ethical being, being for the Other, and the "love of man and the decrease of suffering" shared by religion and psychoanalysis alike.[41] Thinkers have turned to bearers of the Freudian tradition, most notably Jacques Lacan, to argue for what James DiCenso terms "*a reciprocal impingement of religiously derived concepts and issues upon psychoanalytic theory.*"[42] As Lacan noted, the subject of religious experience was for Freud, "literally a dead letter.... Yet ... that letter was nevertheless definitely articulated."[43] Lacan systematically addressed the question of "the monotheistic foundations of Western subjectivity as a set of discursive ruptures" through which the modern subject was forged.[44] The emphasis on Lacan has enabled a rethinking of the relationship between psychoanalysis and "religious and ethical selfhood."[45] In short, Lacan's method "is to bring psychoanalysis into *proximity* with both philosophy and religion," while acknowledging that "religion can give expression to the ethical potentiality for being of the subject."[46]

The Mystic Fable

Within the analytic tradition, mysticism, as a subset of religious belief and practice, has retained a peculiar importance, and for some, an exalted status. Freud himself, according to Ernest Jones, "regretted having ignored 'the rarer and more profound type of religious emotion as experienced by mystics and saints,'" having focused instead on the religious belief of the common man.[47] As Marion Milner points out, Freud discussed mysticism in precious few references.[48] In the introduction to *Civilization and Its Discontents* Freud discussed a letter from Romain Rolland in which his friend described an affective or psychic state termed "oceanic feeling":

> It is a feeling which he would like to call a sensation of "eternity," a feeling as of something limitless, unbounded—as it were, "oceanic." This

feeling, he adds, is a purely subjective fact, not an article of faith; it brings with it no assurance of personal immortality.[49]

Freud ultimately concluded that oceanic feeling was a form of primary narcissism, a residual effect of the ego-feeling of "limitlessness and of a bond with the universe."[50] Oceanic feeling represented a sort of primitive survival in the domain of mental life—an early phase of ego-feeling.[51] According to Ranjana Khanna, Freud's conception was part of a larger progressivist and civilizational discourse "seen not as evolution but as a history in which those whom he understood to be savages really did *await treatment*."[52]

In discussing oceanic consciousness, Freud noted that the affect caused him "no small difficulty." "I cannot," he continued, "discover this 'oceanic' feeling in myself. It is not easy to deal scientifically with feelings."[53] William Parsons has shown that Freud's thirteen-year correspondence with Romain Rolland was beset with ambivalences and that his view of mysticism was far more nuanced than received accounts would have us believe. So much so that the Freud-Rolland debate foreshadowed philosophical arguments found in contemporary debates about mysticism, setting forth the possibility of a "new dialogical position that grants legitimacy to mystical modes of knowing."[54] In sum, we find "an ambivalent Freud who ... oscillated between an ill-informed, dismissive reductionism ... and a more open appreciation of mystics as 'intuitive psychologists' whose ecstatic and artistic utterances, properly interpreted, might lead us to new forms of psychological knowledge."[55]

Beyond the appreciation of such new forms of knowledge, thinking *alongside* mysticism has arguably deepened the analytic tradition and enabled a reconsideration of the ethics of the human subject. Lacanian psychoanalysis, oftentimes through its engagement with mysticism, places ethics at the core of man's relationship to the good, as an unconscious dialectical relationship between the subject and the law mediated through enjoyment (*jouissance*). As Marc De Kesel argues, Lacan breaks with Aristotelian ethics in terms of *content* (as for example, in the cultivation of virtuous habits), but retains the central *form* of ethical judgment in the subject's mediation between the pleasure principle and the reality principle.[56] And yet within Lacan's framework the good is not imagined as the moral universe of general values (neither "the moral 'ought' of the superego," nor the Kantian categorical imperative), but rather a positive orientation toward what lies beyond the formal law, "an antimoralistic ethics."[57] Classical ethics is consequently decentered while its core form is retained.

Lacan devoted particular attention to mysticism, conceived in the style of courtly love, as exemplifying an erotics centered on the love of the "good old God."[58] For Lacan "religion in all its forms" consisted in avoiding a constitutive emptiness (a vacuole) at the heart of the human subject that he terms, following Freud, *das Ding*, conceived as a radical evil, a death drive, around which man must keep his distance and yet ethically orient himself.[59] The entire process of sublimation, to which Lacan devotes much attention, relates to this confrontation between man and "the deathliness of his drive."[60] Religion, like art, sublimates *das Ding*, encircling it in order to conceive it; it is "a gap always in abeyance (a béance) of religious men and mystics."[61] For Lacan "all mysticisms, all that Kant disdainfully calls the *Religionsschwärmereien*, religious enthusiasms.... What is all this except a way to rediscovering the relation to *das Ding* somewhere beyond the law?"[62]

In this book, I explore Islamic mysticism, or Sufism, as a particularly fruitful point of entry for thinking about the relationship between Islam and psychoanalysis in terms of the theorization of the relations among ethics, eros, and the unconscious. Like Michel de Certeau, I find that mystical religious literature often shared an epistemological alignment with psychoanalysis. Pursuing the functional analogy between psychoanalysis and mysticism, de Certeau analogizes these two discursive formations as inaugurating the question of the subject, conceiving the body as itself a symbolic language, establishing a dialectic between the hidden and the shown, and asking what remains of the spoken word, all the while authorizing "a critical analysis by establishing a space (be it 'mystical' or 'unconscious') posited as different but not distant from the configuration organized by those founding principles of the historical system."[63]

It is perhaps, then, not accidental that Lacan had referenced the Muslim Andalusian mystic and philosopher Ibn 'Arabi on a number of occasions, going so far as to note his own alignment with Ibn 'Arabi's position on symbolic knowledge over the rationalism of Averroës.[64] Nor, too, is it incidental to find that Moustapha Safouan, a preeminent member of Lacan's inner circle in Paris, had originally trained with Ibn 'Arabi scholar and translator Abu al-'Ala' al-Afifi, whose doctoral thesis elaborated on the medieval mystic's conception of psychology.

Psychoanalysis and Islam: A Tale of Mutual Understanding?

The first Arabic translators of Freud rendered "the unconscious" as *al-la-shu'ur*, a notion deeply resonant within the Islamic mystical tradition and evocative of the work of Ibn 'Arabi.[65] Contemporary scholars have revisited this link between psychoanalysis and Islam by focusing on Ibn 'Arabi's rendition of the Qur'anic story of Abraham, in which Abraham dreams that he is sacrificing his son and believes it to be a divine commandment. According to Ibn 'Arabi:

> God said to Abraham while he was speaking to him: "In truth, O Abraham, you believed in a vision," which is not to say that Abraham, be-

lieving he had to sacrifice his son, was faithful to the divine inspiration; because he has taken the vision literally, while every dream demands a transposition or interpretation.[66]

As Jean-Michel Hirt notes, the Abrahamic trial confronts us with "whether to believe or to interpret one's dream," in which the "error is to give in to the manifest meaning of the dream, to reduce it to action, instead of hearing its latent signification."[67]

Tunisian analyst Fethi Benslama elaborates further: Ibn 'Arabi interprets the dream not as the desire to sacrifice the son, but rather as "the desire to kill the child in the father."[68] Abraham is " 'not-conscious' (*bi lā chu'ūr*) of the true object of the desire for sacrifice," nor of the divine interpretation of the dream, of which he "was not conscious (*la yach 'ur*)."[69] Ibn 'Arabi continues, "Because God is never unconscious (*bi lâ Ch 'ur*) of anything, while the subject is necessarily unconscious of such a thing in relation with such other."[70] Man is therefore not conscious of the multiplicity of things (for example, in Abraham's dream) and their transmutation into multiple forms, Benslama continues, "forms to which man does not have full access since there is an unconscious."[71] As Benslama states, "Ibn Arabî's unconscious is not the Freudian unconscious, even if it often comes close to it. It is the condition of the spiritual veiling and unveiling of the multiple forms of man."[72] While it may ultimately be true that Ibn 'Arabi's unconscious differs from the Freudian unconscious, it was epistemologically resonant with it, much in the same way that Ibn 'Arabi's notion of the imaginal world (*hadrat al-khayal*) resonated with Lacan's Imaginary, albeit conceptualized as a theophany, as I elaborate in chapter 2.[73]

Fethi Benslama's reading of Ibn 'Arabi takes place in the context of an "exploration of the texts and symbolic constructions of the Islamic religion in relation to the hypotheses of psychoanalysis."[74] In particular, he seeks to redress Abdelkebir Khatibi's claim that "*Islam is an empty place in the theory of psychoanalysis.*"[75] His parsing of the Abrahamic story of sacrifice is an attempt to situate the "primal fictions of Islam and the workings of its symbolic systems" in terms of the Freudian role of the father in the establishment of the monotheistic religions.[76] Yet in focusing on the "repressed elements of Islam's founding narrative," Benslama's writings have been motivated, in part, by a concern for political Islamism as a return of the repressed.[77] Islamist movements, he notes, are "haunted by the question of origins," the heart of a "tormented present."[78]

Benslama is not alone in his use of psychoanalytic concepts and tools in order to understand the means and motives of Islamic religious phenomena. There is, in fact, a large psychoanalytic literature that seeks to understand contemporary Islamism as well as an alleged Arab and Islamic hostility to psychoanalysis.[79] In striving to explore the psychic reasons for an assumed Islamic resistance to psychoanalysis, such thinkers have proffered explanations of an

Arab culture "dominated by the figure of the persecuting Master outside its ranks and the paternal Master within them."[80] Even when such explanations purport to be historical, they fail to take into account the specific history through which "Islam" and "psychoanalysis" became iconic symbols representing allegedly distinct civilizations and political positions. Such debates reduce theoretical models to political signifiers largely evacuated of meaning (a Western self signified by psychoanalysis and an Eastern self signified by Islam). Joseph Massad has criticized this body of literature on psychoanalysis and Islam by arguing that it represents an "uninterrogated conjunction of a reified psychoanalysis and a reified Islam," with the psychoanalytic insights of Benslama functioning as mere "invocations of liberalism."[81] The attempt to stage an interlude between psychoanalysis and Islam reproduces "the avatars of colonial thought with regard to the matter of the psychic being."[82] Indeed, as Alberto Toscano eloquently states, the "idea of transforming psychoanalysis into a secular clinic aimed at diagnosing the phanstasmatic impasses that prevent 'Arabs' or 'Muslims' from becoming the properly pathological subjects of modernity (rather than fanatics stuck between crumbling tradition and fear of 'Westoxification') leaves itself open to the accusation that psychoanalysis might constitute yet another stage in that cunning of Christianity which has often taken the name of 'secularism.'"[83] Such is an implicit danger of Gohar Homayounpour's spirited defense of *Doing Psychoanalysis in Tehran*, where she rebuts claims of an Islamic resistance to psychoanalysis, but only by virtually effacing Islam's presence in the Islamic Republic of Iran, with the exception of a few offhand references.[84]

The Arabic Freud actively refutes the secular civilizing mission of certain strands of psychoanalysis by bringing psychoanalysis and Islam into dialogue with each other and yet at the same time it does not take Islamic scripture, theology, and tradition as an ahistorical object of psychoanalytic inquiry. As such, I do not use psychoanalysis as a theory through which to understand the origins of Islam as a religion, or its allegedly attendant civilization, for example, by exploring the role of the father in the Qur'an (by analyzing the dramatic import of the story of Abraham, Sarah, and Hagar and so forth).[85] Rather, I explore specific intellectuals who theorized the self by drawing on both Islamic and psychoanalytic idioms, and reconstruct historical interactions, such as an interlude between Sufism and psychoanalysis in mid-twentieth-century Egypt, in which thinkers read classical Sufi philosophers such as Ibn 'Arabi, alongside, in concurrence with, and in distinction to Freud.

I thus join a body of work that takes seriously the relationship between psychoanalysis and Islam as mutually transformative, without succumbing to a secular liberal universalism or cultural imperialism. Stefania Pandolfo has referenced the relationship between Islam and psychoanalysis as representing the possibility of an opening, of "cultivating an ethical attitude in which one risks one's concepts, and oneself, in the opening to other traditions—welcoming, in the process, the transmutations of psychoanalytic knowledge."[86] Sigi Jöttkandt and Joan Copjec have likewise argued for the need to stage an "encounter between Islam and psychoanalysis in their mutual opening to the field of the impossible."[87] What is crucial to note here is that to instantiate the dialogue between psychoanalysis and Islam is to admit "to a modern subject whose freedom and finitude, responsibility and praxis are articulated in relation to God, on a transcendental axis where the soul/self must be trained and equipped, in this world, to become the addressee of divine discourse; and who simultaneously ... is ethically active in relation to others in a community."[88] Allowing the encounter between Islam and psychoanalysis to exert pressure on psychoanalytic thought may therefore be productive and generative of new forms of psychoanalytic knowledge.[89] The idea, of course, is not to collapse the distinction between the two traditions, but rather to allow each to view the other as an aperture within which a certain form of lucidity becomes possible.

In contrast, then, to the so-called tale of mutual ignorance between Islam and psychoanalysis asserted by Benslama and others, I trace a tale of historical interactions, hybridizations, and interconnected webs of knowledge production between the Arab world and Europe. A series of interactions, I might add, in which there was as an ethical engagement between psychoanalysis and religion, and in which the two terms were not assumed to be a priori distinct. The result, I hope, will be part of the project of understanding psychoanalysis ethnographically, not simply by provincializing psychoanalysis's European provenance, but rather by demonstrating the non-Western traditions and individuals who contributed to psychoanalysis as a body of knowledge that was always already hybridized with the discourse of the other.[90] The coproduction of psychoanalytic knowledge across Arab and European knowledge formations definitively demonstrates the outmoded nature of historical models that presuppose originals and bad copies of the modern subject—herself so constitutively defined by the presence of the unconscious.

Decolonizing the Self

No discussion of psychoanalysis and Islam can avoid the question of colonialism and the relationship between Islam and the West. Gayatri Spivak has gone so far as to suggest that "institutional psychoanalysis can be a latter-day support of ... epistemic violence," while Jacques Derrida has noted "the psychoanalytic colonization of a non-American rest-of-the-world."[91] Referencing colonial Algeria, he suggests that "it was altogether exceptional and untypical for psychoanalysts to raise the question of their own practice in its political, ethno-psychoanalytical and socio-institutional dimensions."[92]

And yet, as Ranjana Khanna has detailed, psychoanalysis has been widely used by theorists of decolonization ranging from Aimé Césaire to Frantz Fanon, remarking that it was not possible to "think of selfhood entirely independently of psychoanalysis."[93] In fact, she continues, the political stakes of decolonization "demanded that subjectivity come to the fore in consolidating a theory and practice of political commitment."[94] Nevertheless the presence of non-Western analysts raised the pressing question of *"Who* can legitimately lay claim to psychoanalytic knowledge?"[95] Kalpana Seshadri-Crooks examines "the manner in which psychoanalysis ... has served to exclude the non-Western analyst from theory or has demanded a reinscription of his/her subjectivity in consonance with Freudian (cultural) ideology."[96] Far from advocating a rejection of psychoanalysis, Seshadri-Crooks proposes it as a tool with which to understand "the historical ruptures and the epistemic violence engendered by colonialism, with regard to the (re-)inscription of subjectivity as such."[97] Indeed, countless texts of postcolonial critical theory and history have attended to the historicization of such epistemic ruptures and realignments of subjectivity.[98]

At the same time, conventional narratives of Arab intellectual history focus on colonialism as a formative rupture that split twentieth-century thought (and subjects) into liberal secular and religious trends. Moroccan historian Abdallah Laroui and Egyptian political theorist Anouar Abdel-Malek, for instance, expound the twentieth-century Arab intellectual as the product of the struggle for the reconquest of identity in the face of a constitutive self-alienation created by the colonial encounter.[99] For Laroui and others, the intelligentsia's response to colonialism and European hegemony led to two dominant trends, traditionalist Islamic thought and modernist thought—the former characterized by a repetitive recitation of the past or an alienation through time, and the latter by an eclecticism characteristic of ideological backwardness, or an alienation through space.[100]

My concern here, however, is of a decidedly different nature. Rather than assume the rigidity, mimesis, or univocity of "traditional" and "modern" thought, I explore the ways in which writings on the self drew from both psychoanalysis and the Islamic discursive tradition, understood as convivial bodies of knowledge subject to continuous reinterpretation. Further, in thinking about the routes of psychoanalysis in postwar Egypt, I attend to what endures of precolonial ontologies and epistemologies, to the continuities rather than ruptures, and to the trace rather than the cut. If as Pandolfo says, "psychoanalysis ... developed at the margins of European modernity, from the debris of minor or obliterated traditions, and in the form of a counter-move," then so too did postwar Arab writings on the self.[101] What intellectual exchanges, conceptual translations, and encounters between traditions took place between Islam and psychoanalysis?[102]

In fact, theoretical literature on the anthropology of Islam, such as Katherine Pratt Ewing's insightful ethnography of Sufism in contemporary Lahore, or Amira Mittermaier's anthropology of the imagination in Egypt, have eschewed simplistic interpretations of postcolonial Muslim personhood as caught between the fetters of tradition and modernity.[103] Most pertinently, Javed Majeed has compellingly argued that the Sufi poet Muhammad Iqbal might be seen as a possible landmark "in which Islamism and Western critical theory can be considered, not as oppositional discourses, but together, with overlapping concerns, as critiques of and responses to colonial modernity."[104] Similarly, Naveeda Khan explores Iqbal's engagement with philosopher Henri Bergson in order to demonstrate his recasting of Islam as an "open religion with possible futures as yet uninstantiated."[105]

Referencing psychologist Yusuf Murad, leading Egyptian literary critic Mahmud Amin al-'Alim referred to him as the consummate "philosopher of integration."[106] Rather than the "tale of mutual ignorance" that some have claimed to exist, for example, between Islamic and Western theories, debates in the formative postwar period in the Middle East did not view eclectic blendings, in Frederick Cooper's phrasing, as "personally destabilizing, as intellectually contradictory, or as threatening to [one's] sense of cultural integrity: *in between* [was] as much a place to be at home as any other."[107] For example, in postwar Egypt, an entire generation of scholars and their students began to teach the social sciences in Arabic at Egypt's national university, establishing an Arabic language lexicon for fields such as sociology and psychology within a university that had heretofore been dominated by French and British influence. Scholars created synthetic visions that combined Durkheimian sociology with Ibn Khaldun's theory of civilizations, or the dialectical dynamism of psychoanalysis with the mystical philosophy of Ibn 'Arabi, all the while uncovering epistemological resonances between modern European and Arab discursive traditions and demonstrating the contemporaneity of classical Arabic and Islamic texts. Whether scholars were translating Bergson and Fanon, reading Freud, or rethinking Qur'anic ethics, European philosophy was simply not to be dismissed.

And yet even as they were in dialogue with various strands of European thought—existentialism, socialism, and Marxism, to name but a few—postwar intellectuals often agitated for complete political and cultural decolonization. As Yoav Di-Capua has detailed, the postwar period was dominated by a concern for the creation of a "new Arab man"—sovereign, authentic, and free—and on the elaboration of a postcolonial ontology centered on being rather than essence.[108] The 1940s and 1950s constituted the beginnings of a "working through" of the constitutive self-alienation of the colonial era (and hence the focus on the *nafs* or psyche) and a negotiation of the oftentimes divergent agendas of intellectuals and the state. The drive toward national liberation and social justice led to an ambivalent relationship to the postcolonial state, viewed at once as the avatar of national independence and an apparatus of political repression.

In particular, psychoanalysis could not be completely divorced from the attempts to professionalize psychology in the postwar period while putting its views and findings at the service of medicine, criminology, and state social engineering in the hope of creating the postcolonial "new man." At times, psychoanalysis was harnessed to postwar concerns centered on youth and sexual deviance, or on crime and psychopathy, for instance. This was particularly the case given the fact that psychoanalysis itself had made only negligible inroads into clinical practice. Inevitably, such attempts led to tensions between philosophical and ethical orientations and pragmatic political concerns that emerged when intellectual objectives became tethered to postcolonial political programs.

Homo psychoanalyticus was thus not characterized by "the neutralization of ethics and of the political realm" and a dissociation of the "psychoanalytical sphere from the sphere of the citizen or moral subject in his or her public or private life."[109] Rather, psychoanalysis presented the possibility of enjoyment in the use of the other as an instrument or object, while at the same time offering a means of undermining that sovereign pleasure, precisely by critically analyzing one's own psychic implication in it. Simply put, psychoanalysis oscillated between ethical ideals centered on the opacity of the human subject (her resistance to intelligibility and understanding) and the belief in the transparency of humans and the possibility of their instrumentalization. Such divergent views marked the difference between the prospect of a psychoanalysis that would be at "*at the service* of those who suffer, and not an instrument of power or mastery over them."[110]

More specifically, the trajectory of psychoanalysis in Egypt indicates a tension between a notion of the human subject as conceptually opaque, as only incompletely knowable to itself or others due to the existence of the unconscious, and as operationally transparent as the erstwhile object of postcolonial projects of social reform and amelioration. This tension, one internal to psychoanalysis, has often been discussed in terms of the divide between certain strands of Freudian or Lacanian psychoanalysis that posit a "radically unknowable, radically incalculable" subject and those of American ego psychologists that aim for the adaptation of the human subject to his environment.[111] This latter tradition has been criticized for its amenability to projects of human engineering that render the human subject whole, transparent, and calculable, in effect leading to a psychologized subject who becomes the object of Foucaultian biopower.[112]

Among those who drew on psychoanalysis, we observe that the key term of reference was never the ego, but rather always the polysemic Arabic term *nafs* (soul, spirit, psyche, self), a concept implying a spiritual core, alongside the presence of the unconscious (*al-la-shuʿur*) as a place where God could be manifested. Such domains far exceeded the operations of the ego while simultaneously grounded in the praxis of ethics. It would be reductive, then, to think that intellectual and ethical concerns could simply be mapped onto political agendas, and questions beyond postcolonialism and nationalism deeply engaged thinkers concerned with the science of selfhood and the soul. I therefore eschew an analysis that would view psychoanalysis as merely yet another technology of the late colonial state or of postcolonial nationalism, or as epiphenomenal to larger political developments in the Arab world. Psychoanalysis found outlets in theoretical and philosophical debates where thinkers elaborated on the conceptual history of the unconscious and of desire, while attuned to the ethical contours of the subject. At the same time, the exigencies of postcolonial politics often rendered psychological theories in the service of disciplinary projects and prescriptive visions of the postcolonial subject. *The Arabic Freud* traces the movement of these two components of psychoanalytic thought, outlining how these two strands—the philosophical and the pragmatic—intersected and diverged in various ways within the history of analytic thought within twentieth-century Egypt.

Structure, Method, and Argument

By exploring the formation of modern discourses of subjectivity in fields as diverse as psychology, Islamic philosophy, and the law, this book demonstrates that psychoanalysis was a tradition with deep and varied roots in the Egyptian postwar setting, not only among psychologists and mental health professionals, but also among Islamic thinkers and legal practitioners. At the same time this is not a reception history; it does not in any way seek to exhaustively assemble together all those who wrote about or approached Freud's ideas in Egypt, nor does it catalog Arabic translations, commentaries, and exegeses of Freud. Rather, I both stage and historically reconstruct a philosophical encounter between psychoanalysis and Islam, one in which Arab intellectuals emerge as producers of philosophy and theory rather than merely as objects of study or the simple products of their political context.[113] As Edward Baring notes, we should be wary of "a mode of history that reduces philosophical texts to their contextual moment. One should not see biographical, political, or cultural background as an 'origin' for philosophical ideas."[114]

We will encounter Arabophone writings on the self by a variety of scholars virtually unknown to a Western audience, all of whom were in conversation with a range of figures of psychoanalysis, such as Sigmund Freud, Karen Horney, Henri Wallon, and Ian Suttie. Such a dialogue was enabled by a longstanding engagement with the classical Arabic tradition of scholarship on the soul or *nafs*, one that included key luminaries of Islamic thought, al-Ghazali and Ibn 'Arabi, as well as lesser-known thinkers, such as Ibn 'Ata' Allah al-Sakandari.

I mobilize both sets of writings, those on psychoanalysis and those of classical and contemporary Islamic thought, as theoretical frameworks and objects of philosophical analysis, shuttling back and forth, much as my own historical actors, between frameworks. At the same time, my analytical orientation is not confined to those of the scholars that I study, and I draw freely from the psychoanalytic tradition, drawing on scholars such as Jacques Lacan who were at times at odds with the theoretical formulations of my historical actors. I do so with the intent of emphasizing certain affinities, while highlighting key differences between these traditions, rather than a dogmatic fidelity to a particular psychoanalytic orientation.

Part I, "The Unconscious and the Modern Subject," explores postwar intellectuals' engagement with psychoanalytic theory in philosophical and ethical debates on the nature of the soul, the self, and the psyche. Part II, "Spaces of Interiority," explores the more pragmatic concerns that emerged with the professionalization of psychology, particularly within the psychology of sexuality and youth and criminal psychology. Traversing literatures minor and major, ranging from scholarly texts on psychoanalysis to lay literature on self-healing, the following chapters address many of the key questions of psychoanalysis and its intersection with multiple traditions, Islamic and otherwise, by exploring, in turn, the modern subject of consciousness, ethics, sexuality, and the law within mid-twentieth-century Egypt.

Chapter 1, "Psychoanalysis and the Psyche," considers Freudian itineraries in postwar Egypt through an exploration of the work of Yusuf Murad, the founder of a school of thought within the psychological sciences, and the journal he coedited from 1945 to 1953, *Majallat ʿIlm al-Nafs*. By training a generation of scholars, Murad left a wide-ranging legacy on psychology, philosophy, and the wider academic fields of the humanities and the social sciences. Melding key concepts from psychoanalysis with classical Islamic concepts, Murad elaborated a psychological theory of the subject as an integrative agent, embodying a complex synthesis of unity and multiplicity. Theorizing the temporality of the subject, the epistemology of psychoanalysis and the analytic structure, and the *socius*, Murad both drew upon and departed from European psychoanalytic thought, while often insisting on the epistemological and ethical heterogeneity of different theories of the self.

Chapter 2, "The Self and the Soul," reconstructs a historical interlude between Sufism and psychoanalytic psychology in postwar Egypt. How might we think through the relationship between psychoanalysis and the Islamic tradition, while respecting the "ontological stakes" of the latter, namely, the belief in divine transcendence and divine discourse? I address this question through a detailed exploration of the writings of Abu al-Wafa al-Ghunaymi al-Taftazani and his mentor Muhammad Mustafa Hilmi, both prominent Egyptian intellectuals who expounded Sufi ideas for a broader reading public, beginning in the 1940s. Situating these figures within the larger intellectual and religious context of mid-twentieth-century Egypt, I explore the elective affinities between Sufism and certain strands of psychoanalysis in terms of a dialogical relationship between the self and the Other, as mediated by the unconscious.

Chapter 3, "The Psychosexual Subject," traces the intersection of psycho-analysis and the invention of the psychosexual subject in postwar Egypt. Following a set of discussions on Freudian theory and sexuality in *Majallat 'Ilm al-Nafs*, as well as a series of popular and didactic books, I explore newly emerging languages of desire and ethics and their relationship to gender and sexuality. In sharp contrast to the alleged incommensurability between psychoanalysis and Islam, postwar psychoanalysis was able to breathe new life into an earlier premodern classical literature centered on desire and the appetites and on the ethical cultivation of the child. The invention of the psychosexual subject, in other words, did not necessarily entail a simple shift of pleasure and desire away from the theological pastoral toward secular science and medicine as some scholars have asserted.

Between June 1947 and February 1949, a series of articles in *Majallat 'Ilm al-Nafs* debated the heuristic value of Freud's ideas, particularly surrounding the Oedipus complex, for an understanding of criminality. Chapter 4, "Psychoanalysis before the Law," traces this debate spawned by professor of criminal psychology Muhammad Fathi, while paying particular attention to the social role of the criminal at midcentury. I argue that the convergences or divergences found between psychoanalysis and the law were in part related to disputes regarding the causal nature of crime. Further complicating these debates was the juridical status of psychoanalysis itself as it struggled to assert its autonomy as a field of therapeutic practice within the Egyptian legal system. At the center of all of these arguments lay the criminal, himself increasingly enmeshed within new legal and forensic practices, as well as multiple legal regimes over the course of the twentieth century.

In the epilogue, I return to the central question of this book—what does it mean, *now*, to think through psychoanalysis and Islam together as a creative encounter of ethical engagement? Addressing recent scholarly interventions, such as those of Julia Kristeva, that operate within larger civilizing mission narratives that couple psychoanalysis with the secularization of Judeo-Christian legacies, I question the notion of psychoanalysis as the purview of any singular civilization. What might it mean to rethink the secular ends of analysis and open ourselves up to an ethical encounter with the Other?

PART I

The Unconscious and the Modern Subject

CHAPTER ONE

Psychoanalysis and the Psyche

Well now, this year I am proposing not simply to be faithful to the text of
Freud and to be its exegete, as if it were the source of an unchanging truth
that was the model, mold and dress code to be imposed on all our
experience.

—JACQUES LACAN, *ETHICS OF PSYCHOANALYSIS*

ON FRIDAY MORNINGS in Cairo in the mid- to late 1940s and 1950s, scholars and students of all disciplines would assemble at the house of psychology
professor Yusuf Murad.[1] Gathered to discuss the latest intellectual trends in
psychology and philosophy, at those meetings, we are told, the attendees' concerns revolved around two central questions: how can the scholar be a philosopher and how can the teacher be a mentor?[2] Through a capacious body of
work that touched on subjects as diverse as the epistemology of psychoanalysis and the analytic structure, and Abu Bakr al-Razi's medieval treatise on
spiritual medicine, Murad developed what he termed an integrative (*takamuli*) psychology based on the fundamental philosophical unity of the self. Presenting Freud's discovery of the unconscious as a "Copernican revolution" to
his audience, Murad identified psychoanalysis as the dialectical synthesis of
philosophical introspection, positivism, and phenomenology.

Responsible in large part for the formalization of an Arabic language lexicon of psychology and psychoanalysis, Murad introduced the Arabic term
"*al-la-shu'ur*," a mystical term taken from the medieval Sufi philosopher Ibn
'Arabi, as "the unconscious" into scholarly vocabularies.[3] Translating and
blending key concepts from psychoanalysis and the French tradition of philosophical psychology with classical Islamic concepts, Murad put forth a dynamic and dialectical approach to selfhood that emphasized the unity of the
self, while often insisting on an epistemological and ethical heterogeneity
from European psychological and psychoanalytic thought.

The coterie of students in attendance at Yusuf Murad's Friday morning salon were born sometime between 1920 and 1930, making them the generation that would later become instrumental in transforming the role of the intellectual and of knowledge production within Arab postcolonial polities.[4] Among the regular attendees were several scholars training in philosophy: Mahmud Amin al-'Alim, who was to play a decisive part in the fierce debates over existentialism and the role and purpose of literary production for decolonizing political action; Yusuf al-Sharuni, the meticulous and socially conscious short story writer and literary critic who was active in the avant-garde post–World War II literary groups that formed in Egypt; and Murad Wahba, the author of philosophical commentaries on Averroës, Kant, and Bergson, and of a large body of work on philosophy, civilization, and secularism. Other attendees included Mustafa Suwayf, later a well-known psychology professor at Cairo University (and father to novelist Ahdaf Soueif); Sami al-Durubi, the Syrian translator and diplomat, who wrote on psychology and literature and translated Henri Bergson's *Mind-Energy* and *Laughter*, as well as Frantz Fanon's *Wretched of the Earth* and numerous Russian novels, such as Fyodor Dostoevsky's *Brothers Karamazov* and Mikhail Lermontov's *A Hero of Our Time*; and Salih al-Shamma', the author of texts on childhood language and on the semantics of Qur'anic ethics, later a professor of psychology and head of the philosophy department at the University of Baghdad.[5]

Translating the Unconscious

Yusuf Murad (1902–1966) founded a school of thought within the psychological and human sciences in Egypt and the Arab world, best thought of as part of a shared Arab intellectual heritage of blending traditions, of which Murad represented an exemplary "philosopher of integration."[6] Training a generation of thinkers who then went on to become literary critics, translators, university professors, and mental health professionals in Egypt, Syria, and Iraq, he left a wide imprint on psychology, philosophy, and the wider academic field of the humanities and the social sciences. As one of his former students, Farag 'Abd al-Qadir Taha, noted, Murad's mark on psychology in Egypt was thought to be so great that the majority of Egyptian professors of psychology had studied under him either directly or indirectly through his textbook, a popular handbook of psychology published in 1948 that went through at least seven editions.[7]

Murad was himself well versed in the traditions of experimental psychology as well as in European psychoanalytic and neo-psychoanalytic approaches. Born in Cairo, he studied philosophy at Fu'ad I University (later Cairo University), graduating in 1930 and traveling to France where he received his doctorate in psychology in 1940 from the Sorbonne.[8] Upon his return, he taught psychology in the philosophy department at Cairo University, and was the first to do so in Arabic, eventually becoming chair of the philosophy department between 1953 and 1957.[9] Murad, along with his colleague Mustafa Ziywar, a psychoanalyst who had trained in philosophy, psychology, and medicine in France in the 1930s, founded the *Jama'at 'Ilm al-Nafs al-Takamuli* (Society of Integrative Psychology) and the Egyptian *Majallat 'Ilm al-Nafs* (Journal of Psychology) in 1945, and supervised the translation and publication of numerous works of psychology.[10] *Majallat 'Ilm al-Nafs*, the first psychology journal published in the Arab world, was illustrative of the emerging disciplinary space of psychology in Egypt in the 1940s; it was understood as a science of selfhood and the soul (*'ilm al-nafs*) rather than delimited as the empirical study of mental processes.[11] The journal, which ran from 1945 to 1953, served as a wide-ranging platform for academic psychology and was meant to serve as a bridge between the psychological sciences and philosophy, while introducing its audience to the major concepts of psychoanalysis and psychology.

In the inaugural issue of *Majallat 'Ilm al-Nafs*, Yusuf Murad introduced a dictionary that provided the Arabic equivalents to English, French, and German terms in the fields of psychology and psychoanalysis.[12] Murad was himself a member of the Academy of Language for the committee on psychological terms and was therefore crucial in the creation and standardization of an Arabic lexicon of psychology. Emphasizing the difficulty and importance of precise terminology, he remarked that in some instances multiple terms were needed to convey the meaning of a single word and to adumbrate the different interpretations of terms by different schools of thought in psychology.[13] Murad's dictionary was likely partly inspired by his former university professor André Lalande, and his *Vocabulaire technique et critique de la philosophie*, a text known for its analytical rigor.[14] Notably, Murad observed that he often returned to classical Arabic texts in order to create new translations for words and clear, precise, and capacious meanings.[15] Murad's felicitous translations were oftentimes closer to the German spirit of Freud's terms than the standard English translations, as for example in his choice of Arabic terms for psyche (*nafs*), ego (*al-ana*), and superego (*al-ana al-a'la*).[16]

Majallat 'Ilm al-Nafs presented to its academic readers a rich and scholarly understanding of psychoanalysis, drawing on the entire corpus of Freud's work, which many had read in English, and to a lesser extent in French. Beyond that, authors integrated a multitude of diverse conduits of psychoanalytic thought, from the United Kingdom (John Flügel, Ian Suttie, James Wisdom); France and Switzerland (Daniel Lagache, Henri Wallon, Charles Odier); and Hungary (Sándor Ferenczi, Franz Alexander). Yet, in so doing, psychoanalysis in Egypt emerged not simply as an importation or "a derivative exercise" but rather "a reflexive process of appropriation."[17]

This chapter explores the work of Yusuf Murad, the founder of a school of thought within the psychological and human sciences, and provides a close study of the journal he coedited from 1945 to 1953, *Majallat 'Ilm al-Nafs*. I offer not a literal history of Freud in Egypt but rather a history of ideas and debates spawned by Freudianism as a multivalent tradition. I analyze the dense interdiscursive web that constituted the field of psychological inquiry in postwar Egypt, tracing historical interactions and hybridizations between and within traditions of psychological inquiry. Moving away from models of selfhood as either modern or traditional, Western or non-Western, I examine the points of condensation, divergence, and the epistemological resonances that psychoanalytic writings had in postwar Egypt.

More specifically, I explore the coproduction of psychoanalytic knowledge, across Egyptian and European knowledge formations, through the concept of the *point de capiton*. For Jacques Lacan quilting points are signifiers around which dense webs of meanings converge, thereby providing ideological cohesion to discursive formations.[18] In what follows, I draw attention to a number of quilting points that sutured the discursive field of psychology and psychoanalysis in midcentury Egypt. Such *points de capiton* were, quite tellingly, terms or concepts that were pregnant with epistemological resonances drawn from pre-psychoanalytic discursive formations, such as from Ibn ʿArabi's metaphysics or Aristotelian philosophy. I focus on a number of concepts: integration and unity as central both to the self and to knowledge formations (*wahdat al-nafs, wahdat ʿilm al-nafs*, or *ʿilm al-nafs al-takamuli*); insight and intuition (*firasa* and *kashf*) as a mode of knowledge production distinct from positivist or empirical epistemology; and the *socius* or community of/in the other (*al-nahnu, al-akhir*).

The Integrative Subject

Yusuf Murad's corpus embodied an approach he termed *integrative psychology*, which presented the self not solely as a body, or a psyche, or even a psyche added to a body, but rather as "*wahda nafsiyya, jismiyya, ijtimaʿiyya*," the unity of psychic, bodily, and societal aspects.[19] Murad's integrative psychology both constituted and was constituted by the larger sociopolitical context within which it was embedded, namely, Egypt's emergent postcoloniality. If, as Jan Goldstein has demonstrated, Victor Cousin provided a postrevolutionary psychology and pedagogy that enabled the production and reproduction of bourgeois subjectivity in nineteenth-century France, then Murad provided the contours for what we might term a postcolonial subjectivity for twentieth-century Egypt.[20]

Murad's integrative curriculum was part of a larger intellectual context that spanned French philosophical and empirical psychology, psychoanalysis, Aristotelian philosophy, and medieval and modern Arabic thought. Murad's integrative subject was not equivalent to the split subject of postwar Lacanian psychoanalysis, but nor was it the instrumentalist subject of American ego-psychology.[21] In fact, rather than the ego, the key term of reference for Murad and his cohort was the Arabic term *nafs* (soul, spirit, *âme*), a term etymologically imbued with a primordial divinity.[22] In particular, the emphasis on integration can be seen, at least partly, as a response to the events of World War II in the postcolonial context of decolonization, which arguably led to differing notions of selfhood in the former colonies, and within Europe as well.[23] If we take that exemplar of anticolonial thought, Frantz Fanon, we see that the political question that was most pressing for him was how to reconstitute the psychic life of the colonized indigenous subject from the scattered and fragmented elements that remained after colonialism.[24] In contrast, then, to the decentered self that was in part the product of France's interwar cultural crisis and embodied in the Lacanian notion of the split subject, Murad's integrative subject was an agent of synthesis, embodying a complex unity of multiplicity and heterogeneity.[25]

In another Middle Eastern context, Stefania Pandolfo has detailed the emergent locus of subjectivity under the shadow of colonialism as situated within an interstitial zone, both a limit and an entredeux. The modern postcolonial subject emerged in the aftermath of the trauma of colonization, to quote Moroccan novelist Driss Chraibi as an "arabe habillé en français"; the interstitial zone where encounter became possible (between East and West, past and present, modernity and tradition) was also the space of subjectivity.[26] Murad's integrative subject was dialogically constituted across the space of social and cultural difference and embodied translations and borrowings from Europe while maintaining an irreducible heterogeneity from the emphasis on the dissolution of the self in postwar French philosophy. In so doing Murad theorized a new relationship to temporality, progress, and the social body, which I discuss in turn.

At a lecture delivered at the Dar al-Salam Center in Cairo in December 1946, Murad discussed the psychological foundations of social integration.[27] Murad's notion of bio-psycho-social integration was embedded in a complex notion of the temporality of the psychological subject and a rejection of monocausality. Biological, psychological, and social factors were to be considered not in terms of a superimposition, "but of mutual penetration on a convergent concourse of these three factors."[28] By "social" Murad referred to the social order and the individual's integration within the community, and more fundamentally, the order of language in the *socius*; "psychological" referred to memory and consciousness; and "biological" to the nervous and circulatory systems. Each level, he noted, operated according to different laws but taken together functioned, ideally, harmoniously.

Criticizing conventional classifications that categorized human psychology in terms of affect, cognition, and behavior, as static and artificial in character, Murad argued that from an integrative perspective an emphasis on movement—whether generative or degenerative, was essential.[29] Stated differently, an integral perspective was eminently genealogical and connective—

concerned with the past and present bio-psycho-social development of man as brought to bear on his future orientation. Further, rather than a linear temporal conception of human personality or social progress, Murad's conception was helicoidal (fr. *hélicöidal*), an ascending spiral or corkscrew temporal movement that he referred to as "*haraka lawlabiyya*."[30] That is to say, that personality involved, like lived time, "partial regressions in the course of the process of maturation, thereby preparing for new progress and a new differentiated level of emergence."[31] Consequently, even radically opposing and contradictory tendencies could be integrated into a psychosocial personality. Movement, contradiction, and struggle, rather than stasis and stability, were at the heart of his conceptualization of human personality.

Murad's conception of temporality as radically heterogeneous yet holistic was reminiscent of Bergson's notion of duration, with which Murad would certainly have been familiar. Several of Murad's students, Mustafa Suwayf, Murad Wahba, and Sami al-Durubi most notably, had written extensively on or translated Bergson's works.[32] Bergson provided what Suzanne Guerlac refers to as a "dynamic ontology of irreversible time."[33] Temporality as conceptualized by Bergson was dynamic and synthetic, embodying qualitative progress and a radical heterogeneity.[34] For Murad, the past was significant, but not in terms of a mere repetition of the same; rather, in the way in which the repetition of the past was experienced in the present bearing its future orientation in mind.[35]

This noncontinuous view of psychic history as marked by the lack of a simple linear progressive evolution was, of course, itself partially derived from psychoanalysis. As Murad noted, psychic development was neither linear, nor cyclical, but rather involved partial regressions and latencies. In the course of the process of maturation, a new differentiated and complex level of psychic development arose out of the preservation of a previous stage, or to use Murad's turn of phrase, each level of psychic development emerged "because of and in spite of" the previous level of development.[36] This radical critique of unilinear progressive temporality is itself nestled within the Freudian status of the event. Progressive time is continuously disrupted by the time of repetition and the *après coup* (*nachträglichkeit*).[37] The temporalization of psychic reality was thus distinct from Hegelian teleology, while other elements of Bergsonian idealism remained in Murad's conceptualization of integration, most notably in the idea of psychic integration and social holism. Suffice it to say that the operations of mental syntheses, or the interpenetration of multiple states of consciousness, resulted in an organic whole, one that Murad referenced as bio-psycho-social integration—"realized most perfectly in the voluntary act or act of will."[38]

Admittedly, integration within the social body would be polymorphous due to the multiplicity of social situations within which the individual was immersed. Social integration, according to Murad, attempted to bridge differences while realizing the unity of goals and the harmony of means, "a community of ends" that excluded total domination, exaggerated particularism, obstinacy, aggression, and servitude.[39] What I term Murad's "pastoral optimism," namely, the possibility of social integration, was rooted in a rejection of Freud's discussions in *The Future of an Illusion* and *Civilization and Its Discontents*.[40] According to Freud, Murad argued, true integration was impossible, as a fundamental variable in all social conduct was aggression, a mask for frustration. The role of fear and guilt in the relations between individuals and nations would lead one to conclude that civilization contained the seeds of its own destruction, and that the final word rested with the death drive.

In contrast to this philosophical pessimism, Murad juxtaposed the ideas of other psychoanalysts, such as Ian Suttie, Karen Horney, and Ranyard West.[41] For Suttie, the love of others comes into being simultaneously with the recognition of their existence; accordingly, Freud's infantile narcissism has no real existence. Freud, he argued, denied "the existence of love as a primal and independent need for expression and response," viewing the individual as an absolutely separate entity, rather than acknowledging love as constitutive and primordial.[42] As such, love may be given in its total capacity, constituting the premier resort of social conduct; it is the contingencies of milieu that give rise to the diverse emotions and sentiments that divide humanity. Suttie's ideas functioned for Murad as a counterpoint to Freud and, like Suttie, Murad repudiated the death drive.[43]

The analytic experiences of Horney and West, he noted, justified this optimism, with the social instinct geared toward the mitigation of aggression. But if social integration were possible, the means of its realization remained to be found. Murad was particularly concerned with what he termed the "bedrock of collective life," which could only be sought by overcoming fear and allowing the discovery of the common goal that transcends individuals and nations to live in the community of the other, without subjecting them to the will of the other. The integrative curriculum was one that embraced sociopolitical optimism and a dynamic temporal coefficient of movement; it critiqued egocentricity and put forth the self in the community of the other as a model for social integration and cohesion, thereby envisioning a harmonious totality whose intersubjective nature was suited to the imagined postcolonial polity to come.

Unity and the Philosophical Self

What were the intellectual wellsprings of Murad's philosophy? Conceptually it can be argued that the overarching concept, the quilting point, both in the integrative curriculum and in Murad's conceptualization of the significance of psychoanalysis, was the notion of *wahda* or unity. What was the overarching significance of *wahda*? The Gestalt theorists to whom Murad was indebted retained residual elements of absolute idealism in their concept of holism—which entailed a fundamental unity in the perception of objects and in the synthesis of experience. There was, however, another older reference point for unity, namely, the writings of Ibn ʿArabi that Murad had actively relied upon during his doctoral research in the 1930s. For Ibn ʿArabi unity was "the Lord's gift to mankind."[44] Threaded throughout his work, and in particular his treatise on *Divine Governance of the Human Kingdom*, which Murad had consulted in manuscript form in Europe, was the idea that "division is incidental, unity is principal," a unity created from the apparent multiplicity of man.[45] Ibn ʿArabi elaborated on the dual aspects of unity: "One is the absolute oneness of all and everything. The other is personal unity and oneness." The former "applies to everyone" and "has the power to defeat everything false, everywhere, at all times." The latter is "the goal of all men of wisdom and knowledge and of their people: an attempt at unity and oneness to be created from the apparent multiplicity in man."[46] According to a commentary on Ibn ʿArabi:

> The unity of essence is the concept that there is only one existence, one cause—inconceivable, unknowable, yet responsible for the existence of all and everything. The quality, the characters, the attributes, the identity of all and everything are the manifestation of this one cause. . . .
>
> Everything is from God, and yet is not God. He is before the before and after the after He is the outer and the inner, the visible and the invisible. His outward manifestation is the unity of everything, and still He is hidden in his Oneness.[47]

For Ibn ʿArabi, "God is the One/the Many (*al-wahid al-kathir*)"; "God is one through his Essence (*dhāt*) and 'many' through his differentiated knowledge" or through the manifestation of his Names.[48] Arguably, Murad's interest in Ibn ʿArabi was rooted in an intense personal spirituality; he had converted from Greek Orthodoxy to Roman Catholicism in his early twenties and remained in close contact with Dominican and Sufi religious leaders in Cairo throughout his life. This abiding interest in Islamo-Christian metaphysics, and a firm belief in the salvific power of *agape*, had led him to believe, much like Ibn ʿArabi, in the underlying spiritual unity of all religious traditions.[49] This complex conception of the "unity of manyness" and the "manyness of the one," or of unity and alterity within Ibn ʿArabi's thought, was further echoed in Murad's conception of psycho-social integration.

Yet clearly Murad's emphasis on unity was not derived solely from the holism of Ibn ʿArabi. Murad's training at the Sorbonne had entailed a blend of academic philosophy and empirical psychology, most notably through the writings of Théodule-Armand Ribot, Pierre Janet, Henri Wallon, and Henri Piéron.[50] The reigning paradigm in experimental psychology at the time of his studies was *Gestalttheorie* or *psychologie de la forme*, imparted through "the exceptional personality" of his dynamic advisor Paul Guillaume.[51] *Gestalttheorie* had maintained an organismic view of experience and is most famously known for the idea that the whole constitutes more than the sum of its parts:

> Taken together, the fundamental theses of *Gestalttheorie* are an expression of that systematic view which regards experience as an organic whole or, at least, as made up of organic wholes.... Wholes, and—if *Gestalttheorie* goes all the way with absolute idealism—ultimately the single whole which constitutes the total system of reality, are not mere collections of parts, but are organized in such a way that their parts necessarily derive their natures from the relations in which they stand.[52]

While holism is clearly fundamental to *Gestalttheorie*, in point of fact, its emphasis was on empirical experiments and demonstrations rather than the elucidation of a general philosophical structure.[53] But some have argued that Gestaltists, adamant in their critique of atomism, shared elements of idealism and monism, particularly, in their account of experience as a single systemic whole or in Guillaume's discussion of the inherent order of experience.[54] Murad's emphasis on the fundamental unity of the self and its integrative nature, as well as his refusal to abstract selfhood from society or biology, was in keeping with *Gestalttheorie*, but he departed from *Gestalttheorie* in his overarching philosophical concerns, which as will soon be clear, were of an idealist nature. It would be a mistake, then, to conclude that his research was dominated by concerns of an empirical sort.[55]

Bearing in mind the diversity of his influences we could say that Murad's general orientation toward psychology was in keeping with larger trends within the French academy, namely, the enduring impact of eclectic spiritualism. Eclectic spiritualism, founded by Victor Cousin, combined eclecticism (the preservation of what was best in any philosophical doctrine, or what John I. Brooks refers to as a bricolage), spiritualism (the recognition of a thinking substance; a notion of the moral sciences—ethical and spiritual) and scientism (the science of observation), and was emblematic of the French philosophical tradition in the human sciences.[56] Brooks has examined the relation between academic philosophy and scientific psychology, demonstrating strong interconnections between the two in the early Third Republic, through figures such as Ribot, Janet, and Durkheim, although the two disciplines began to diverge by 1914.[57] Simply put, the importance of academic philosophy to the human sciences created a philosophical discourse that included empirical psychology. Murad very much embodied this tradition of combining academic philosophy and psychology, and in the Egyptian postwar context where the territorial division of the human sciences within the academy had not yet solidified, there was no reason to keep the two fields separate.[58] In fact, Murad had founded the Association of Philosophy Graduates in 1947 with himself as president and devoted a substantial part of *Majallat 'Ilm al-Nafs* to publishing philosophical works.

The Epistemology of Psychoanalysis and the Analytic Structure

The disciplinary divide between psychology and philosophy was not as pronounced in postwar Egypt as it was elsewhere, and epistemological questions in the production of psychological knowledge were of great importance to the founding figures of psychology. In fact, Yusuf Murad directly addressed the question of psychoanalytic epistemology in a series of articles, dividing knowledge between deduction or analogical reasoning (*istinbat*) and conjecture or intuition (*hads*). Characterizing psychology as a branch of metaphysics concerned with the question of the human psyche, he posited intuition as a direct window into the substance of the soul (*nafs*).[59]

Murad outlined three possible modalities for conceptualizing psychological inquiry and, by extension, the structure of analytic experience: introspection, positivism, and phenomenology, each of which emerged dialectically from the critique of the other. Overviewing introspection, or what he termed "psychology in the first person," he noted that its status as a means for direct knowledge of the self had been critiqued by Comte and led to the emergence of positivist or experimental psychology ("psychology in the third person") in the forms of behaviorism and *Gestalttheorie*, most prominently.[60] Murad argued that the positivist perspective remained unable to grasp human complexity, viewing selfhood as an object among other material objects.[61] It could not capture being or thinking, and above all it elided the relationship between the self and the other (or the self and the we), and the way that man knows himself through the other. This critique of positivism led to "psychology in the second person," or phenomenology and existential psychology.[62] Arguing that, ultimately, phenomenology could not overcome the difficulties faced by introspection and empiricism in psychological inquiry, he noted the need for a deeper and more comprehensive and explanatory view. Such a view was to be found in psychoanalysis, which entailed the perspective of the observer, the speaker, and the one spoken to. It was a journey that began with Freud and Breuer in 1895 and that entailed the analyst and analysand, the intersubjective discourse of the unconscious of both, and their conflicts within the self.[63] Or, as Lacan noted, in the analytic situation "there are two of us—and not only two."[64] Lacan argued that the interanalytic situation was best understood as triadic, or a three-term relation (if speech were understood as a central feature). Murad's use of the grammatical first-, second-, and third-person constructions underscores this linguistic component so central to analytic discourse.[65]

Murad considered the position of psychoanalysis with respect to the three major forms of psychological inquiry: positivist, phenomenological, and introspective.[66] Murad's aim was nothing short of demonstrating the way in which psychoanalysis had provided a synthesis of the three epistemologies, and so demonstrated its unification (*tawhid*) of psychology itself.[67] Murad outlined this synthesis by approaching the development of psychoanalysis genealogically, showing how it emerged and transformed itself over time, dialectically working though each of these distinct methods. Murad's portrait of Freudianism emphasized its initial emergence out of a materialist and positivist framework of physiology, laboratory work, and neurology. He emphasized Freud's enduring interest in the reciprocal causality of biological and psychological factors, his insights from anatomy and philosophy, leading to his view of man as a total unity (*al-insan ka wahda kamila*). This exposition was levied at those who accused psychoanalysis of being drawn from the "fabric of dreams" (*nasij al-khayal*). Above all, he emphasized how psychoanalysis began as an experimental treatment for psychopathological phenomenon, before becoming a general theory of psychic phenomena and personality.[68]

Freud's "Copernican revolution," however, lay in the discovery of the unconscious, of that which is not available to consciousness (*ghayr mashu'ur*).[69] Through his research into abnormal phenomena, whether of abnormal individuals or abnormal or subnormal activity in normal individuals (such as dreams, forgetting, slips of the tongue), the unconscious could be accessed. According to Murad, the *Interpretation of Dreams* was Freud's most important work, and it demonstrated the workings of the unconscious and all of the major defense mechanisms. It represented his abandonment of hypnotherapy for free association, dream interpretation, and a more dynamic conception of the unconscious. Further, Freud originally conceptualized the unconscious as dominated by two drives: sexual and self-preservative. Later, after World War I the exigencies of life and death led Freud to shift his emphasis from sexual factors to an emphasis on social antagonisms and aggression. Murad posited the psychoanalytic study of the formation of personality as a dynamic and comprehensive view that integrated three trends: biological, civilizational, and psychological.[70]

It was, however, in the analytic experience itself that the shortcomings of other methods and the advantages of psychoanalysis became clear. Introspection, Murad noted, was required for the recollection of memories and the description of feelings. The use of language by the analysand would not only exceed description passing into interpretation by necessity, but it would also be insufficient. The individual's knowledge of himself would be influenced by various unconscious factors, most notably the presence of the other within the unconscious, leading to a variety of defense mechanisms. In sum, introspection, or self-analysis, was impossible in practice.[71] Murad went further, by drawing on his own clinical experience. Introspection, he pointed out, most often became an impediment to analysis, which needed to rely on a less willful, more free-flowing discourse characterized by less organization, preparation, and critique. The analyst must lessen the justificatory introspection of the analysand. He noted the difficulty in his own practice of moving patients away from an enumerative litany of negative experiences stored in memory toward experiencing them in the clinical situation, which would function as a proxy for childhood experience.[72]

Turning to phenomenology, which at first glance appeared to be closest to the psychoanalytic school, Murad asked to what extent could the analyst apply self-knowledge to his patient? Stated differently, to what degree was there an identification between the analyst and the analysand, given the fact that the distinctiveness of psychology itself rested on the similarity between the observer and observed. Identification, however, could not signify a unity of the two persons, which would lead to a loss of all therapeutic value. Simply put, it is not possible to say in the session, "I am you, and you are me."[73] In fact, the question of identification led Murad directly into a discussion of transference, or the unconscious redirection of affects toward the analyst. The analysis of transference would lead to one of the greatest resistances encountered in therapy, which he argued distinguished psychoanalysis from second-person psychology. Transference enabled the transformation from phenomenology to a third-person position, without eliminating the other two approaches. The shift that occurred in the analytic experience from imagined experiences to lived experiences, enabled transference and other experiences that phenomenology could not account for.[74] The analyst, Murad noted, must remember that the patient lies to himself and his analyst from a place that he knows not (*min haythu la-yadri*) even when he tries to be as authentic as possible. As Lacan put it, "at the level of the unconscious the subject lies, and his lying is a way of telling the truth of the matter."[75]

Murad anticipated Paul Ricoeur's juxtaposition between phenomenology and psychoanalysis by over a decade, by arguing that the analytic method was unique in its emphasis on technique and the fact that analytic experience unfolds in the realm of speech.[76] The primacy of technique over interpretation left analysis radically distinct from phenomenology. It was in the *durcharbeiten*, the working through of the analytic situation as an intersubjective technique that encompassed the analytic encounter itself, as well as past dramas as they unfold within it (resistance, transference, repetition), that insight was attained, as well as through the practice of the frustration of transference love.[77] For Murad, the analyst must then embody several roles at once: that of a researcher collecting evidence, contemplating possible interpretations of the collected materials, subjecting them to verification during analysis; that of a screen onto which the analysand projects his experiences, complexes, and problems; and that of a caregiver who represents the reality principle against the pleasure principle, the cause of new deprivations and sustenance.[78] Murad envisioned the analytic situation as one in which the individual's psychic energy could be freed from repetition, enabling a renewed psychic energy, eventually leading to integration. "Thus we see the analyst in the position of the scientist who deals with his patient as an interpretative bloc in the web of a total situation that envelops the patient, his environment, and his analyst in a single instance."[79] In sum, we can see that despite acknowledging the constitutive alienation of the subject, "the ego as other and the unconscious as the Other's discourse," Murad still held out the promise of unity at multiple levels: the unity represented by the synthetic vision of psychoanalysis as well as the unity represented by the possibility of psychosocial integration.[80] Such a conception of unity was, as we have seen, in part derived from the complex metaphysical world of Ibn 'Arabi wherein unity is conceived of as both one and many.

If the previous discussions have seemed, in a certain sense, to be too similar to the letter and spirit of European psychology, it is in the discussion of specific modalities of understanding that Murad exemplifies the points of contact, and the epistemological resonances with earlier pre-analytic traditions. We turn now to a discussion of the significance of insight and intuition in psychological understandings as an epistemological mode that exceeded the limitations of psychoanalysis and other epistemological formations.

Insight and Hermeneutics

Behold, in this are signs for those who, by their insight, do understand.

—QUR'AN 15:75

It is because of this mixture of truth and error, good and evil, that the old art flourished so well, and will continue to reappear under new forms, as long as men's souls are hidden in strange bodies.

—GEORGE SARTON

Yusuf Murad's thesis on Fakhr al-Din al-Razi (d. 1209), an annotated translation of *Kitab al-Firasa* (*The Book of Physiognomy*),[81] was intended to be of interest not only to Orientalists but also to historians of science as part of a larger series of translated Arabic medico-psychological texts.[82] Murad's interest in al-Razi was part of his concern for the recuperation of the Arabic tradition as part and parcel of the history of the human sciences, and was also evident in his translations of psychological terminology in which he consistently chose terms that had resonances in an earlier Arabic literature. Murad's choice of physiognomy as a vehicle for the communication of Arab science to a Western audience may appear a strange one to contemporary sensibilities. Physiognomy, however, enabled him to trace Greek influence and the significance of Arab culture in scientific traditions as well as locate numerous points of convergence between the newer psychological sciences and the medieval Arab scientific art of *firasa*.[83] *Al-firasa* or the science of judging internal meanings from external forms (how to discern the unknown from the known) was transmitted through the pseudo-Aristotelian text the *Secretum Secretorum* or *Kitab Sirr al-Asrar*.[84] The text, widely attributed to Aristotle in the medieval Arab world, although of dubious authenticity, was constructed as an epistolary book of advice to Alexander, a compendium of useful knowledge. Philosophically the text illuminated the strength of the Greek tradition in Arabic. The first printed edition was edited in 1954 by ʿAbd al-Rahman Badawi, a philosopher who was a student of Alexandre Koyré at Fuʾad I University and one of the main transmitters of the existential tradition into Arabic, most notably through Heidegger.[85]

Considered a conjectural science and often disputed—al-Ghazali considered it a natural science while Averroës thought it was closer to the divinatory or occult sciences—physiognomy was so widely practiced in the High Middle Ages that Hanbalis used it juridically to determine culpability, and al-Shafiʿi was reputed to have practiced it.[86] *Sirr al-asrar* asserted the veracity of physiognomy and was transmitted through numerous writers, including the medieval Sufi master Ibn ʿArabi.[87] In its mystical translation by Ibn ʿArabi, *al-firasa* undergoes something of an alchemic transformation, which Murad argued was among the most original and productive forms of thought on physiognomy.[88]

According to Ibn ʿArabi there were two forms of *firasa*: natural *firasa* and divine *firasa*, the latter a divinatory power that God granted to saints and mystics. Mystical *firasa*, sometimes referred to as *al-firasa al-dhawqiyya*, was only given to a few; whereas the physiognomist learned how to judge character or temperament from exterior signs such as physical appearance, the mystic judged spiritual essence.[89] Divine or spiritual insight was like a divine light that illuminated the consciousness of the believer and was therefore infallible; with it one could judge the hearts and souls of men. Al-Qushayri (d. 1072) recounted *al-firasa* or spiritual insight as etymologically related to the prey of a wild animal, and like prey, the human heart cannot oppose the flashes of insight that strike it no matter how hard it tries.[90] In the words of Ibn ʿArabi:

> Know that insight is a light shed by the divine light, with which the faithful find their way to reach salvation. That light also makes visible all that there is to see in the material world. If we could see the real realities, they would become signs and proofs of the existence of the Creator, and teach us divine wisdom.

The natural, inborn, human insight enables us to identify and iso-
late these realities, one by one, while the insight taught by religion sees
all as a whole, because religion has come upon us as a divine order and
mercy from the one and unique God.[91]

Ibn ʿArabi argued that natural insight based on intellectual operations such
as associations, theories, past experience, and logic were "but veils which can
only be lifted by true spiritual insight."[92]

Murad's interest in Ibn ʿArabi was echoed in some of the precepts of *Gestalttheorie*, one of his early and enduring interests. For Murad *Gestalttheorie*
had introduced form and structure into empirical psychology and was nothing short of a study of human spirit that offered the possibility of reconstructing psychic life in its totality and dynamism. Following Koffka, he noted that
if we were to abandon our scientific attitudes and join poets and artists (and
mystics he added), we would strengthen our perception of the world.[93] Drawing the analogy between Sufism and *Gestalttheorie* further, Murad analogized
Gestalttheorie's concept of *einsicht* to *firasa* as sagacity, intuitive intelligence,
and illumination. *Firasa*, consequently, was not a pure act of the intellect but
a combination of feeling, sentiment, and knowledge.[94] For Ibn ʿArabi *firasa*
was the interior light that illuminated the spirit much in the same way that
vision was the organ of perception for the visual world.[95]

This defense of mystical or philosophical intuition as a valid means of
knowing was in many ways analogous to Bergson's attempt to critique neo-
Kantian positivism, and perhaps accounts for his popularity in Arabic writings.[96] Bergson is taken by many to be the consummate philosopher of intuition.[97] And as Guerlac rightly points out, intuition need not be viewed as a
symptom of fuzzy thinking or a mere ruse for mysticism, but rather a vigorous
effort of abstraction.[98] Like the Sufi thinker Abu al-Wafa al-Ghunaymi al-
Taftazani's discussion of Sufi intuition, Bergsonian intuition also relied on the
immediate data of conscious experience, but in a manner that may best be
described as prelinguistic, resisting symbolization absolutely.[99]

In an article on the notion of the unconscious in Bergson, Murad Wahba
discussed the significance of Bergson in terms of his critique of materialism,
and his rethinking of the relationship between spirit and matter.[100] His re-
versal of materialism and his emphasis on vitalism, Wahba argued, was a welcome change from the dominance of materialism, as was his precise use of
language.[101] In particular, it was Bergson's emphasis on the use of intuition to
understand duration, or the struggle to understand the interiority of exterior
signs (*batin al-zawahir*) that was appreciated and that made the philosopher a psychologist by necessity.[102] Providing a detailed discussion and comparison of Bergson's notion of duration with Freud's notion of the unconscious, he analogized duration not to the Freudian unconscious but to the
preconscious.[103] Wahba was not alone in his meditation on the significance of

Bergson to psychoanalytic theory, and there were others who engaged Bergsonian thought, particularly as related to the question of social integration and egocentricity.

The Socius: *Self and Other*

A central topic that emerged in mid-twentieth-century psychological discourse was the question of the relation between self and other, and by extension the *socius*. Egyptian critiques of the egocentricity of Western philosophical notions of the self led authors to expand on notions of the self in the community of the other. For example, Mustafa Ismaʿil Suwayf critiqued Bergson's egocentricity.[104] Suwayf situated Bergson's critique of science and his development of the notion of intuition through an analysis of its sociohistorical context, namely, the loss of faith in science and the identification of science with mechanical conceptions. Overviewing his emphasis on intuition over rational thought and his positing of *élan vital* as the highest principle, Suwayf questioned the psychological bases of social integration in Bergson's thought. He argued that Bergson insisted on egocentricity as man's first and most profound characteristic, namely, that we are first individual egos and acquire social egos later, which are superficial and dictated from without (here referencing Bergson's notion of the two selves, one fundamental and the other a social projection). Suwayf took Bergson to be Jean-Paul Sartre's forerunner in many respects and critiqued his social theory for the elevation of stability to its highest principle, its dichotomous view of relations between the individual and his social environment, its absence of any dialectical conception, and, ultimately, despite its vitalism, its lapse into mechanism.

Tellingly, Egyptian writers preferred thinkers who lauded the collective nature of selfhood, such as the Socialist psychologist Henri Wallon and the Christian existentialist Gabriel Marcel, to those who championed an ontological egocentricity. The research of Henri Wallon (from whom Lacan had derived his idea of the mirror stage), whose writings were widely read and translated in Egypt, is instructive in this regard. Prior to Wallon, work in child psychology had emphasized the primordial constitution of an "I" prior to the child's acknowledgment of the other. The wildly popular work of Jean Piaget was, of course, exemplary in that respect. Wallon, by contrast, contested the view of the child's self-generated autotelic consciousness, arguing instead that self-consciousness itself was the effect of the encounter with the other, whether the mother or the child's own mirror image.[105]

In his foundational text, "The Role of the Other in the Consciousness of the Self," which was foregrounded in the October 1946 issue of *Majallat ʿIlm al-Nafs*, Wallon stated, "there is no more widely held assumption in psychology than the notion that the subject must become conscious of his own ego before being able to imagine that of the other person."[106] Critiquing Piaget's widely held view that the child's consciousness passes from autism to egocentrism, Wallon posited the shaping of the child's individual consciousness by the collective milieu, pointing to Freud's own view of consciousness as delimited by species-being.[107]

> The ego as it seeks to particularize itself, cannot avoid treating society as opposed to it in the shape of a primitive and larval *socius*—to use Pierre Janet's term. The individual, when he apprehends himself as such, is social in his essence. He is social not as a result of external contingencies, but by virtue of an internal necessity, by virtue of his *genesis*. The *socius*, or *other*, is the ego's constant partner in mental life.... The relations between the ego and its indispensable complement—the internal other (*autre intime*) [*al-akhir al-khafi*]—can thus be used to explain or identify basic states or complexes of consciousness ranging from the normal to the pathological. In this way the normal development of a personal consciousness in the child can be seen in its connections with the entire range of attitudes making the human being in his innermost essence a *social* being.[108]

The dialectic of self and other resembled the Hegelian dialectic but emphasized non-antagonistic reciprocity rather than the dialectic of mastery and submission.[109] In a similar vein, numerous authors in *Majallat 'Ilm al-Nafs* approached the question of self-consciousness as a problem of self and other.

Zakariyya Ibrahim Buqtur, discussing the problem of consciousness, argued that Descartes and other philosophers had incorrectly elevated self-consciousness to a primary state. In fact, social life, he argued, facilitated self-consciousness. We experience *ourselves in the mirror of others*. Hence, he noted, self-consciousness was belated in psychological life, and cogito was not a primary state.[110] Above all, however, it was in his engagement with Sartre that Buqtur departed most decisively from the idea of egocentricity as a primary and natural state of man.[111] Focusing on the gaze, he argued that it embodied "being for the other." Recapitulating, in essence, Wallon's argument, he noted that for children and parents the gaze establishes the other, or more precisely existence for others, *wujud li-l-akhirin*. Or stated differently one cannot have being for self (*wujud li-l-dhat*) without being for the other (*wujud li-l-ghayr*).

Viewing the gaze as a sociopsychological phenomenon, much like language, Buqtur contested Sartre's notion of the gaze. According to Sartre's exposition in *Being and Nothingness*, it is through the gaze of the other that one can confirm his external existence as an object, while the other is free to pass judgment upon him—I am then the object of the other's freedom, which is not my freedom; this objectification in turn robs us of our freedom as a subject. "It is in this sense that we can consider ourselves as 'slaves' in so far as we appear to the Other."[112] Buqtur critiqued, in particular, Sartre's generalization of shame (which he translated as *khajal*) as a medium through which the self is created as an object. He argued, instead, for a more contextually specific argument in which the other shapes us even when not present, in other words as possible presence. In particular, he noted that the gaze of the other does not in all cases reduce one to the status of an object, as for example in the case of love, a sentiment that, he observed, presented extreme analytic difficulty for Sartre. Sartre must reduce love to its most instrumental manifestation (love as seduction) in order to make the case for a relationship of a self to an object, rather than a relationship between two selves. For Buqtur, "the gaze," in other words, "signals the deepest sign of humanity."[113]

The gaze, of course, has numerous intellectual genealogies, of which Sufism provides perhaps one of the most sophisticated and elaborated conceptions. Within Sufism, the differential economy of the gaze exists within an alternative understanding of relations between the lover and the beloved.[114] Analogous to Ibn 'Arabi's distinction between the two types of *firasa*, is the Sufi distinction between *basar* and *basira*, or mere eyesight and spiritual insight. Within this latter economy of the gaze, the beloved's form may be imprinted on the very existence of the lover, "that image of the beloved which resides in the innermost recesses of the secret heart."[115] What, indeed, could be further from the Sartrean conception of the gaze as the objectification of the other, from his absolute refusal, in the words of Martin Jay, "to posit a redemptive notion of the visual"?[116]

Conclusion

Majallat 'Ilm al-Nafs and the debates contained within it represented, in part, the attempt to develop an integrative science of the self and psyche. According to leading literary critic Mahmud Amin al-'Alim, Yusuf Murad influenced a generation of thinkers in philosophy, literature, and psychology through his integrative curriculum, which sought nothing less than the exploration of "the secrets of the human soul." Rather than a view of individuals as atomistic units, monocausally determined by biological, sociological, or psychic factors, Murad envisioned the *nafs* as an assemblage of overdetermined factors that functioned, ideally, within a unified totality whose boundaries were porous both to the outside world and to the discourse of the other. This porousness of the self to the other was embodied in the coproduction of psychological knowledge across European and Arab knowledge formations, sutured through quilting points drawn largely from pre-psychoanalytic discursive formations. Thus may we better understand Murad's epistemological pluralism; his predilection for the dynamism of psychoanalysis, the holism of *Gestalttheorie*, and the eclectic spiritualism of Janet and Cousin, echoed in the philosophy of Ibn 'Arabi, all of which lent itself to his reading of personhood best conceived of as a multiplicity in unity.

Above all, for Murad, the psyche was forged in the vortices of the social body. Devoting considerable attention to the *socius*, the social element introjected into the self since childhood in an unconscious fashion, he espoused a view of community without subjection or domination in his integrative conception of selfhood. In his own writings, Murad's pastoral optimism was geared toward the achievement of psychic integration. Yet perhaps somewhat surprisingly, it would also provide a structure for the integration of psychology into the governance of everyday life and labor. The young Free Officers who led Egypt's 1952 revolution readily absorbed Murad's integrative psychological theory. Murad had presented a series of lectures to the Higher Military Academy beginning in December 1946 on topics such as the importance of applied psychology and the use of psychological testing in the selection of army officers and pilots. So inspired were the young officers that they enlisted his services immediately following the revolution, in August and September of 1952, in order to introduce psychological and intelligence testing into the military, and to create psychological clinics alongside medical clinics.[117]

It is easy to understand why the Free Officers might have found Murad's theories appealing, in part due to the "belief that psychological theory could be pressed into the service of sociopolitical engineering."[118] After all, in the aftermath of the 1952 revolution the regime strongly identified itself with the language of science and rational planning, relying increasingly on the armature of social scientific expertise for the formulation and implementation of its major schemes, such as land reclamation.[119] The themes of psychological unity and harmonious totality were echoed in the revolution's call for national unity in the aftermath of colonization and its desire to create a "happy family of workers and peasants." Murad's integrative framework anticipated the totalizing framework of social welfare that was to become the hallmark of Nasserism, a framework meant to encompass social, political, and psychological factors at one and the same time.[120]

In sum, the Free Officers lifted the language of integration, harnessing the psychic to the cause of building productive, national, and socialist citizens while discarding and disarticulating other elements of Murad's integrative psychology, most notably the revival of hermeneutics and ethics as well as the critique of instrumental rationality, positivism, and progressivism. The translatability between the political programs of the postcolonial state and Murad's psychological theories should give us pause, demonstrating the dangers of a belief in the transparency of human behaviors and motives, which would render psychoanalysis "ethically monstrous."[121] It marks the difference between the possibility of a psychoanalysis that would be "*at the service* of those who suffer, and not an instrument of power or mastery over them."[122]

At the same time, as Ranjana Khanna has noted, the political stakes of decolonization "demanded that subjectivity come to the fore in consolidating a theory and practice of political commitment."[123] The tensions between a postcolonial political program whose singular goal lay in the creation of a decolonized national subject, on the one hand, and the radical critique of the present and of the subject offered by psychoanalysis and philosophy, on the other, would become clearer over the course of the 1950s and 1960s. While Murad would increasingly distance himself both from the regime and from the language of socialist realism, these tensions were embodied in the intellectual trajectory of some of his students. For example, Mahmud Amin al-ʿAlim, as Yoav Di-Capua and others have detailed, would become one of the main literary proponents of existentialism and Sartre's notion of *engagement* (*iltizam*), recast in terms of the committed Marxist intellectual in opposition to colonialism, the postcolonial regime, and the literary old guard.[124]

Al-ʿAlim's generation, the generation of the 1920s, was keen on the ideological politicization of intellectual and cultural programs. The role of the militant intellectual, newly conceived and inspired by intellectual figures such as Sartre and political figures like Che Guevara, both of whom had visited the Middle East, was to radically remake society from within.[125] Yet al-ʿAlim's appropriation and dissemination of the figure of the committed leftist intellectual who stood in an antagonistic relationship to the state, increasingly "came to mirror the authoritarianism and didacticism of the regime's political discourse" and quickly turned into a "critical 'terrorism'" of a Stalinist sort, underscoring the hazards of a Sartrean ontology entailing "a consciousness of the other that can be satisfied only by Hegelian murder."[126]

Mahmud Amin al-ʿAlim's dogmatic take on existentialism as part of an arsenal in the fight against colonialism and the oppressive elements of the postcolonial state was a far cry from the nuanced discussions of Sartre as they appeared just a few years earlier in *Majallat ʿIlm al-Nafs*. Najib Baladi's thoughtful 1949 essay on "Freedom and the Past" analyzed the dense metaphysical and ethical questions posed by Sartrean existentialism, concluding that existentialism took anguish (*angoisse, hasr*, angst, anxiety) as a sign of individual liberty, while simultaneously cutting off the individual from the depth of the past as both a lived reality and historicity; it remained therefore imprisoned as a symptom of the historical moment it purported to analyze.[127] This brief juxtaposition, between an existentialism reduced to political commitment and an existentialism critiqued as part of a dialogue with the other, is meant to underscore the types of tensions that emerged between critical philosophical orientations and pragmatic political concerns once intellectual agendas became tethered to postcolonial political programs.

Born in 1902, Yusuf Murad was intermediately placed between the old guard literati, intellectual luminaries who were proponents of an enlightened liberal literature molded in the image of Europe, and the younger generation of vanguardist radicals, for whom decolonization, existentialism, *engagement*, and socialist realism were the new intellectual currencies. By and large, questions of an epistemological and ethico-philosophical nature predominated in his work and generated a set of concerns that were a far more novel site of engagement than the mere production of national or socialist citizen subjects so prevalent in the postcolonial world. As noted, Murad and other founding figures of psychological and psychoanalytical schools of thought in Egypt engaged in blending key psychoanalytical concepts with central concepts of classical Islamic thought, drawn from Ibn ʿArabi, Avicenna, al-Ghazali, and al-Razi. Thinkers remained preoccupied with metapsychological questions concerning the nature of the soul, the self, the subject, and consciousness, concerns that came prominently to the fore in discussions of the psychology of Sufism, to which we now turn.

CHAPTER TWO

The Self and the Soul

All is essentially in the Breath,
As light is, in essence, in the dark before dawn.

—IBN ʿARABI, *BEZELS OF WISDOM*

Divine Breath

According to Qurʾanic lore the Lord breathed the spirit into Adam and into Mary mother of Jesus, imparting the primordial Breath (*Nafas*) into the dark matter.[1] For the medieval mystical philosopher Ibn ʿArabi, the root *nafasa* "clearly denotes the living reality of God, His living consciousness, which as the active pole inflates, inseminates, irradiates, and informs the dark passivity of primal substance, of original Nature."[2] The *Nafas Rahmani*, or Breath of Divine Compassion, gives rise to an existentiating Cloud, "which the Divine Being exhaled and in which He originally was ... and at the same time *gives* beings their forms."[3] The mystic comes "to know that the very substance of his being is a breath (*spiritus*) of that infinite Compassion."[4] The Arabic term *nafs* (soul, spirit, âme, psyche) is thus imbued with this primordial divinity. Psychology itself is referred to in Arabic as the science of the "*nafs*" (*ʿilm al-nafs*) and is intimately bound up with preexisting meanings, its genealogical reach extending into classical Islamic invocations of the term such as those of Ibn ʿArabi and others.

A well-developed tradition of Islamic thought centers on the *nafs* and its relationship to the body and the spirit. In particular, Sufism provides a complex theory and topography of the human soul that resonates with psychoanalytic thought. As Stefania Pandolfo has argued, "it is in the field of theological argumentation and spiritual practice" that some of the core preoccupations of Islam and the psychoanalytic tradition converge.[5] And yet exploring this convergence would mean moving away from the generalized assumption of "the non-religious, radically atheistic, anti-metaphysical foundations of psychoanalysis."[6] As a result of this, Christian Jambet asserts that "psychoanalysts who have sought to account for the meaning and depth of Islam have had difficulties finding their marks," in large part because "they treat as miscognition something the believer ... holds to be the real par excellence, God, the Unique, whose speech heralds a promise and issues commandments, the essential conditions of salvation."[7]

What might it mean to think through the relationship between psychoanalysis and the Islamic tradition, while respecting the "ontological stakes" of the latter, namely, the belief in divine transcendence and divine discourse?[8] In this chapter I look at Sufism as an especially apt point of entry into the relationship between psychoanalysis and religion. In thinking about the interconnections between Sufism and psychoanalysis, I approach modern Sufism as a "theoretical stance in its own right," one that encompasses an ethico-philosophical orientation and a phenomenological pathway of subjective experience at one and the same time.[9] Reconstructing a historical interlude between Sufism and psychoanalysis in mid-twentieth-century Egypt, I explore how articulations of selfhood were an innovative synthesis of Islamic ethics (the human kingdom as the path toward the divine kingdom) and Western psychoanalytic psychology, that was at once "self-realizing and other-directed."[10] Islamic thinkers in the postwar period emphasized points of contact between Freud's interpretation of dreams and Islamic dream interpretation, as well as between the manifest and latent content of religious knowledge, and they noted that the analyst-analysand relationship and the shaykh-disciple relationship of Sufism were nearly analogous. If Freudian theories of the self had successfully decentered the subject from autonomy, self-mastery, and rational consciousness, Sufism had similarly posited a heteronomous subject and deemphasized man's relation to his own rational faculties.

I provide a detailed reading of a number of intellectuals who expounded Sufi ideas for a broader reading public beginning in the 1940s, such as Abu al-Wafa al-Ghunaymi al-Taftazani, a young shaykh of the al-Ghunaymiyya Khalwatiyya Sufi Order and later a scholar and professor of Islamic philosophy and Sufism at Cairo University, who had received his master's degree in philosophy in 1955 with a thesis on the mystic Ibn 'Ata' Allah al-Sakandari (d. 1309) and a doctorate in 1961 on the Andalusian philosopher Ibn Sab'in (d. 1270).[11] Simultaneously embedded within the Islamic discursive tradition and modern social scientific thought, al-Taftazani published widely on the relationship between psychology and Sufism and situated himself at the intersection of multiple discourses—Sufism, the orthodox Islamic theological tradition, and Freudianism, to name but a few.

Situating figures such as al-Taftazani within the larger intellectual and religious context of mid-twentieth-century Egypt illustrates that we must remain attentive to the ways in which differing discursive traditions and their subjects come into contact, rather than the presumption of hermetically sealed

traditions, Western, Islamic, and otherwise.[12] Thinkers who situated themselves within an Islamic tradition often articulated selfhood as an innovative
synthesis of Islamic ethics and Western psychology.[13] In particular, I explore
the elective affinities between Sufism and certain strands of psychoanalysis in
terms of a dialogical relationship between the self and the Other, as mediated
by the unconscious; a human subject at once heteronomous and autonomous,
constituted by a heterogeneity at the core of the self; a radical theory of self-
knowledge; a preoccupation with eros and love; and, finally, a vast and highly
specialized vocabulary of the self and its topography.[14]

It is important to note that such epistemological resonances between Sufism and psychoanalysis were not related solely to the "infiltration" of Western
ideas into the Middle Eastern world. They were related, as well, to the nature
of psychoanalysis itself. Kenneth Reinhard has argued that "scripture is the
unconscious of psychoanalysis, at once its model of dream interpretation, its
grammar of law and desire, and its treasury of unspeakable words and absurd
commandments."[15] More contentiously, David Bakan has noted that psychoanalysis can be seen as deeply embedded in the Jewish mystical tradition.[16]
While many have argued that psychoanalytic theory and method need not be
reduced to Jewish mystical theology and Talmudic scholarship, the argument
can be made that the relationship was at least partially constitutive.[17] Further, even if Bakan's contentions regarding the interconnected nature of psychoanalytic interpretative techniques and the Jewish mystical tradition (such
as the use of manifest and latent content in textual interpretation) are specu-
lative, such connections were often made by Sufis as well.[18] The ease then
with which analogies between Sufism and psychoanalysis were made in midcentury relates, in part, to this controversial yet arguably central feature of
Freud's thought.

Perhaps more directly, we may note that mysticism has continued to play
a role within analytical theory as a nexus for understanding the relationship
between the self and the Other. We find that Jacques Lacan had referenced
Ibn ʿArabi on a number of occasions, by way of the analysis of the renowned
French Islamic studies scholar Henry Corbin.[19] Lacan's writings on the "good
old God," on the love of God and its relationship to courtly love, and on the
jouissance of mysticism, all attest to his own self-proclaimed alignment with
Ibn ʿArabi's position on symbolic knowledge over the rationalism of Averroës.[20] As Lacan noted, "these mystical ejaculations are neither idle gossip
nor mere verbiage, in fact they are the best thing you can read." [21] Nor, too, is
it incidental to find that Moustapha Safouan, a preeminent member of Lacan's inner circle in Paris, had originally trained with Ibn ʿArabi scholar and
translator Abu al-ʿAlaʾ al-Afifi, whose doctoral thesis elaborated on the medieval mystic's conception of psychology.[22] Here I continue this tradition of staging an encounter between Sufism and psychoanalysis, in the hope that it may
prove to be a mutually transformative experience.

The Topography of the Self

In a 1950 article published in *Majallat 'Ilm al-Nafs* on the "Psychology of Sufism," a young shaykh eagerly presented an account of Sufism to the budding psychologists of the midcentury Arab world. Let us recall his audience, namely, the twentieth-century psychologists, psychoanalysts, psychiatrists, and medical doctors who made up the readership of the Egyptian *Majallat 'Ilm al-Nafs*. The journal itself provided a platform for the hermeneutical, rather than positivist, tradition of the human sciences, and yet few authors had addressed religion directly from the perspective of the practicing and believing subject.

Al-Taftazani's intervention was to bring a discussion of the psychology of Sufism to an audience concerned with the human sciences. In so doing, he was part of a larger lineage of academic inquiry into the philosophical tradition within Sufism, one that had been established in part due to the efforts of Mustafa 'Abd al-Raziq (d. 1947), an Azhari-trained scholar known as the "great master" and "perfect philosopher" who had challenged secular currents and played a formative role in the reintroduction of Islamic philosophy into modern Egyptian intellectual life.[23] 'Abd al-Raziq can be viewed as the intellectual progenitor of modern Egyptian studies of Sufism and its integration into mainstream academic and religious thought, and he was himself the mentor of al-Taftazani's own mentor, Muhammad Mustafa Hilmi.[24]

This intellectual genealogy of teachers and students ('Abd al-Raziq, Hilmi, and al-Taftazani) was part of a wider trend that sought to integrate Sufism within both mainstream orthodox Islam and academic discourses. Such a project was, in part, a response to the trajectory of anti-Sufism in early twentieth-century Egypt.[25] After World War I the Sufi orders had experienced a period of decline, during which they had not responded to reformist critics and in which they lost members to Islamic voluntary organizations such as the Muslim Brotherhood (established in 1928 by Hasan al-Banna).[26] Secular and religious critics alike accused the Sufi orders of promulgating irrational ideas and an atavistic antimodern worldview not suited to the goals of social and intellectual liberation from colonialism, while Islamic reformers accused them of heterodox innovations.[27]

Al-Taftazani began publishing in the heady days of the late 1940s and early 1950s, during a period of intense struggle over the proper place of Islam in the public sphere. From 1935 to 1954 the Sufi orders faced varying degrees of pressure to reform and reorganize from al-Azhar, from the government, and from the Muslim Brotherhood, which had gone so far as to seek the prohibition of the orders in 1953.[28] Egypt's 1952 revolution by the Free Officers brought an unexpected element into the growing confrontation between the Muslim Brothers and the Sufi orders. The government of Gamal Abdel Nasser banned the Brotherhood in 1954, concerned that their organization threatened the hegemony of the new regime. Simultaneously, the Free Officers became actively interested in the Sufi orders as a potential counterbalance to the Brotherhood and a bulwark against more radical political strains of Islam.[29]

Al-Taftazani, operating within this complex political milieu, strove to recuperate Sufism as part of the orthodox tradition, creating what Andreas Christmann terms an "Islamic Sufism" in postcolonial Egypt, one that portrayed Sufism as part and parcel of a universal mystical religious experience, while wresting the subject away from Orientalists and combating secular and radical militant religious ideologies.[30] Al-Taftazani sought to reintegrate controversial figures such as Ibn ʿArabi, Ibn ʿAtaʾ Allah al-Sakandari, and Ibn Sabʿin into the canon of orthodox mysticism (*al-tasawwuf al-sunni*) through psychological theories that excluded their more heterodox formulations as the product of peak or ecstatic experiences for which they were not reasonably responsible.[31]

Likewise his mentor, Muhammad Mustafa Hilmi, a professor of Islamic philosophy and Sufism as well at Cairo University, had published widely on the relationship between orthodoxy and Sufism in order to demonstrate that many orthodox Islamic writers had Sufi backgrounds.[32] As Hilmi noted in his 1945 preface to *Ibn al-Farid and Divine Love*, Islamic mysticism had long been an object of inquiry for Orientalists such as Louis Massignon and Reynold Nicholson, but had been neglected in the Arabophone literature.[33] Hilmi recuperated the significance of the philosophical tradition within Sufism for a local audience. In a favorable review of Hilmi's work titled "Sufism and Psychology," Ibrahim Abu Ghurra praised the text for taking Sufism, gnosis, and affective states seriously by highlighting their proximity to contemporary psychological theories.[34]

Five years later, in a 1950 article, Abu al-Wafa al-Ghunaymi al-Taftazani outlined a unique Sufi perspective on the architecture of the self, narrating the composition of the self as an interconnected network of self or soul (*nafs*), spirit (*ruh*), heart (*qalb*), and mystery or inner secret (*sirr*).[35] Taken together these components constituted the soul or the human "seat of subjectivity."[36] In many ways analogous to the "topographical aspect" of Freud's model of consciousness and the unconscious as "systems in the mind that are superimposed one upon another," such psychological topographies similarly had little to do with anatomy.[37] Rather than a straightforward concern for "regions in the mental apparatus" however, al-Taftazani's topography concerned the very nature of man's soul, that which enables a being to "bear what is intolerable in this world."[38]

Sufi notions of the self are comprised of multiple forces, varying in number depending on the thinker.[39] Within al-Taftazani's fourfold typology, the *nafs* (soul, self, or psyche) is perhaps the most complex to grasp. In premodern ontologies, the term could be used to refer to "the subject of multiple desires,

the seat of true freedom, and the essence of the individual person."[40] According to al-Ghazali:

> The term *nafs* has two meanings. The one relates to that entity in man
> in which the power of anger and the power of desire are found. This
> use is the most prevalent among the Ṣūfīs. For them *nafs* means the
> element in man that includes all the blameworthy qualities.... The
> second meaning is [that of] the subtle entity ... that is man's true real-
> ity, soul (*nafs*) and essence.[41]

For al-Taftazani, the *nafs* retained this polysemic meaning, but he emphasized
its reference to the lower self as the seat of the passions and base instincts, in
a manner that was commensurate with the broader Sufi evaluation of the
nafs and complementary to Freudian understandings of the id.[42] Within this
Sufi ontology the *nafs* was a specified evil—representing the locus of base instincts and reprehensible acts.[43] This was in keeping with the "overriding
negative view of *nafs* in Sufi mystical psychology" and pietistic literature.[44]
According to al-Qushayri (d. 1074), "the soul is nothing but darkness; its secret [heart] is its lamp; and the light of this lamp is Godspeed. Whoever is
not accompanied by God's assistance in his secret [heart], lingers in total
darkness."[45] Quoting the thirteenth-century Andalusian mystic Ibn ʿArabi, al-
Taftazani stated, the "*Nafs* is all that which is sick in the servant [of God]."[46]
However, the *nafs* itself was subject to both degradation and elevation, index-
ing a theosophy of light; all humans were connected to a Satanic force located
in the *nafs* that rejected truth, but the relative darkness of the soul could be
illuminated by the divine attributes in an "ascending, luminous, and angelic"
movement.[47]

Al-Taftazani further expounds upon this malleable aspect of the *nafs* in
his treatise on the spiritual cosmology of the Shadhliyya mystic Ibn ʿAtaʾ
Allah al-Sakandari.[48] The *nafs*, although singular in essence, was multiple in
its existential manifestations, mapping onto a bipolarity of the body (darkness) and the spirit or heart (luminosity).[49] As a spiritual essence the *nafs*
was distinct from the body, a Neoplatonic presence that existed previously in
another world (ʿalam al-amr, the world of Divine command) outside of time
and matter.[50] Yet in its earthly manifestation it was trapped in the prison
house of the body, a source of evil.[51] The *nafs* thus oscillated between its
bodily and spiritual manifestations, functioning as a *barzakh* or isthmus between spirit and matter. This spectrum of darkness and luminosity expressed
itself in a tripartite conceptualization of the *nafs*, derived from the Qurʾan
and loosely echoed in Aristotle's treatise *On the Soul*.[52] The three modalities
of the *nafs* mentioned in the Qurʾan were *al-nafs al-ammara bi-l-suʾ*, the self
commanding to evil, which leaned toward the body, commanding pleasures,
desires, and vile deeds; *al-nafs al-lawwama*, the rueful or reproachful self,

ambivalently placed between the body and the heart (the seat of the human spirit), and partly lit up by the latter, such that every time darkness overcame it, divine light illuminated it and it reproached itself for its evil desires; and finally, *al-nafs al-mutma'inna*, the tranquil self, continuously illuminated by the heart and freed from the prison house of the body.[53]

Al-Taftazani was careful to emphasize the key similarities and differences between al-Sakandari's system of thought and that of modern psychology. Sufism and modern psychology, he noted, were far from antithetical endeavors but rather oftentimes complementary systems of thought and practice. Al-Taftazani cited work on the psychology of mysticism as evidence that Sufis were not characterized by psychosis but rather by a concern for interiority, introspection, and the *batin*, or the realm of hidden meanings, and the inner reaches of the unconscious.[54] Although both Sufism and modern psychology took self-knowledge as a cornerstone of their philosophy and practice, he noted, for Ibn 'Ata' Allah self-knowledge (*ma'rifat al-nafs*) was understood not as an individualistic self-exploration but rather as part of a path of knowledge leading directly to God, *'irfan*. Ibn 'Ata' Allah, he argued, studied the *nafs* not as an object of research but as an ethical means for attaining moral perfection, while separating the body completely from the *nafs*, features that marked his distance from modern psychology.[55] One could argue, nevertheless, that all Sufis such as al-Sakandari were, in part, psychologists because they mobilized an introspective method (*manhaj al-istibtun*).[56] Further, he continued, they did not engage with the manifest content of the *nafs* but with its latent content—content often marked by sexual desires, a domain referred to by psychoanalysts as the unconscious (*al-la-shu'ur*).[57] The Sufi shaykh, much like the analyst, must ascertain from his novice (*murid*) that which they know not (*la-yashu'urun bihi*).[58]

Within the larger typology of the self, the spirit (*ruh*) was the beginning of life, pure, clean, and free of the negative sovereignty of the *nafs*—it surpassed the understanding of the intellect and, al-Taftazani opined, "you will note that many Sufis do not even speak of it."[59] For many Sufis the soul (*nafs*) represented the ego-affirming self, while the spirit (*ruh*) affirmed the Other (God), but the two could be merged in the heart.[60] According to al-Taftazani the heart (*qalb*) was the location of *ma'rifa*—gnosis or mystical knowledge of God—and was the seat of perception of the divine Reality.[61] *Sirr* (literally, secret or mystery), the final, and perhaps the most esoteric of the faculties, has been variously translated as the "inner secret" of the heart or "divine mystery."[62] Al-Taftazani referenced *sirr* quite simply as that which was safeguarded between the servant and his Lord, citing Ibn 'Arabi's elliptical phrasing, "the secret of the secret is that which the Lord imposes [impresses] upon his servant."[63] The secret represents "the individual's reality as known by God himself."[64] A key to its existence is its specular quality, an aspect that was in fact specific not to Islamic discourses but rather to Sufism. Al-Taftazani states, "if the heart is the seat of knowledge or intuitive knowing; then the *sirr* is the seat of seeing (*mushahada*)."[65] Seeing, rather than knowing through reason, constituted an epistemologically distinct "stage beyond the intellect," a point to which I will return.[66]

Within this psycho-cosmological view of the self, al-Taftazani sought to emphasize that which rational argumentation and modern science could not provide—true knowledge of God and of man's soul.[67] As Lacan once remarked, "I fail to see why the fact of having a soul should be a scandal for thought—were it true," and one might add for psychoanalytic thought in particular.[68] The Sufi model of the self explicitly provides insights into the "invisible dimension of human being," a realm of being between God and man, and accordingly "into the Muslim understanding of human consciousness," resonating with psychoanalytic models and at the same time provincializing them.[69]

A Phenomenology of Mysticism

Al-Taftazani's discussion of the Sufi typology of the self and the various levels of consciousness was far from merely theoretical; it embodied both a *modus loquendi* and a *modus agendi*, "a *space* and an *apparatus*."[70] "Unseen realities were defined" in order to "be experienced as distinct levels of consciousness by the traveler on the path to God."[71] As Ibn ʿArabi notes, "Sufism is the path leading to the most beautiful of secrets, leading to the conversion and transformation of your state."[72] The delineation of a subjective pathway enabled Sufi travelers to imagine their own psychic and spiritual journey within the "ocean of the soul" (*bahr al-nafs*).[73] Despite the esoteric nature of these faculties, al-Taftazani encoded them within a series of stages. As a result he argued that a Sufi might move beyond his *nafs*, removing all base instincts and allowing his heart to be filled with faith and righteousness, then he could shift to the spirit, and finally once his spirit was able to see, he moved on to the *sirr*.[74] This transformation of the self is best conceptualized not as a sequential progression but as a process of harmonization.[75] This virtually alchemic transformation of properties, from the blameworthy to the serene, known as *tabdil al-akhlaq* (the exchange of virtues), was thought to take place in this world through the transformation of inner subjective life.[76]

Al-Taftazani argued that the psychological states associated with mysticism were common across all religions. Although religions differed in their philosophical or moral outlooks, he noted, they were similar from a psychological perspective.[77] This assumption of a unified psychology for mankind was tempered, however, by his emphasis on the particularity of Sufi affective states. It is in his discussion of the various affective and psychic states induced by Sufism that the analogies between mystical experience and the language of modern psychoanalysis become clearest.

Psychic or affective states (*al-halat al-wijdaniyya al-khassa*), such as the annihilation of the self or mystical union with God, constituted the psychological core of mystical experience.[78] *Hal* (sing., *ahwal* pl.), meaning state, refers to a "transitory affective condition experienced from time to time, regarded as a special grace from God."[79] Al-Taftazani carefully pointed out that such states could not be solely subject to empirical psychological interpretation or scientific experimentation. Such objective methodologies had to be combined with knowledge of the intuitive sciences and a wide range of human sciences: theology, linguistics, comparative literature, history, and philosophy.[80] Such a broad-based hermeneutical approach, we might note, was compatible with the capacious intellectual reach encouraged by psychoanalytic thought within both the Freudian and Lacanian traditions.

The first psychic state discussed by al-Taftazani was what he termed a psychological tendency toward Sufism. In a fascinating discussion that mobilized the examples of al-Ghazali and Saint Augustine, he defined tendencies toward Sufism largely in terms of existential crises and affective states such as doubt, anxiety, depression, deep sadness, fear of the unknown, and a desire to know the truth of existence.[81] This analysis was rendered in modern psychological theory to the extent that al-Taftazani noted that psychological traumas might often be the reason behind such a tendency toward Sufism.[82] Such a stage began with physical and psychological weakness and psychological anxiety and ended, ideally, with a calmness of the self and soul (*nafs*).[83]

The next state was that of the "Sufi affect and its construction," which occurred once the Sufi knew the annihilation (*fana'*) of the world and was a prelude to the Sufi path of love.[84] Only then would the Sufi come to know the good, truth, and beauty and accept worship as a craving and longing for God. Love was the principle affective state upon which all the others were built—it was the highest-order affect. Or, one might wonder, "if the soul be not love's effect."[85] According to al-Taftazani, it was the pillar of Muslim and Christian mysticism alike. As such, renunciation of the world and spiritual exercises were a means toward that end, as were the settings in which they took place—monasteries and Sufi lodges. Sufi love focused on the goal of reaching God and perceiving the truth of existence.

In order to reach God, however, various stations had to be attained. *Maqam* (sing., *maqamat* pl.) referred to the "level one had achieved in one's training and personal growth: patience, for instance, or faith or certainty."[86] Muhammad Mustafa Hilmi noted how the soul passed through several successive stages in order to reach enlightenment, and through which it was possible to understand the psychic life of the mystic.[87] According to al-Qushayri the stations proceeded from knowledge to certainty, to confirmation, to sincerity, to direct witnessing, and then full obedience; faith was the word that combined all of these.[88] Similarly, al-Taftazani referenced repentance, asceticism, patience, thankfulness, love, and gnosis as stations (*maqamat*), while joy, sadness, and simplicity were deemed affective states (*ahwal*).[89]

The end goal of such stages and levels was the love of God, which as we know, "has held a certain place" within philosophy, "a fact of great import which, if only indirectly, psychoanalytic discourse cannot afford to ignore."[90] Citing 'Abd al-Karim al-Jili's exposition of Ibn 'Arabi in *al-Insan al-Kamil* (*The Perfect Human Being*), al-Taftazani outlines the phases of love within Sufism.[91] The Sufi will first see the name, and then the description, and then the essence (*dhat*) of God. This love will vary in its intensity and its mode of expression, but in the final stage, when the lover sees the Beloved, there will no longer be any difference between the lover and the Beloved. Al-Taftazani was conveying what Michael Sells terms the dialectic of love in Sufism, historically articulated as an affective experience of God that expresses the infinity of desire as eros.[92] Such a mystical union of lover and Beloved had "the power to manifest the 'angelic function of beings.' "[93]

The love of God as a particular form of *jouissance*, "which goes beyond," is heavily theorized within the psychoanalytic tradition.[94] As Lacan notes, "the first being of which we are aware is our own being, and everything which is for our own good will, by dint of that fact, be *jouissance* of the supreme Being, that is, of God. In short, in loving God it is ourselves we love, and by first loving ourselves ... we render to God the appropriate homage."[95] This is deeply resonant with the *hadith* oft-quoted by Ibn 'Arabi, "He who knows himself [his *nafs* or his soul] knows his Lord," and refers neither to an impersonal self nor to an impersonal, self-subsisting Lord.[96] Rather, to quote Corbin, a mystic knows oneself in order to know one's God, because "his 'soul' (*nafs*), is the reality of the Real Being, manifesting himself in this form—such a man knows his Lord."[97] The relationship between I and Thou is what Corbin terms a "syzygic unity."[98] Likewise Ibn 'Arabi relates, "When you have entered into my Paradise, you have entered into yourself (into your 'soul,' *nafs*) and you know yourself with another knowledge."[99] One could easily see this, as did Freud, as a mythological and religious view of the world in which "*nothing but psychology* [is] *projected into the external world*."[100] Yet Sufism has a highly complex view of the relationship between God and the internal and external relationship of his vassal to the world. Whereas within the theophanic imagination "the work of prophetic inspiration is a projection of the inner soul upon the outside world," it is not a projection of the inner workings of the unconscious mind.[101] Rather, the individual form of the soul is itself imprinted with the divine attributes, which it must discover and apprehend.[102] This is the secret of the secret, the correspondence between the two selves, that of the divine Lord and his *fedele* (devotee), as manifested in the very self of his vassal.[103]

Al-Taftazani elaborated further by noting that this syzygic unity of love entailed a final level or station, which Sufis referred to as the annihilation of the self (*fana'*).[104] Such an annihilation had to do with the individual's lack of a sense of self (*al-ana*, "I," "ego"), an existential state of "lack of consciousness of an individual of himself or of any of his needs."[105] According to Corbin, the term *fana'* (annihilation) was "a cipher" or symbol that evoked the "passing away of the forms that appear from instant to instant and their perpetuation (*baqā'*) in the one substance that is pluralized in its epiphanies."[106] The mystic's experience of God as a sublime excess, first as annihilation and then as remainder or residue, is best characterized as *jouissance*, an ecstatic surplus at the heart of the mystical experience, something more, something "which goes beyond."[107]

Self-Struggle (Jihad al-Nafs)

The attainment of psychic states on the path to the Divine, however, could not be accomplished unguided.[108] Such states and stations required a particular path, a *tariqa*. The term refers both to the path tread by Sufis as well as the orders to which Sufis belong. Such a path could not be traveled alone but required a "knowing guide to aid the way."[109] Muhammad Mustafa Hilmi described Sufism as situated between two poles: *askesis* and taste (*al-riyada wa-l-dhawq*); these two aspects, practical exercises and drills, on the one hand, and spiritual and intuitive experiences, on the other, were inseparable.[110] Arguing that Sufism had formulated rules for ethical self-attunement (*tahdhib al-nafs*) that were based on self-knowledge, Hilmi presented Sufism as an ethics founded on the psychological analysis of the *nafs*.[111]

The cornerstone of Sufi ethics was the relationship between the shaykh and his disciple. According to al-Taftazani the *murid* (Sufi disciple) must confide all of his personal psychological issues to his shaykh or *murshid* (spiritual master). The nature of the relationship was intimate, entailing instruction in the secrets of the *batin* (the inner hidden meaning of words and things, their latent content). Al-Taftazani went so far as to state that the shaykh was in effect a psychologist, who turned to psychoanalysis in order to know the *nafs* of his initiate, and who diagnosed and healed its illnesses.[112] Once the shaykh knew the psychology of his *murid*, he drew a path for him, often through heterosuggestion, specific in its discipline (*riyada*) and struggle (*mujahada*). Al-Taftazani references al-Ghazali's magisterial *Revival of the Religious Sciences*, in which he states the shaykh must create a unique path for each *murid*, in the same way that a medical doctor must treat each patient individually. He must look into the specificity of his *murid*'s illness. The self-struggle (*al-mujahada al-nafsiyya*) that the *murid* undertakes, emptying himself of impurities of the senses, was the first step on the Sufi path.[113] As Ibn 'Arabi notes, "what is the process of the cleansing of the mirror of the heart? It is an unending battle with one's ego, whose purpose is to distort reality."[114] Thus cleansed, the heart can then reflect, as in a polished mirror, the Divine itself.[115]

Dhikr, or the remembrance of God through rhythmic repetition, was for al-Taftazani a quintessential technique of the self, functioning as "a mirror to the heart revealing its imperfections" and enabling the purification of the self as well as knowledge of God through intimate tasting (*dhawq*).[116] *Dhikr,* as in the thought of his intellectual progenitor Ibn ʿAtaʾ Allah al-Sakandari, was of the tongue, heart, and secret (*sirr*), a means for divine knowledge, opened through the heart. Beyond this, it represented a metaphysical witnessing, a recognition of the one true Being. The wholeness of the universe was realized in one utterance, epistemological, phenomenological, and metaphysical at one and the same time.[117]

Katherine Pratt Ewing refers to the relationship between the shaykh and *murid* as one of attunement, the "subtle meshing of interaction behavior" in which the "experiencing subject [i]s moving among different modalities and an array of desires."[118] Historians of the premodern Sufi orders have been careful to assert that the *murid*'s path along the way not be confused with modern forms of analysis since Freud. For example, Marshall Hodgson argued that the Sufi was "not attempting a general scientific study of personality," and that he was not concerned with the "complex individual personality, but with universal human potentialities in which individual variations were likely to prove a mere hindrance." He continues:

> Nor was the Sufi even concerned with therapy for ill personalities, despite analogies to modern psychotherapy since Freud. Elementary therapy might help a person blocked in his self-exploration by repressive fears, but the moral and emotional discipline of the Sufis was primarily intended to develop normal personalities to abnormal levels. The analysis, then, was intended as an aid to understanding the psychical states of those upon the Way, and also, incidentally, to making sense of the human place in the universe.[119]

Hodgson's analysis is laden with normative judgments regarding the normal and the pathological, equating Sufism with the creation of pathological or abnormal personalities, precisely the interpretation that al-Taftazani and others had sought to combat. On the contrary, Rifaʿat Abou-El-Haj and Sudhir Kakar have discussed the relationship between the mystic and disciple as one of healing, with a potential psychotherapeutic function.[120] Kakar has further noted that it might be productively viewed, following Ferenczi, as an arena for good transference and for the resolution of pathogenic parent-child relationships.[121] In other words, the shaykh may function as part of an alchemic idealizing transference. This perspective is far more in keeping with al-Taftazani's understanding of the transformation of the self within Sufi practice.

Significantly, al-Taftazani couched his entire discussion of *jihad al-nafs* in psychological terminology. He discussed self-struggle as an expression of the inner wish of humans to know their faults—and the treatment of these faults was built on biological and psychological principles. The origin of self-struggle was the repression of the instincts.[122] He further pointed out that his use of the term *repression* was somewhat different from that of Freud's. For Freud, repression was largely unconscious, whereas for Sufis it referred to the willful suppression of unconscious impulses uncovered in introspection. Further, Sufis acknowledged that every biological struggle had psychological antecedents. The Sufi life was about constant struggle, based on the battle between noble and ignoble tendencies. The Sufi aimed to repress, in a conscious manner, tendencies in conflict with the noble moral and spiritual principles that he wished to fulfill. The Sufi's behavior was willful, distinguished by the ability to inhibit instincts through a focusing of attention in a specific place. Al-Taftazani explicitly referred to self-struggle as a form of sublimation, thereby directly engaging the psychoanalytic tradition.[123] Hence, he concluded that Sufis were concerned with the psychological and moral aspects of human behavior, and so guide their disciples toward ethical being. In sum, unconscious desires and thoughts were meant to be analyzed with the shaykh, and the disciple was to forage his unconscious.

Similarly, according to Muhammad Mustafa Hilmi, the mystical shaykh applied the intuitive sciences to the formation of the *nafs*. In sum, he argued that Sufism was simultaneously a spiritual exercise, an inquiry into existence, and a social order, thereby emphasizing the affinity between Sufism and psychology in terms of the exploration of inner affects or emotions (*shu'ur batini*) and the use of what he termed the esoteric program, *al-manhaj al-batini*.[124] The shaykh's direction, education, and knowledge of the human heart and experience allowed him to know the *nafs* of the novice, and their unconscious desires. Mysticism was presented as a form of therapy and catharsis. According to Islamic philosopher 'Abd al-Halim Mahmud, "every Sufi master is a 'psychotherapist,' so to speak."[125] Hilmi concluded with a discussion of the value and experience of the mystic. It was not, he argued, to be viewed as pathological but as an effort at the purification of the *nafs* and the intuition of the truth. Muslim mystics were attached to the study of the human *nafs*—they clarified the secrets of the self, its faculties, illness, and its treatment. They probed its movements, thoughts, desires, passions, and multiple states of consciousness and analyzed the diverse sentiments: absence, presence, love, desire, ecstasy, repentance, anguish. Above all, the science of mysticism was not simply learned and transmitted, but lived, experienced, and intuited.[126]

An understanding of the shaykh-*murid* relation requires that we revisit the concept of the *nafs* from the Sufi perspective. The *nafs* or lower self was viewed as an enemy that must be combated, a process referred to as *jihad al-nafs*, or the greater *jihad*.[127] Sufis targeted the *nafs al-ammara bi-l-su'*, the commanding self that leaned toward the body, commanding pleasures, desires, and vile deeds.[128] Its evil qualities, such as pride, envy, hypocrisy, must

be removed through a battle against the self. The *jihad* of the self was a crucial step for the disciple, since the lower self was a prison house that the Sufi
must escape. Sufi texts often delineated the path of struggle needed to defeat
the commanding self and attain knowledge of God. According to al-Taftazani,
self-struggle contained two major components: bodily (hunger, sleepless-
ness, thirst) and psychological, which aimed for self-correction from an ethical standpoint—to remove envy, pride, malice, and other negative qualities,
by contemplating God's characteristics and attempting to emulate them.[129] It
was the latter form of moral accounting of the self that Sufis considered more
difficult.

Stefania Pandolfo has noted that the concept of *jihad al-nafs* (struggle of
the soul / battlefield of the self) attests to the presence and activity of an ethical subject.[130] It is in keeping with Qur'anic or pietistic cures that see harm
as internal to the self (unlike vernacular cures that see harm as external), and
she compares it to a Freudian intimate enemy (death drive) or Lacanian exti-
macy that it is to be encircled.[131] As such, she notes evil is an ontological challenge and the *nafs* is the space of freedom and radical heterogeneity.[132] If, as
she suggests, *jihad al-nafs* is seen as a complex and unending struggle with
heterogeneity, then the entire concept of *jihad al-nafs* is emphatically not
about the perfectibility of the soul.

Selfhood within the Sufi tradition entailed a highly complex conception of
the self, at once autonomous and heteronomous and simultaneously characterized by unity and division or heterogeneity. The heterogeneity of the self—
its internal division into the lower self and its more luminous counterparts—
mirrored "the unity of the One God *and* of His necessary pluralization in
His manifestations."[133] As Christian Jambet notes, this enables us to think
through "the question of unity not as a misrecognition of primordial fantasy,"
but rather "unity, unicity, unification" are ontological prerequisites "which
we find at every stage of Muslim thought."[134] At the same time, we must conceive of a unity *in potentia* that neither contradicts nor effaces heterogeneity
and alterity. As Julien Maucade asks, "can religion remedy the division of the
subject? There is something in Islam that tends towards this unicity of the
subject and which does not cease to insist, in order to remedy the division of
the subject without ever attaining it."[135] It is precisely this internal alterity or
self-division of the subject, *jihad al-nafs* or self-struggle, as the counterpart
to a divine unity (understood as the discursive underpinning of the Symbolic
order) that resonates with psychoanalytic theories.[136]

Noetic Knowledge and das Ding

Despite such elective affinities between psychoanalysis and the Sufi path, there
remained, of course, heterogeneities of both a theoretical and experiential
nature, for ultimately, the unique and singular purpose of Sufi ontology was

to know God (*al-ma'rifa bi-Llah*).[137] *Ma'rifa* or gnosis was mystic knowledge or an illuminative cognition that "is life in the memory of God" in which the human partakes of the Divine, as in a mirror "when he looks at it, his Lord shines there for him."[138] To attain this goal of knowledge of the Absolute, the Sufi must follow a strict spiritual regimen of bodily and psychological exercises in order to attain the passionate love of God (*'ishq*), and yet such passion was not the intrinsic goal of Sufism itself, but a state that preceded the full perception of God.[139] Knowledge of God, al-Taftazani argued, could be gained through the intuitive sciences (*al-'ulum al-laduniyya*). The term *laduni*, which refers "to knowledge imparted directly by God through mystic intuition," is perhaps best translated as noetic.[140] These sciences enabled individuals "through exploration and the sharpening of their perception to directly know God and his characteristics, the secrets of being, and the hidden meaning of the *shari'a*."[141]

The "hidden meaning" al-Taftazani references relates to the Sufi interpretation of Qur'anic discourse—one related to the outer shell of language (its literal meaning or apparent form, *zahir*) and one related to the inner hidden meaning of words (*batin*).[142] Sufis were characterized precisely by this concern for the *batin*, or the realm of hidden spiritual meanings.[143] This was part of a larger distinction between exoteric and esoteric knowledge (*'ilm al-zahir* and *'ilm al-batin* or *'ilm al-haqiqa*).[144] Exoteric knowledge related to the forms of knowledge and practice laid down in the *shari'a* and was encapsulated in worship. The type of knowledge that it required, according to al-Taftazani, was *'aql* and *hiss*, or rational knowledge and sensate data. Esoteric knowledge, however, related to the heart and was encapsulated in the idea of witness.[145]

Al-Taftazani put forth esoteric knowledge (*'ilm al-batin*) as an advanced epistemological form, citing in particular the medieval mystic Ibn 'Arabi.[146] *Ma'rifa*, or gnosis, thus moved from the exoteric to the esoteric—from the description to the essence of God.[147] Such a juxtaposition between the exoteric and esoteric meaning of words and things was a key cornerstone of Sufism embodied in the process of esoteric hermeneutics. Symbolic understanding or esoteric hermeneutics "is the only means of signifying what is to be signified."[148] Signification itself is based on the play of difference between the manifest and the latent content. Similarly, within Sufism, Henry Corbin reminds us, the "symbol announces a plane of consciousness distinct from that of rational evidence; it is the "cipher" of a mystery" that "cannot be apprehended in any other way."[149] What is made manifest in the mystical encounter with the unconscious is "the inner, hidden, meaning of a prophetic revelation."[150]

And yet knowledge of God was not simply hermeneutical but rather entailed the direct experiences of *kashf* and *dhawq* or unveiling and taste.[151] According to al-Taftazani, Sufis distinguished between knowledge gained through deduction and sense data (*connaissance discursive*) and knowledge gained through intuition (*connaissance intuitive*). While al-Taftazani did not denigrate *connaissance discursive*, he asked those who berated Sufism to move toward the world of the soul in order to explore what lay behind and beyond the sensate world. Al-Taftazani distinguished between multiple types of intuition: direct rational perception (*idrak ʿaqli mubashir*), such as Descartes's *res cogitans* ("I think therefore I am") and direct *affective* perception (*idrak wijdani mubashir*) or gnosis, which was found among Sufis. Although both types of knowledge required intuition, Cartesian knowledge was intellectual and intuitive, yet deductive, whereas Sufi intuition was the result of examination and *vision*, a direct result of the psychological struggles and the passionate states that the Sufi inhabited.[152]

Illumination, epiphany, or mystical intuition, *kashf* referred to "the lifting or tearing of the veil (which comes between man and the extraphenomenal world)."[153] *Kashf*, according to al-Ghazali, was the light God placed in your heart.[154] In al-Taftazani's formulation, *kashf* enabled one to enter "into the light of certainty from the darkness of doubt."[155] Such an unveiling or *intuition mystique* was analogous to Spinoza's notion of *connaissance adéquate*.[156] Metaphorically, al-Taftazani elaborates, the process is akin to the lifting of the veils such that one's vision of God is, as it were, the vision of the eye.[157] *Kashf* was intimately linked to witnessing (*shuhud*), that is to say, bearing witness to God's majesty.[158] Accordingly, al-Taftazani argued that *ʿaql* or reason, logical demonstrations, as well as sense data were deficient for knowledge of the divine Essence. Rather, what was required was a form of knowledge unique to Sufis, located in the heart (*qalb*)—the organ of intuition, "a secret force or energy," and "the center of mystical physiology" that produces true knowledge.[159] The heart both mirrors and projects God; the "Gnostic's heart is the eye by which God reveals Himself to Himself."[160] As a point of comparison, *darshan* within the Hindu tradition functions as an analogous theophanic state. Sudhir Kakar discusses *darshan* as visions that are like dreams that have found their way into waking life, unconscious visions that are irreducible to language, or in the words of Octavio Paz, as a return to the world before the existence of language.[161]

Within this mystical unveiling, direct affective experience of God was possible, in particular through "seeing" and "intimate tasting."[162] The Sufi concept of *dhawq*, direct personal experience or "intimate taste," deserves special consideration.[163] Al-Taftazani argued that *dhawq* referred to an ecstatic state among Sufis, rather than intuition itself. It was an experience that demonstrated the truth of the intuitive sciences. *Dhawq*, in other words, was a passing ecstatic state, and not an end point in itself, but rather an experience that constituted the only proof of intuitive knowledge—and which could not be expressed to people in ordinary words.[164] Quoting Ibn ʿArabi's discussion of how to deal with an individual who asks for evidence and proof (*dalil wa-burhan*) of the divine secrets that the Sufis speak of, "he said to him in reply—what is the proof of the sweetness of honey? This is knowledge that can only come through *dhawq*."[165] Similarly, al-Taftazani continued, "how can we prove that there are intuitive sciences unless we tread the Sufi path? And therefore, we may say that the intuitive sciences are achieved through *kashf* and the proof of their existence is only through *dhawq*."[166]

Ibn 'Arabi's example of "knowing the sweetness of honey" is illustrative because empirical claims about knowledge (say, the sugar content of honey), do not negate a form of knowledge that can only truly be known through experience. Ibn 'Arabi elaborated in *The Meccan Revelations*:

> The Prophet said, "*There is a knowledge that has the guise of the Hidden* [hay'at al-maknûn]; *none knows it but those who have knowledge of God. When they speak of it, none denies it but those who are deluded about God.*" Such is the situation, yet this is a knowledge that can be spoken about. So what do you think about their knowledge that cannot be spoken about? For not every knowledge can be expressed. These kinds of knowledge [that cannot be expressed] are all sciences of Tastings (*'ulûm al-adhwâq*).[167]

Dhawq encapsulated the possibility of the direct experience of God within the Sufi worldview.[168] Noetic knowledge through mystical intuition (*kashf*) and the experience of intimate tastings (*dhawq*) was thus epistemologically and ethically distinct from psychoanalysis. Within psychoanalysis the mystic mistakes the Symbolic for the Real, or in Freudian terms the "obscure recognition ... of psychical factors and relations in the unconscious is mirrored ... in the construction of a *supernatural reality*, which is destined to be changed back once more by science into the *psychology of the unconscious*."[169]

At the same time, the psychoanalytic tradition acknowledges the opaque core of the subject, something *beyond* the unconscious and *beyond* symbolization, known as *das Ding*—a chasm, an impossible primordial object around which the subject circumambulates, a "traumatic particle of internalized exteriority."[170] As a commentator on Lacan notes, *das Ding* is "a gap always in abeyance (*a béance*) of religious men and mystics."[171] The mystic inhabits this gap in abeyance, in anticipation of the Divine. In being ineluctably drawn to the Divine, he approaches *deus absconditus*, veiled as in the well-known Sufi parable, by seventy thousand veils that separate the world of matter from the world of the One reality. The Sufi path provides an apocalypse of the seventy thousand veils and a mode of knowing that enables a human soldering to the Divine.[172] Unlike psychoanalysis, then, Sufism is a "psycho-cosmology."[173]

Conclusion

In thinking about the work of Abu al-Wafa al-Ghunaymi al-Taftazani I have emphasized the ability of his work to move between and translate across Sufi and psychoanalytic bodies of knowledge. The shifting between psychoanalytic and Sufi registers enabled the knowledge of the *nafs* developed in the science of the soul, *'ilm al-nafs*, to contribute to the knowledge of God, *ma'rifa*. Far from being simply an epistemological question, knowledge of the *nafs* could never really be an abstract epistemological problem, and ethics was a central preoccupation for both psychoanalysis and Sufism. In an important sense then, the self-knowledge of the subject could never be divorced from the ethical dispositions, embodied practices, and sensory capacities of the Sufi traveler. By highlighting the elective affinity between Sufism and psychoanalysis in terms of the relationship between the realms of manifest and latent content (the *zahir* and the *batin*), we see that Sufism, like psychoanalysis, was itself an ethical encounter with the Other mediated by the domain of the unconscious. And yet, rather than relegate the mystical to a simple projection of the unconscious, or a form of *méconnaissance*, we have instead sought to engage mysticism in conversation with psychoanalysis while preserving its ontological and epistemological stakes. The key desideratum for Sufism was *ma'rifa*, or knowledge of God, attained through noetic experiences of the syzygic unity of the lover and his Beloved.

Al-Taftazani marked a melding of premodern and modern, Islamic and psychoanalytic discourses, presenting a human subject at once heteronomous and autonomous and constituted by a radical heterogeneity at the core of the self. In this he did not differ vastly from psychoanalytic ethics insofar as both were removed from the Kantian notion of ethical autonomy embodied in the concept of "conscience," the inner sovereign seat of moral functioning determining the subject's ability to judge "that which is good."[174] In comparison to Kant, Freud's work offered "a more somatically, socially, and historically grounded approach to the formation of rational and ethical capacities."[175] A Lacanian perspective elaborates further on Freudian ethics, salvaging "from the discounted sphere of theology a principle of heteronomy in two senses: it insists both that *the law is other*, not the autonomous distillation of reason apart from revelation, and that *there is something other than the law*, a transgressive enjoyment or *jouissance* in excess of the prohibition that produces it."[176]

In fact, it is instructive to think about the interplay between autonomy and heteronomy within al-Taftazani's view of ethics. Al-Taftazani shared with his medieval predecessor al-Ghazali a view of the self as an obstruction on the path toward the Divine, while at the same time integrating Freudian insights, particularly regarding the sublimation of instincts and passions as emanating from within the subject. Psychological subjecthood was conceptualized in al-Taftazani's model in a way that was compatible with the model of a partially autonomous subject who consciously breaks his own vile will in order to regain his footing on the path toward God.

What is uniquely modern, indeed, mid-twentieth century, about al-Taftazani's discussion was the way in which he psychologized the Sufi subject;

the way in which he situated Sufi epistemology among other epistemologies, albeit privileging the Sufi path as *the* way to attain knowledge of God. Tracking the transformation from premodern orthodox religious discourse on the sources of the self to psychologized notions of the subject is not as straightforward an enterprise as it may seem. It is not about the alleged modern presence or medieval absence of interiority, nor a simple narrative of modernity's claim to individual autonomy in the face of medieval heteronomy. Rather, what one finds in the modern period is a coexistence of autonomy and heteronomy, of the traditional practice of ethical self-attunement (*tahdhib al-nafs*) and the modern science of psychology (*'ilm al-nafs*). For instance, the medieval Sufi notion of *tahdhib al-nafs* or *al-mujahada al-nafsiyya* could be combined with, or more precisely translated into Freud's idea of sublimation, to arrive at the positive consequences of certain forms of repression. Thus the modernist Freudian ethic was not antithetical to Islamic discourse, but in fact complementary to it.

PART II

Spaces of Interiority

CHAPTER THREE

The Psychosexual Subject

Firstly, there is the power of the instinct [gharīza] which lies at the root of one's temperament, together with the length of time for which it has been present: the capacities for desire, anger and pride are [all] present in the human creature; however the most difficult to deal with and the least susceptible to change is that of desire, which is the oldest capacity in man. For it is the first thing to be created in a child, to be followed, perhaps after seven years, by anger, and finally, the power of discretion.

—AL-GHAZALI, *ON DISCIPLINING THE SOUL*

Freud does remind us all the time that in order to follow the track of the accumulated experience of tradition, of past generations, linguistic inquiry is the surest vehicle of the transmission of a development which marks psychic reality.

—JACQUES LACAN, *ETHICS OF PSYCHOANALYSIS*

ABU-HAMID AL-GHAZALI'S *On Disciplining the Soul*, from his medieval magnum opus *The Revival of the Religious Sciences*, arguably one of the most widely read religious texts in the Muslim world until this day, introduces the category of instinct in the context of a discussion of good and bad character and the susceptibility of character traits to change through discipline.[1] Intriguingly, al-Ghazali's use of the term instinct (*gharīza*) was reworked in twentieth-century discussions of the psychosexual subject in relation to Freudian theories of infantile sexuality. Within the pages of *Majallat 'Ilm al-Nafs*, and in a variety of psychological texts on gender and sexuality written for a lay audience, connections were made between the premodern religious and ethical sciences and the modern psychoanalytic study of sexuality. Both psychoanalysis and the premodern discourses on sexuality, one might argue, centered on the question of desire.

Dror Ze'evi has argued that premodern Ottoman texts on sexuality emphasized sexual pleasure and desire within a Rabelaisian discourse that was devoid of the rigid sexual norms and sanctimonious nature of public sexual discourses of the last few decades.[2] And yet "as the nineteenth century progressed, the Ottoman Middle East seemed to shirk almost all prevalent forms of text-based sexual discourse and to retreat into embarrassed silence."[3] Further, by "the beginning of the twentieth century the transformation was complete. A veil of silence had descended on sex in Middle Eastern culture."[4] Ze'evi maintains that contrary to the West, where, as Foucault argues, an entire set of discursive practices hailed sex "as a unique signifier and as a universal signified," no such new set of discourses replaced the old in the Ottoman Middle East, at least until the nation-state culture of the 1940s.[5] Liat Kozma contests this interpretation, noting that such discourses were not replaced by silence, "Rather a scientific medical discourse seeking to regulate sexual contacts and pleasure according to new domestic bourgeois and bureaucratic modes replaced the earlier discussion of pleasure and desire described by Ze'evi and others."[6]

And yet the emphasis on pleasure and desire was never fully displaced in the twentieth century, whether by silence or by scientific sexology and medical discourses. Tracing the invention of the psychosexual subject in postwar Egypt, I argue that in sharp contrast to the alleged incommensurability between psychoanalysis and Islam, postwar psychoanalysis was able to breathe new life into an earlier premodern classical literature centered on desire and the appetites and on the ethical cultivation of the child. Psychoanalysis as a theory of pleasure and desire thus functioned as a supplement to Islamic discourse. The invention of the psychosexual subject, in other words, did not necessarily entail a shift of pleasure and desire away from the theological pastoral toward secular science and medicine as Michel Foucault and others have asserted.[7]

Following a set of discussions on Freudian theory and sexuality in the Egyptian *Majallat 'Ilm al-Nafs*, as well as a series of popular and didactic books, I make several further interconnected arguments. First, I argue that the postwar science of sex shifted toward psychoanalysis and psychology away from earlier discourses prevalent from the fin-de-siècle through the 1920s and 1930s that had focused on biomedicine. Such discourses remained adjacent to, yet analytically distinct from, biomedical and psychiatric nosology. Second, the postwar period was marked by the increased problematization of the gendered body, whether of the female body and psyche, or the improperly gendered male body.[8] As Carolyn Dean asserts in the French context, "female deviance came to symbolize a crisis of male authority which began in the late nineteenth century" and intensified, in the Egyptian context, in the postwar period.[9] Finally, I explore the implications of the neo-psychoanalytic approach to gender taken by Egyptian authors in midcentury, one that diverged in significant ways from Freud and had dramatic implications for understandings of human gendered sexual difference and normative sexuality.

Languages of Desire

In the inaugural issue of *Majallat 'Ilm al-Nafs* and the first installment of the "Dictionary of Psychological Terms," an extensive discussion of the term *ghariza*, rendered in English as instinct, appeared.[10] *Ghariza* has been variously translated in contemporary dictionaries as impulse, urge, drive, and nature.[11] In his midcentury dictionary, editor Yusuf Murad noted that he often returned to classical Arabic texts in order to create new translations for words and clear, precise, and capacious meanings.[12] The term *ghariza* has a long pedigree of usage among premodern figures such as Avicenna and al-Ghazali, where it frequently signified disposition or faculty. Murad informed his audience that the term had too often been used in English with a lack of precision, but that it entailed multiple, and at times distinct or overlapping, meanings. One meaning was the life force (*al-dafi' al-hayawi*) that propelled living creatures to maintain their existence. It could denote a natural instinct or innate tendency that directed the animal to act toward a specific objective or need (for example, to maintain existence, defense, nutrition, or reproduction).

Standing as a supplement to this meaning of *ghariza* was the compound term the instinctual drive (*al-dafi' al-gharizi, al-mil al-gharizi*, or rendered in the original German, *trieb*), defined as the necessary mover or impetus of human activity, entailing instinctual, acquired, and intellectual behaviors, at one and the same time.[13] Murad was drawing out the distinction between instinct and drive for his readers. A distinction that, as Jean Laplanche noted, lay "not between the somatic and the psychical but between, on the one hand, something that is innate, atavistic and endogenous and, on the other hand, something that is acquired and epigenetic but is by no means less anchored in the body for all that."[14]

Murad concluded with a final possible meaning, *ghariza* could be seen as analogous to Avicenna's "estimative faculty" (*al-quwwa al-wahmiyya*), one of a fivefold classification of the internal senses, that which receives the intentions inherent in what is perceived by the common sense.[15] In this manner, Murad continued, one could understand *ghariza* as an innate faculty that negotiated between the world of the internal senses and the external world. Moving on to a slightly later usage than Avicenna, we find that al-Ghazali referred to "the power of the instinct [*ghariza*] which lies at the root of one's temperament," a faculty that included, among others, anger and desire, the latter being "the most difficult to deal with and the least susceptible to change." Crucially, al-Ghazali continues, "What is required is not the total extirpation of these things, but rather the restoration of their balance and moderation which is the middle point between excess and defect."[16] In al-Ghazali, we see *ghariza* as inextricably linked to both desire and childhood. No wonder, then, that Murad, well versed in the Freudian idiom, used the term for instinct and instinctual drive.

Afsaneh Najmabadi has drawn our attention to the significance of charting the linguistic contours of genealogical excavations of sex and gender. Taking the Arabic-Persian word for sex/genus (*jins*), she asks how does *jins* come to mean sex and how does this matter? Exploring *jins* as a trafficking sign, that is, its polysemic usage as an adjectival modifier between male and female, often meaning gender (masculine/feminine), genus (type), and at times sexuality (a modifier of desire), she notes that "an effect of the diffusion of meaning among these many registers is that *jins* is never just sex. Nor can genus be innocent of sex."[17] Likewise, Joseph Massad notes the "hegemonic impact" of Western cultural encroachment on language, with *jins* coming to mean sex at some point in the early twentieth century, carrying with it not only new meanings of biological sex, but also retaining its old meanings of type and kind, among others.[18]

In shuttling between the premodern and the modern, Najmabadi rightly reminds us that "the re-articulation of earlier concepts is already a grafting of new ones."[19] Here, however, rather than emphasize the novelty of concepts, I shift our attention toward the epistemological resonances between older classical concepts and texts—understood as living traditions subject to continuous reinterpretation—and newer usages of terms of reference surrounding sex and gender. Indeed, it was through a semantic expansion of an already existing linguistic mold that a term like *ghariza* retained its polysemic valence, in part through a reinvigoration of the concept of desire by way of a reimagining of the Freudian corpus and a retention of classical concepts.

The Sexual Drive

In a discussion of the mental growth and personality development of the child, Yusuf Murad addressed the significance of infantile sexuality, elaborating for his audience the school of thought initiated by Sigmund Freud and his followers.[20] As previously noted, Murad hailed Freud's discovery of the unconscious as a "Copernican revolution" that brought to bear the central significance of the unconscious, psychic repression, the mechanisms of forgetting, as well as their psychic, affective, and material effects. Despite a predominantly positive evaluation of the Freudian corpus, Murad was nevertheless critical of the overarching significance of the sexual instinct within Freudian metapsychology and of the overvaluation of intrapsychic forces.[21] Like much of object relations theory and relational psychoanalysis, he preferred a focus on the relational nature of early childhood and its concomitant psychic effects.

Murad credited Freud with what Jean Laplanche termed "the enlargement of the sexual" (the "*sexual*") "enlarged beyond the limits of the difference between the sexes and beyond sexual reproduction. It is the sexuality of the component drives, connected to erogenous zones and functioning on the model of *Vorlust*." [22] Further, in his elucidation of the manifestations of infantile and childhood sexuality—oral, anal, and phallic—Murad emphasized the "primal 'enigmatic' inscriptions of the other."[23] That is to say, the concentration of the libido within erotogenic zones was coterminous with the discovery of the "other," who functioned as a source of passion or sexual and affective attachment.[24] This was in keeping with the work of Henri Wallon, whom Murad had translated into Arabic, that asserted "the *socius*, or *other*, is the ego's constant partner in mental life."[25] In the words of Laplanche, "What psychoanalysis teaches us—which seems utterly foreign—is that in man the sexuality of intersubjective origin, that is, drive sexuality, *the sexuality that is acquired, comes before the sexuality that is innate. Drive comes before instinct, fantasy comes before function*; and when the sexual instinct arrives, the seat is already occupied."[26]

More specifically, moving through the phases of infantile sexuality, the child initially does not distinguish between the self and the not self, then distinguishes that which is from the self, but still not self (for example, feces), while directing the sexual drive outward, and finally the crisis of the constitution of the self (*dhat* or *ana*) takes place within an initial framework of narcissism, a crisis that is recapitulated during adolescence.[27] Crucially, the "phases of development of the sexual organization" do not transpire according to a simple progressive evolution. The drive both drifts and derives from the instinct while simultaneously *preceding* the instinct.[28]

The Oedipus complex (*al-'uqda al-udibiyya*) was the phase that received the most attention by Murad as well as in the wider media in postwar Egypt. Readers would have been familiar with the complex both from popularizations of Freud in print media and from the Sophoclean plays; the first scholarly Arabic translation of *Oedipus Rex* had appeared in 1939 by Egyptian belle lettrist Taha Husayn, and two adaptations appeared in 1949 alone, one by Tawfiq al-Hakim and the other by Ali Ahmad Bakathir.[29] Further, readers of Naguib Mahfouz's 1948 *The Mirage* (*al-Sarab*) would have solidified their understanding of the Oedipus complex graphically portrayed in the novel, by immersing themselves in the world of its protagonist, Kamil, pathologically erotically attached and fixated on his possessive mother.[30]

The Oedipus complex was presented by Murad as a bipolar situation—one in which the child maintained dual and ambivalent feelings of love and hatred toward both parents.[31] Taken together, the castration and Oedipus complexes and their resolution or irresolution had implications for gender identity, as well as homosexuality and heterosexuality, and the so-called normal (*sawi*) development of the child.[32] Specifically, Murad focused on the period of sexual latency as having the greatest impact on the development of the psyche and the emotions, the one in which the capacity for love and the desire for the other reach maturation through the romantic attachments of same-sex friendship.[33] Murad argued that it was the absence of such intense same-sex romantic attachments that should be considered abnormal.[34] While Murad's emphasis on same-sex romantic attachments may appear to bolster the distinction Khaled El-Rouayheb draws between passionate infatuation (*'ishq*) and sexual lust in the early Ottoman era, a closer reading demonstrates that attachment and affection need not be separated from the perspective of an enlarged conception of sexuality.[35] I will return later to the question of homosociality, homosexuality, and heterosexuality and the new social type with which those categories were most closely associated, namely, the adolescent (*al-murahiq*).

Read in a cursory or superficial fashion, Murad's analysis may be viewed as merely a sophisticated gloss on Freud's own theories and observations. Examined more carefully, however, with attention to the intertextual elements inside the text, he provides a hybridization of Freudian thought and theory with classical Islamic ethics. Metapsychology, in other words, was inextricably linked to ethics. For instance, referencing the law of recapitulation (*qanun al-i'ada*), or the way in which the concentration of pleasures during childhood recapitulate themselves in adolescence, Murad emphasized the significance of an intervening ethical training.[36] In the interplay between the pleasure principle and the reality principle, *tarbiya* (or the proper upbringing, education, and cultivation of the child), played a central role, a point that I now turn to.

The Spiritual Physick

Our first clue to the significance of ethics and the formation of the ethical subject within Murad's metapsychology is a mention made of the Epicurean *Spiritual Physick* (*al-Tibb al-Ruhani*) by the ninth-century Abu Bakr Muhammad bin Zakariyya al-Razi.[37] Like the *Spiritual Physick*, Murad treated "ethics as a kind of psychic medicine or clinical psychology."[38] Indeed, he would have agreed with Epicurus's statement, "Empty is that philosopher's argument by which no human suffering is therapeutically treated. For just as there is no use in a medical art that does not cast out the sicknesses of bodies, so too there is no use in philosophy, unless it casts out the suffering of the soul."[39] Within al-Razi's framework, the excessive pursuit of the passions to the point of addiction became the equivalent of neurosis and compulsion.[40]

Epicureanism, as is well known, places pleasure, or more properly *ataraxia*, at the forefront of its vision for psychic and ethical well-being. Referring to the careful control of desire, and the casting out of suffering, it warns against the amassing of the appetites and pleasures, or in the words of al-Razi, the excesses of "pleasureless addictions."[41] For al-Razi, "Pleasure consists simply of the restoration of that condition which was expelled by the element of pain, while passing from one's actual state until one returns to the state formerly experienced."[42] Pleasure thus entailed the reduction of unpleasure.[43]

Jonathan Yahalom has argued that "psychoanalysis is situated within the Epicurean tradition, despite Freud's failure to fully recognize it."[44] Mobilizing Derrida's characteristically playful reading of Freud's forgetting of Gassendi (a seventeenth-century scholar well known for reintroducing Epicureanism) as indicative of the erasure of the Epicurean debt within psychoanalysis, Yahalom develops an interpersonal theory of the drive and emphasizes the relationally constituted features of the psyche already present in Freud.[45] I am decidedly less interested in the question of the provenance of Freud's ideas or his unacknowledged debts and cryptamnesia. Rather, what intrigues me is the way in which the Epicurean concern for *ataraxia*, like the Aristotelian concern for human flourishing (*eudaimonia*), as reimagined in classical Islamic texts, is combined with the psychoanalytic emphasis on pleasure and desire, and by extension excess. As Jonathan Lear has noted, the "Freudian approach to the human psyche gives us a new way of inheriting the ancient philosophical legacy," one in which the pleasure principle and the reality principle may be seen as *"essentially ethical in nature."*[46]

While Aristotelian and Epicurean philosophies differ in their views of the relative health of society, the significance of communal attunement, the role of dialectical philosophy, and the depth of their analysis of the passions, both were similar in their emphasis on inner worlds and the need to transform thought and desire, and both evidenced a preoccupation with education, understood along a medical model of ethical inquiry.[47] In his 1943 text, *Shifa' al-Nafs* (Healing the Psyche)—a clear nod to Avicenna's Aristotelian *Book of Healing*—Murad noted that the problem of the self, and in particular the question of engaging the faculty of reason in order to lead a life of balance and engagement, had been a philosophical preoccupation since the time of Socrates.[48] Further, the Greek injunction to know oneself was complicated by the fact that individuals dissemble from a place from which they know not, even when trying to be as authentic as possible.[49]

What, then, were the techniques of the self that best led to *eudaimonia* or *ataraxia*, particularly for those souls who suffered?[50] For Murad, there were three principal means, purification, introspection, and a reintegration of the personality.[51] "Art purifies the passions" (*al-fann yutahir al-shahawat*), Murad commented, paraphrasing Aristotle. Theater and tragedy had the ability to portray the emotions and contradictory passions, leading to identifications and reflections on the self and other through catharsis.[52] "Frank talk" of past emotions, dreams, and repressed desires were, from a Freudian perspective, part of the secret of healing.[53] Introspection was a significant means for the individual to reflect upon the marks of the past; most importantly, it allowed him to separate his fantasy of desire from what he desired in actuality.[54] And finally, the reintegration of personality would help the patient expand his powers of analysis and discernment (*tamyiz*: a faculty Murad placed great emphasis upon and to which I will return), with respect to his motives and desires in relationship to ethics, leading ideally to knowledge of the self and others.[55]

The Epicurean notes in Murad's analysis are clear: the emphasis on the chimerical nature of desire and motivation, confession as a technique of the self, the significance of practical reasoning, and the use of repetition in rehabituation. Yet there was one way in which his analysis was more Aristotelian than Epicurean, namely, the emphasis on education and communal attunement. Murad's use of terms such as *tadbir al-nafs*, *dabt al-nafs* (self-management, self-control, adjustment, rectification), and *tahdhib al-akhlaq* (ethical attunement), were clearly indicative of the importance of repetition, habituation, and the ethical attunement of the self.[56]

Of particular interest is the way in which Freud's theory of psychosexual development was hybridized with ethical attunement. Murad asserted that the superego was the domain of *tarbiya*.[57] In discussing the need to modify the pleasure principle, Murad asserted that the reality principle must enter under the influence of *tarbiya* (upbringing, education) and *tadrib* (training) whether in weaning the infant or in toilet training.[58] Stated differently, between infancy and adolescence lay ethics, or more precisely ethical training. For Abu Hamid al-Ghazali ethics were crucial in the formation of dispositions, good or bad, and the *nafs* (psyche or soul) required constant processes of training and disciplining the soul (known as *riyadat al-nafs* or *tahdhib al-nafs*), and governing the body (*siyasat al-badan*) in order to attain a synchrony of the interiority and exteriority of the self, similar to the Aristotelian notion of entelechy.[59] At the center of this ethical training lay the child.

Murad's use of the term *tarbiya* was very much in keeping with that of al-Ghazali. In his core text *'Ihya 'Ulum al-Din* (*The Revival of the Religious Sciences*), al-Ghazali outlined the proper guidance for children during the early stages of life.[60] Al-Ghazali's discussion is noteworthy in several respects: first, pedagogy was understood as a primarily ethical education—one which created dispositions and so was crucial in the formation of the child's character. Its main purpose was to ensure the salvation of the child's soul, and parental responsibility for the child's education was to be understood as a religious duty. Second, al-Ghazali's conceptualization of the modes of training appropriate for children before the age of discernment (*tamyiz*) was one of *ta'wid* (or roughly habituation), and entailed the disciplining of the body and the cultivation of the senses in order to inculcate the appropriate dispositions toward good deeds; morally upright behavior; religious practice; moderation in the sensory stimulation, instincts, and pleasures of the body (food, drink, sleep); and revulsion toward evil deeds and morally reprehensible actions. The process of *ta'dib* was to be developed by the cultivation of shame and shyness and the elaboration of the faculty of distinction or discernment (*tamyiz*).

Crucially, for al-Ghazali, "the power of lust, should it become excessive, is called gluttony.... If it is deficient, lethargy, dastardliness, and dishonor (come). When it is in balance, it is called temperance; from it come modesty, contentment, patience, tolerance, grace, wit, and approval." Each of these extremes was to be avoided, "but the medium is good and praiseworthy. That medium, between these two extremes, is narrower than a hair. That medium is its Straight Path. It is as narrow as the Bridge of the Hereafter."[61]

Throughout history, Murad opined, doctors and philosophers had demonstrated the inseparability of psychological health from ethical health, as readily demonstrated by the *Spiritual Physick* by al-Razi.[62] A concern for the ethical well-being of the child, then, was crucial to later psychological well-being. Most psychological illness, which could be traced back to early childhood, signaled a lack of integration of the personality and the disintegration of its components. The effects of a negative familial environment and improper *tarbiya*, he discoursed, could lead to disruptions of the self and psychological illnesses.[63] The circumvention of disintegrative selfhood was best accomplished, therefore, through proper *tarbiya*, infused with a philosophical spirit. The cultivation of the sensory and mental abilities of the child through the inculcation of the Delphic injunction to know oneself and the cultivation of a spirit of scientific doubt and critique led to the possibility of integrated selfhood, all within the domain of ethical training.[64]

The Psychology of (the Female) Gender

The question of virtue ethics, understood in a predominantly Aristotelian and Epicurean fashion, permeated Murad's exposition of Freudian notions of infantile and childhood development. For Freud the question of childhood, whether in his discussion of the Oedipus or castration complex, was inextricably linked to the constitution of sex and gender difference. Likewise, in *Sikulujiyyat al-Jins* (The Psychology of Sex-Gender), published in 1954 as part of the popular *Iqra'* (Read) series, Yusuf Murad outlined for a lay audience the gendered male and female as a psychosexual subject whose complex psyche was formed at the intersection of unconscious sexual impulses rooted in childhood and societal norms of Egyptian gender relations.[65] Compared to earlier Arabic writings on sexuality, *Sikulujiyyat al-Jins* was less of a medicalized discourse on sex and gender than a treatise on the *psychological constitution* of sex and gender.[66] *Sikulujiyyat al-Jins* was peppered with case studies and dialogues drawn from students and patients, thereby providing an enlivened psychology for its readers.

The text illustrates quite unequivocally that sex had not vanished from Arabic-language public discourse. Rather, the postwar science of sex shifted away from earlier discourses prevalent from the fin-de-siècle through the 1920s and 1930s that had focused on biomedicine and moved instead toward psychoanalysis and psychology. As Hanan Kholoussy has shown, discussions of sexual practices in 1920s and 1930s Egypt centered on monitoring and medicalizing sexuality to produce the normative heterosexual healthy subject as the foundation of a postcolonial nation free of sociomedical ills.[67] Prolonged bachelorhood, female prostitution, and precocious male sexuality were targeted as social ills.[68] Supplemental to this was the larger literature on sexuality and sexual deviance, which by the late 1920s and 1930s, as Wilson Jacob notes, "had become a regular topic of cultural criticism, marshaling the opinions of doctors, journalists, fiction writers, and significantly, enthusiasts of the physical culture movement. This is demonstrated in a wide array of sources—from newspapers, magazines, and pulp novels to police and court records."[69]

By the late 1940s and 1950s psychological and psychoanalytic discourses emerged to supplement this earlier literature. *Sikulujiyyat al-Jins*'s publication in 1954, and its emphasis on female psychology, was not incidental. It appeared at a particular historical moment, in the aftermath of Egypt's 1952 postcolonial revolution and the transition to state socialism. Laura Bier has chronicled how Nasser's postindependence political and social projects sought to integrate women into new discourses and practices of citizenship while mobilizing them in the service of national development, a project termed state feminism by many scholars.[70] Such processes inevitably led to the increased visibility and participation of women in the public sphere, even as it created new anxieties regarding the proper place of men and women in the public and private domains. The emergence of an Arabic-language psychology of gender and sexual difference, then, must be understood within this broader context.

Addressing the question of the psychology of sex and gender differences for a general audience, *Sikulujiyyat al-Jins* contained sections on gender differences in physical attributes, sensory-motor skills, mental abilities, tendencies and aptitudes, and social acclimation. Murad argued that scientific findings had pointed to the significance of societal factors (beliefs, manners, customs, social mores) and *tarbiya* in the constitution of gender difference, rather than inherited traits.[71] Biology, he quickly pointed out, was neither all-explanatory nor mono-causal, and children fulfilled the image that society projected of them. In sum, society (not to mention the history of masculine civilization) and the practices of *tarbiya* were more influential than biology, even as they responded to biological human difference.[72] Further, the influence of societal mores upon upbringing had fomented the mistrust between the sexes.[73]

Drawing on Freud's later writings on femininity and female sexuality, as well as Karen Horney's writings on feminine psychology, Murad emphasized the psychic rather than biological nature of female sexuality and its relative complexity, noting Freud's delineation of three possible paths for women: the suspension of sexual life, a defiant overemphasis on masculinity, and the development of a so-called normal feminine attitude.[74] The comparatively intricate nature of psychic development among females related to the complexity of their genitalia, as well as their need to transfer their love object from mother to father, and the concomitant difficulties in the resolution of the Oedipus complex and castration anxiety. All of this made psychic equilibrium more difficult to attain for females.[75]

For Murad it was only through proper *tarbiya* that the castration complex, a complex suffered equally by both genders, could be successfully resolved. Here Murad noted the possibility of an emerging masculinity or gender complex, in which the girl child (although occasionally also the boy child) felt deprived of the advantages of the other sex, which threatened to destabilize the child's gender identity and self-perception.[76] According to Karen Horney, "the entire complex of feelings and fantasies that have for their content the woman's feeling of being discriminated against, her envy of the male, her wish to be a man and to discard the female role, we call the *masculinity complex of woman*."[77] Through *tarbiya*, Murad opined, "the child-rearer can stabilize (*yuthabbat*) the boy and the girl in their sex/gender (*jins*) and aid them in discriminating between men and women from the perspective of their roles in the family and society."[78]

At the same time, highly sensitized to what he considered the cultural prejudices of his audience and the transitional historical moment in the Arab world, he noted that the differences between boys and girls were greatly exaggerated by their differential upbringing.[79] The castration complex, he observed, was heightened due to cultural factors and the parental preference for males.[80] In the Arab East boys were exalted above girls, and such early experiences left their mark on women's psyches.[81] For example, preferences, aptitudes, and even degrees of social acclimation were related to *tarbiya*. An exemplary *tarbiya* would accord with lofty humanistic principles of justice and love.[82] For Murad neither the distinction between males and females nor the sexual instinct was to be taken for granted. Neither the instinct for heterosexuality nor too the instinct for motherhood was inborn, both of which he argued also required *tarbiya*.[83]

Murad presented femininity as an excessively fragile, almost unattainable ideal, noting that females traversed adolescence only with extreme difficulty. He argued that even when married, females often lacked awareness of the unconscious perverse sexual impulses of their own adolescent years and their negative attitudes toward the opposite sex—attitudes that could lead to frigidity or hysteria during marriage. He ended with a plea for psychological education for youth to help them combat deviant sexual propensities and attain a harmonious married life. Heterosexuality, in other words, needed to be inculcated through psychological education (*tarbiya*) and analysis. In his view, the Egyptian milieu intensified feminine psychological tendencies, such as the perception of lack in comparison to males, which was only reinforced through differential treatment by parents. Similarly, he argued, as females began to experience heterosexual feelings in adolescence, the societal interdictions against male-female interactions led to a conflict between sexual feelings and societal norms. Rather than direct and discipline the female child's feelings (a process he referenced as *tahdhib*), Egyptian parents reinforced the interdiction.[84]

Murad's arguments are best situated within a larger debate within psychoanalysis, namely, the question of whether human sexual difference preexists the creation of the subject. Broadly speaking, scholars who read Freud in a radical fashion emphasize that a Freudian framework erodes normative conceptions of gender difference and sexuality; specifically, they note that "the threat of castration is not something that has been done to an already existent girl subject, or that can be done to an already existent boy subject; it is, as it was for Freud, what 'makes' the girl a girl and the boy a boy, in a division that is both essential and precarious."[85] In the 1920s and 1930s, however, resistance emerged to Freud's "account of sexual difference by analysts specifically arguing *for* women."[86] Such diverse thinkers as Karen Horney and Ernest Jones argued that "men analysts have been led to adopt an unduly phallocentric view."[87] For example, Karen Horney's so-called culturalist stress, which viewed feminine psychology as the product of social and cultural factors, was concerned with female sexuality more than sexual difference. As Juliet Mitchell notes, she assumed "that the human subject could be set apart from society and was not constructed solely within it: the child and society were separate entities mutually affecting each other. For Horney there are men and women (boys and girls) already there; in this she takes for granted what she intends to explain."[88]

Murad's analysis of femininity was thus, broadly speaking, neo-psychoanalytic, placing great emphasis on cultural and sociological factors.[89] He was far from a thoroughgoing Freudian and had critiqued certain aspects of orthodox Freudianism as mechanistic and reductive.[90] His approach to feminine psychology as largely the product of social and cultural factors was far more akin to that of Karen Horney, whom he had cited favorably in other contexts.[91] Accordingly, his analysis suffered from some of the very same flaws, namely, in its "reference to a pre-given sexual difference aimed at securing that identity for both sexes."[92] It subscribed, in other words, "to ideas of how men and women do or should live as sexually differentiated beings."[93]

There was another point upon which Murad's analysis and neo-psychoanalytic schools of thought converged: the question of love. For Murad, Freudian theory emphasized pleasure, understood predominantly as sexual pleasure (even if goal-inhibited), at the expense of an understanding of love as constitutive and primordial.[94] Here his analysis was very much in keeping with Scottish analyst Ian Suttie, for whom Freud had denied the existence of love and depreciated the social significance of the mother.[95] Murad devoted a significant amount of attention to love, increasingly an object of concern for a society in which romantic love and companionate marriage had quickly become the norm over the course of the twentieth century.[96]

For females, Murad noted, love coexisted with competition with respect to the figure of the mother; females maintained two diametrically opposed feelings, one conscious and the other unconscious. This would become a significant factor in the young girl's (and later woman's) psychic struggle. Residual unconscious attachments to the mother might lead to abnormal developments (*shudhudh* or *inhiraf*) or the inability to have a complete emotional life.[97] Murad emphasized the difficulty of attaining the ideal of femininity, but pointed to the significance of *tarbiya*—"all those involved in her upbringing must help her attain her femininity and convert any masculine predilections that she might succumb to."[98]

Murad's text was filled with anecdotal evidence regarding female psychology. He discussed a case study of a female college student recounted to him by a colleague, a young woman who found herself unable to study or concentrate and was jeopardizing her future.[99] Through a Socratic-like method of questioning, she finally confessed to experiencing strange emotions toward a male colleague, namely, love. She found herself unable to make sense of feelings that struck her as dreamlike and poetic, feelings radically inappropriate to the modern era, which required struggle, competition, and an objective spirit. Analyzing her case as one in which the desires of the heart were in conflict with those of society, or in which the ideal-I or super-I split off from the I, Murad went onto an excursus on love and psychoanalysis. Discussing the ideal love relationship as one in which the ego and superego were in agreement, he noted that in cases of conflict between the ego and superego, anxiety and pain would follow.[100] Love from the perspective of analysts, he informed his readers, entailed the transposition of the beloved onto the ideal-I. But this love was not always pure or constant, it had moments of doubt, as if the self needed to torture itself to counter its own happiness. To a degree, he opined, the individual who loved was looking for herself, recapitulating a primary narcissism.

Returning to the case of the college student, Murad argued that she was experiencing a strong tension between the conscious and unconscious elements of herself, and that she tended toward masochism and the denial of her own pleasure. This tension had manifested in the splitting off of the two aspects of love, the bodily and the spiritual or affective.[101] Her assumption, that succumbing to emotions was a form of weakness, and that the bodily aspect of love would be a degradation of her dignity, blocked her from the pursuit of love as the complete realization of both bodily and psychic elements. Murad had posed to his audience psychoanalysis as a venue for understanding love, one that moved beyond the insights offered up by poets and writers, and instead posited love as "an emotional orientation to the world," in short, a psychic structure.[102] Murad presented his audience with love as an ethical ideal, a complete union of the lover and the beloved, representing a desire to restore a lost unity.[103] Such a conception, we will recall, echoes the Sufi notion of the love of God as a unity with the One.

At the same time, love was, to be sure, confounded by the presence of unconscious factors, such as unresolved attachments to mothers or fathers. No doubt, too, that love often took on contradictory aspects of aggression and submission, and individuals often viewed the other as a fantasy imagined according to their own desires or fears.[104] Above all, the imprint of the past made its mark on love. Married couples often projected the imago of their parents onto their spouses, a fact that sometimes steered marriages toward distress and failure.[105] Early childhood experiences also influenced attitudes toward sex and gender. Boys, he counseled his audience, needed to be raised as masculine subjects without contempt for the opposite gender, while girls needed to be raised as feminine subjects without fear of the opposite sex, and without the belief that they were lacking.[106]

Same-Sex Desire

Murad's concern with the gendered upbringing of children was, in part, related to the heteronormative ideals of his time embodied in the possibility of healthy companionate marriage. In another Middle Eastern context, Afsaneh Najmabadi has tracked the modernist presumption of heterosexual desire, driven by a concern with national health, in Iranian biomedical texts, marital advice literature, and most significantly for our purposes, literature on the psyche.[107] Yet Murad's concern lay less explicitly with conceptions of national health and more with notions of self-integration. Throughout *Sikulujiyyat al-Jins*, Murad illustrated numerous incomplete resolutions of psychosexual complexes, drawing on examples from clinical practice and interviews with adolescents or young adults. In keeping with his theoretical emphasis on integrative psychology, he focused on intrapsychic conflicts that emerged between different parts of the self, or between conscious and unconscious impulses, and their intersubjective contours.

Many of Murad's examples illuminated failed heterosexual attachment, for example, in his focus on situations in which females became attracted to and developed romantic attachments to classmates of the same sex. His analysis of homosocial and homosexual female attachment was predicated upon a conflict between societal norms and psychological imperatives.[108] For example, Murad proposed a hypothetical clinical vignette of a girl's abnormal psychosexual development in order to elaborate the negative effects it would have on her future marital life.[109] Initially, the comparison the little girl made between herself and her brother led her to believe that she was lacking in bodily composition. Her parents' behavior reinforced this idea, leaving her with feelings of pain and failure. Then the period of late childhood arrived during which the girl began to orient herself toward the outside world, social activities, and school. During adolescence, nebulous sexual impulses appeared as a natural attraction to the opposite sex, but these came into conflict with social mores and with her parents' limited understanding of these signs of emotional development. Instead of directing her impulses, the parents instilled a sense of danger in the girl, and she searched for an outlet that was not forbidden by societal norms. She looked to her schoolmate who was perhaps a year older than she, and her level of love and affection approached an abnormal depth. The young woman was now romantically attached to a member of the same sex, while viewing the opposite sex with fear, aversion, and repulsion. The young woman might dissociate from her femininity, as her abnormal tendencies from childhood congealed. And so the young woman passed through adolescence with varying degrees of emotional maturity and then agreed to marriage but with tepidity, all the while ignorant of the unconscious abnormal impulses that developed during her adolescence. Unable to purge herself of her negative feelings toward the opposite sex, she found great difficulty in acclimating to marital life. Murad ended the vignette with a plea for psycho-sexual education for both sexes.

The counterpart to failed femininity was the improperly actualized masculine subject, a topic Murad and his coeditor, Mustafa Ziywar, had addressed several years earlier. In a 1948 issue of *Majallat 'Ilm al-Nafs*, two readers wrote in asking the editors to elaborate on same-sex love. One, who signed with the initials "Sin 'Ayn," began by recounting his early childhood years in which his sister dressed him in female clothing and had him play female roles. The structure of his letter was clearly indicative of the extent to which the confessional self-narration of childhood had taken hold among readers of the journal. Sin 'Ayn was perturbed by the fact that as a twenty-one-year-old male he had experienced no feelings of sexual desire toward women. At school he had befriended a good-looking male and was experiencing sexual urges, despite acknowledging that homosexuality was against both custom and law. What should he do, he asked, and how could he combat his urges? The journal's response was extensive and measured.[110] The journal noted the increase of homosexuality (*al-jinsiyya al-mithliyya*) and lamented the absence of any sustained scientific discussion in the Arabic scientific and scholarly press.[111]

After outlining the various types of homosexuality (ranging from actual sexual contact, to sexual relationships without full sexual contact, to sexual desire), and the various psycho-social studies that had estimated the incidence of homosexuality (such as those by Havelock Ellis and Alfred Kinsey), the editors proceeded to discuss in depth numerous psychological theories of homosexuality, ranging from Freud to Adler. Crucial to their argument was the need to move away from entrenched popular perceptions of homosexuality as innate, toward the idea of homosexuality as a psychological phenomenon.[112] If homosexuality could be shown to be due to an abnormal childhood, an inferiority complex, or the separation of the sexes, then it could be resolved through psychological analysis and behavioral or environmental changes.[113] In point of fact, the editors' principal explanatory emphasis was neo-psychoanalytic. Presenting a simplified account of the Oedipus complex, they noted that the lack of proper resolution of the complex was responsible for many instances of homosexuality. In sum, the young reader troubled by his lack of heterosexual urges, they suggested, should seek psychoanalysis.

In a discussion of unconscious childhood psychological complexes, Murad presented another concrete example of same-sex desire "that could only be understood through psychoanalysis."[114] An individual with repressed homosexual impulses decides to marry, and his repressed impulses appear in a distorted fashion as jealousy. Jealousy, he noted, was rooted in the Oedipus complex in which the male child was sexually attached to the mother and jealous of the father. It represented a form of love that was possessive and selfish, one rooted not in reality but in an imaginary figment of the past. Murad noted that jealousy was often the product of a psychological defense mechanism known as projection (al-isqat). For example, a husband's own unconscious repressed impulse for infidelity was projected onto his wife and converted into jealousy within conscious life. His jealous feelings toward his wife indicated a desire for an attractive competitor who could fulfill his own homosexual desires. His unconscious feminine tendencies led to a transmigration onto his wife's personality. It was not enough for him to merely wish for a competitor for his wife's love, but he also desires from a place he knows not (min haythu la-yadri) an attractive competitor, and the creation of a triangulated relationship. Murad assured his readers that although this may seem fanciful, the secrets of the human nafs were deep and hidden.

The production of normalized psychosexual subjects was therefore part and parcel of the development of a psychoanalytic psychology that sought the "normal" resolution of psychological complexes through the inculcation of heterosexual desire and companionate marriage. Yet every step toward normalcy was beset with potentially "pathological" resolutions: from early childhood to marriage, and most acutely in adolescence, homosexual desire threatened to destabilize individual psychology.[115] Although marriage emerged in Murad's account as the telos of proper psychosexual health, the process of adolescent sexual maturation was plagued by hesitations and halting failures. Heterosexual masculinity and femininity emerged in this literature as nearly impossible norms of psychosexual development. The path to normality was as narrow and precarious as the sirat, the straight path, the bridge of the hereafter, a "bridge thinner than a blade or a thread," a metaphor that al-

Ghazali had used to describe the happy medium of erotic desire. Arguably, for Murad homosocial and homosexual romantic attachments were themselves models for erotic desire and the quintessential model for ideal heterosexuality.

Technologies of the Self

The invention of the psychosexual subject was premised on a variety of technologies of the self, most notably introspection, self analysis, and confessional modes of self-narration. Such techniques of the self were perhaps most visible in discussions of the adolescent, newly emerged as a discrete class of person within the consolidated disciplinary space of psychology, one who had all but displaced the family as a central unit of analysis.[116] Adolescence was reconfigured as a psychological stage beset by unconscious sexual impulses that recapitulated childhood configurations of gender and sexuality. Yet the question remained as to how, precisely, to access such interiority.

In fact, throughout the 1940s accessing interiority through diaries, correspondence, questionnaires, psychiatric tests, and observation had become a principal goal of adolescent psychology.[117] In 1945, Murad had laid out a research agenda for the study of adolescent psychology in Egypt and the wider Arab world in which he proposed a questionnaire composed of forty-four questions divided into seven sections: childhood memories, original desires, intimate journals, friendship, philosophical preoccupations, and diverse conflicts and aspirations.[118] Students were asked questions about their childhood years, whether they had any positive or negative memories, their concern with philosophical or religious issues, and whether or not they kept a diary; questions, in short, that required the articulation and elaboration of interior states.

Adolescence, in other words, marked the developmental beginnings of a cavernous interiority and represented a new category of analysis that hailed new modes of being.[119] This process was, of course, not unique to Egypt, it was contemporaneous with the demarcation and research of adolescence as a distinct developmental stage in European adolescent psychology, such as in the writings of Maurice Debesse, a student of Henri Wallon.[120] Wallon, from whom Lacan derived his idea of the mirror stage, was surprisingly popular in postwar Egypt, part of a broader set of interconnections between French and Egyptian psychology. The imprint of Debesse's pioneering 1937 work, *Comment étudier les adolescents*, was clear in Murad's emphasis on diaries as a means of accessing interiority as well as on the unique significance of affect in adolescence.

'Abd al-Min'am al-Miliji, who had taught philosophy in Helwan and psychology in Cairo, took up Murad's research agenda and advocated the use of diaries and memoirs as a research method specific to understanding adolescent psychology. He argued that adolescence could be clearly demarcated as a psychologically distinctive stage of life, marked by a romantic phase.[121] The key attribute of adolescence was the way in which the individual, previously embedded and connected to the outside world, becomes increasingly disconnected and focused on the self while distancing himself from society and social mores. Based on a careful reading of numerous student diaries and memoirs, al-Miliji depicted adolescence as a period of intense turmoil, focusing on the conflicts youth experienced between self and society; these conflicts, he noted, could be resolved in any number of ways, ranging from personal diaries to suicide.[122] Al-Miliji also noted the key attributes of these diaries, namely, secrecy, a focus on self-analysis, and the representation of society as cruel and merciless.[123]

Al-Miliji defined adolescence itself in terms of the emergence of unconscious sexual instincts and the conflict between these instincts and societal or religious mores. For example, in discussing the case of a young man who had begun praying, fasting, and worshipping "to the point of Sufism," he analyzed his extreme religiosity as a form of moral guilt for sexual impulses that had been sublimated into religious impulses.[124] In particular, he explored extreme religiosity as a way for adolescents to deal with inner turmoil and unconscious sexual impulses in a socially sanctioned manner, while noting that it could take forms such as melancholia manifested in constant prayer.[125] In his discussion of the aberrant adolescent (*al-murahiq al-shadh*) al-Miliji depicted the individual in a battle with his negative human self, trying to overcome his sexual impulses through asceticism. Evoking the figure of the Sufi who reached a state of ecstasy and self-annihilation, al-Miliji likened such adolescent responses to an extreme form of religious sickness.[126] Citing examples such as Augustine and al-Ghazali, he argued that such processes of religious conversion (from debauchery to piety, or from doubt to belief) could be understood as the product of unconscious emotional complexes and struggles that came to be resolved through religious experience.[127]

The tormented process that al-Miliji described as akin to psychological illness is referred to in the Sufi tradition as *jihad al-nafs*, in which certain qualities of the *nafs* or self are viewed as an enemy that must be combated. In our previous discussion of the young shaykh al-Taftazani, we saw the entire discussion of *jihad al-nafs* (self-struggle) couched in psychological terminology of the repression and sublimation of instincts.[128] According to al-Taftazani, within the shaykh-disciple relationship, unconscious thoughts were meant to be analyzed, and the process of self-attunement, or *tahdhib al-nafs*, which the young initiate worked through with his shaykh, entailed the repression of sexual instincts uncovered in introspection. The Sufi, he argued, aimed to repress tendencies in conflict with the noble moral and spiritual principles of ethical being. Repression, in this rendering, was seen as a positive, and nonpathological, psychological facet of adolescent life.

What I want to suggest here is that al-Taftazani's discussion of Sufism and its relationship to sexual impulses represents the way in which the drive (*trieb*) may touch on an area of excess, a "something more" beyond an economy of pleasure that cannot be explained through a simple model of the de-tensioning of the sexual instincts. This something more, which Lacan referred to as *jouissance*, was best embodied by mysticism as "one of the available forms of expression where such 'otherness' in sexuality utters its most forceful complaint," a "sexuality in the form of a disturbance."[129] While scholars such as al-Miliji and Murad viewed adolescent psychology as characterized by intensive introspection, the manifestation of unconscious sexual impulses, and a tumultuous interiority, there nevertheless remained an excess that could not be accounted for by certain figures of alterity, such as the excessively devout Sufi, repressed at the margins of public discourse. Such an opacity at the heart of the human subject oftentimes subverted the terms of psychological discourse and demonstrated its inability to fully incarcerate the subject as the homogeneous product of its disciplinary practices and epistemic categories.

Conclusion

The midcentury body of work on the psychosexual subject was directed, by and large, toward a lay audience. Many readers would have been at least vaguely familiar with Freudian ideas, whether through their exposure to Mustafa Ziywar's radio talk shows or through the burgeoning crop of novels and films in the late 1940s and 1950s inspired by psychoanalytic themes. But more than a simple familiarity with Freud was needed to make Yusuf Murad's psychoanalytic interventions into discussions of gender and sexuality comprehensible. What was needed, in fact, was the solidification of a very particular kind of modern individual. As Dipesh Chakrabarty reminds us:

> This modern individual ... whose political/public life is lived in citizenship, is also supposed to have an interiorized "private" self that pours out incessantly in diaries, letters, autobiographies, novels, and, of course, in what we say to our analysts. The bourgeois individual is not born until one discovers the pleasures of privacy. But this is a very special kind of "private self"—it is, in fact, a deferred "public" self, for this bourgeois private self, as Jurgen Habermas has reminded us, is "always already oriented to an audience [*Publikum*]."[130]

It was precisely this formation of an "interiorized 'private' self that pours out incessantly in diaries, letters, autobiographies, novels" that enabled the invention of the psychosexual subject. And yet it would be a grave error to assume "that modernity introduced subjective interiority into Islam," which has long been recognized in the tradition. As Talal Asad notes, "What modernity does bring in is a new *kind* of subjectivity, one that is appropriate to ethical autonomy and aesthetic self-invention—a concept of 'the subject' that has a new grammar."[131] Yet the bourgeois modern individual characterized by a cavernous interiority was not merely replicated in the Egyptian context, nor was he simply characterized by ethical autonomy and aesthetic self-invention.

Rather, as we have demonstrated, such an individual was characterized by both autonomy, understood as the creation of a self-actualizing subject, and heteronomy, understood as the proper cultivation of ethical savoir-faire. In other words, a new grammar of the subject was soldered to older notions of the ethical cultivation of sexual ideals and practices. Hence, Yusuf Murad's writings on sexuality were clearly based on a reading of Freud through virtue ethics. Within this framework, sexual desire was characterized as a happy medium that could be attained by navigating between the dangers of "pleasure-less addictions" and the denial of the sexual drive. Neither fully religious nor fully secularized, this vision of the significance of sexual desire and pleasure for the integration of human being and becoming centered on desire and the appetites and on the ethical cultivation (*tarbiya*) of the child. The invention of the psychosexual subject thus did not entail a simple shift of pleasure and desire away from the theological pastoral; indeed, it was precisely in the interplay between the pleasure principle and the reality principle that *tarbiya* (or the proper upbringing and cultivation of the child) played a central role.

The literature on *tarbiya* drew on the medieval writings of al-Ghazali, demonstrating that psychoanalysis as a theory of desire could function as a supplement to Islamic discourse. The emphasis on *tarbiya* was coupled with a neo-psychoanalytic approach that led Murad to assume that sexual difference preexisted the creation of the human subject and to emphasize the significance of stabilizing gender identity and normative sexuality. And yet, far from a straightforward and medicalized model of homosexuality that wholly pathologized same-sex sexual desire, Murad put forth homosocial and homo-erotic friendship as the ideal model for conjugal heterosexuality. Interestingly enough, civilizational anxieties were nowhere evident in any of Murad's writings; there was no concern for an aberrant contemporary Arab sexuality, no idealization of a past golden age.[132] Rather, the intertextuality that existed with the medieval past was in the form of an engagement with classical era texts, not as a veiled vehicle for critiquing classical, and by extension contemporary, sexuality but as a mode and model of ethical attunement.

CHAPTER FOUR

Psychoanalysis before the Law

*Paradoxical as it may sound, I must maintain that the sense of guilt was
present before the misdeed, that it did not arise from it, but conversely—
the misdeed arose from the sense of guilt. These people might justly be
described as criminals from a sense of guilt.*

—SIGMUND FREUD

IN YOUSSEF CHAHINE'S masterful neorealist film noir classic *Bab al-Hadid*
(*Cairo Station*), the newspaper vendor Madbuli asks Qinawi (played by Chahine himself) to read the day's headlines on the Rashid court case.[1] Knowledge of the sensationalist murder case—in which a decapitated body is found
in a trunk—pushes Qinawi over the edge of sanity as he unsuccessfully pur-
sues his beloved and unattainable love object, the sensual and flirtatious
Hannouma. Qinawi's fragile psyche, compounded by severe sexual repression, leads him to attempt a murder in order to avenge his unrequited desire.
Released in 1958, Chahine's cinematic excursion illustrated the extent to which
the figure of the deranged criminal, beset by psychosexual complexes, had
captured the national imagination at midcentury.[2]

In fact, debates on criminality in postwar Egypt were widespread and intensely focused on the nature of criminal psychology. Perhaps unsurpris-
ingly, vigorous disagreements surrounding the relevance of Freudian theories
developed in tandem with the burgeoning literature on psychology both in
academic journals and the popular press. Lawyers, judges, academic psychologists, and practicing psychiatrists alike mobilized the figure of the criminal
to further their understanding of the nature of normal and abnormal psychology. Theories of innate criminality, such as those of Cesare Lombroso, had
long fallen out of favor, and while some resorted to the language of psychoanalysis, others sought recourse to what they perceived to be more complex and
multicausal models of criminality. In the event, psychoanalysis was repeat-
edly placed before the law at midcentury, whether in the public discussions

surrounding criminal motives in major court cases or in the determination of licensing laws for the practice of psychotherapy.

In what follows, I outline a number of discussions on Freudianism and its relevance to criminology while paying particular attention to the social role of the criminal at midcentury.[3] Tracing a debate spawned by lawyer and professor of criminal psychology Muhammad Fathi, regarding "the problem of psychoanalysis in Egypt," I argue that the convergences or divergences found between psychoanalysis and the law were in part related to disputes regarding the causal nature of crime—deep or proximate depending on one's interpretive position. More specifically, in his defense of psychoanalysis as a methodology for determining criminal culpability, Fathi found himself at loggerheads with a number of academic psychologists, including Mahmud al-Rawi, Mustafa Suwayf, and Sabri Jirjis, some of whom relied heavily on their mentor Yusuf Murad's integrative method of psychology. In essence, the debates turned on the question of whether, in the adjudication of criminal intent, one need consider unconscious conflicts of a distant and infantile past or if, rather, crimes should be viewed as the complex product of psychological, social, and biological disturbances in the present.

Further complicating these debates was the juridical status of psychoanalysis itself as it struggled to assert its autonomy as a field of therapeutic practice. Biomedicine, and forensic medicine in particular, had long held a hegemonic position within the Egyptian legal system, and medical doctors would increasingly become involved in the adjudication of mental states. At the center of all of these arguments, of course, lay the criminal, himself increasingly enmeshed within new legal and forensic practices, as well as multiple legal regimes over the course of the twentieth century. Debates on criminality at midcentury eventually turned to the question of political crime, and especially to political assassinations, which had seen a dramatic increase in the middle of the 1940s. Here, once again, arguments regarding the distant or proximate causes of mental disturbances were revisited, and theories of social and psychological disintegration were explored, particularly with reference to the figure of the psychopath who emerged as a distinct marker of social disintegration, and in some instances of political anomie. In essence, the question of madness was regarded as a social and juridical problem, one that could be addressed, in part, through the psychoanalytical science.[4]

Psychoanalysis, Crime, and Culpability

Between June 1947 and February 1949, a series of articles in the newly founded *Majallat 'Ilm al-Nafs* debated the heuristic value of Freud's ideas, particularly surrounding the Oedipus complex, for an understanding of crime and criminality. Contesting accusations that Freudianism had little to teach us about crime, Muhammad Fathi Bey—then a professor of criminal psychology at the Institute of Criminal Sciences in the School of Law, Fu'ad I University—argued that, quite the contrary, psychoanalysis and criminology were entirely analogous disciplines.[5] Alongside Muhammad al-Babli, the dean of the Police College, Fathi was a founding figure in the field of criminology in the 1930s. His major contribution was in criminal psychology, a topic he began lecturing on in the Faculty of Law in 1933. His magnum opus, which went through numerous editions, was his three-volume *'Ilm al-Nafs al-Jina'i: 'Ilman wa-'Amalan* (Criminal Psychology: Theory and Practice) that was based on his lectures and articles.[6] Fathi thus represented an important strand of thought in midcentury Egypt, one that connected the discipline and practice of the law to psychoanalysis and psychology.

Fathi was, according to the eminent sociologist Sayyid 'Uways, an "ardent advocate of psychoanalytic theory" who "sought to interpret criminal behavior from this perspective through field studies on the detection of criminals, the behavior of police investigators, and the behavior of judges."[7] Fathi was incredibly active in prison reform and retained an administrative and consultative role in legal matters pertaining to criminal law even well after the 1952 revolution, including membership on the board of the National Institute for Criminology. Fathi disseminated his views on Freud and criminology to as large an audience as possible—including numerous articles written for a lay audience in the newspaper *al-Misri* from January to February of 1947.

In an extensive article published in 1948 in *Majallat 'Ilm al-Nafs*, Fathi recounted an awkward conversation that transpired between himself and a colleague who was by training and profession a medical doctor, one who questioned the utility of a Freudian perspective for the law.[8] Drawing a sharp distinction between medicine's approach to nervous diseases on the one hand, and that of the law and psychology on the other, Fathi argued that the former was content with the description of external signs, while the latter strove for analytic interpretation relying on that which was hidden (*majhul*) from immediate understanding.[9] Throughout his writings Fathi would continue to distance psychoanalysis from medicine in the hope of establishing its professional autonomy and validity, particularly in legal contexts.[10]

The homology Fathi drew between criminology and psychology was both epistemological and ontological. Epistemologically, both psychoanalysis and criminology relied on indirect methods of interrogation, "the purpose of which is to lead the accused person to establish his own guilt or innocence objectively."[11] Further, in both psychoanalysis and the law, as Freud asserted, there was a concern for the secret:

> In the case of the criminal it is a secret which he knows and hides from you, whereas in the case of the hysteric it is a secret which he himself does not know either, which is hidden even from himself.... The task of the therapist, however, is the same as that of the examining magistrate.

We have to uncover the hidden psychical material; and in order to do this we have invented a number of detective devices, some of which it seems that you gentleman of law are now about to copy from us.... In the neurotic the secret is hidden from his own consciousness; in the criminal it is hidden only from you.[12]

As Fathi noted, in the analytic session as in the criminal examination, the prosecutor and the analyst encountered resistances that would have to be overcome.[13]

Beyond these methodological similarities, what Fathi found most appealing about psychoanalysis was the way in which it aligned more closely with the model of *nahdawi* (or cultural modernist) learning and erudition than with that of the positivist conception of the law. Psychoanalysis, he pointed out, relied on a model of hermeneutical understanding more akin to a deep art form than to a positivist endeavor such as medicine. It required a vast knowledge base of literature, the arts, mythology, ethnology, ancient history, and the history of civilizations and religious traditions.[14] Why would an approach that was marked by hermeneutics rather than positivism, and holism rather than atomism, be appealing to a lawyer and judge at midcentury?

Elliott Colla has explored the analogous mediatory role that both lawyers and writers occupied in colonial Egypt.[15] The appearance of the novel form, as well as the *effendiyya* (middle-class professionals) to which it was tied, was bound to new forms of secular law, legal advocacy, and the emergence of a legal profession in colonial Egypt.[16] The mediatory role of lawyers between the law and society, between modernity and the past, between Islam and Europe, and between the enlightened theory of law and its unjust practice, led to a fundamental ambivalence about speaking for others before the law and was foregrounded in novelic representations that suggested that the law had little to do with justice. As Colla notes of Tawfiq al-Hakim's 1937 *Diary of a Country Prosecutor*, the "novel suggests more than a simple disconnect between the theory of criminal law and its application. It also argues that the *Nahda* discourse of modernity is contaminated by this irrationality and chaos, that disorder is not a misuse of the law but, rather, a fundamental part of its rule. The point is again related to the function of representative legal agents who speak in the name of society."[17]

Fathi's insistence on psychoanalysis as a supplement to the law may be seen as similar to fiction in that it enabled the redress of social and psychological issues that the law could not address.[18] There was, however, a key distinction between the analogy Colla draws between the law and fiction in Fathi's case. Whereas in both detective fiction and the law the investigator mobilized a combination of inductive and deductive logic to recreate the "narrative" of the crime in a rationalist manner, the criminal-investigator-turned-analyst needed to rely on a more hermeneutical approach based on an often tenuous distinction between a world both real and imagined.[19] This included, by necessity, access to mental associations, dreams, and other "enchanted" modes of evidence that did not align with the instrumental rationality so familiar to jurisprudence.[20] Above all, however, what distinguished a psychoanalytic mode of understanding from a legal perspective was what we might call a concern for deep causality rather than proximal causes. Fathi had favorably noted the *longue durée* perspective of analysis as one in which the modern human was shaped by foundational primitive crimes (maternal incest and patricide), based on forbidden desires, that had transformed into antisocial repressed instincts in the psychic life of individuals.[21]

Beyond the epistemological convergences and divergences between psychoanalysis and the law, Fathi argued that in point of fact the criminal and the neurotic were nearly identical. Pointing to his own legal experiences as a judge, Fathi noted that he had the opportunity to witness firsthand the connections between mental illness and crime. Simply put: "the neurotic is an imaginary criminal and the criminal is a neurotic in practice" (*'asabi 'amali*).[22] Fathi viewed mental illness and crime as two branches of the same root, related to repressed instincts inherited from primeval man. The criminal acted on these impulses in real life, while the neurotic acted on his impulses in the domain of the unconscious; hence the analyst understood neurotic behavior via crime, while the criminologist understood crime via neurotic behavior.[23]

To substantiate his argument, and it is quite clear from his writings that Fathi had to stridently justify his psychoanalytic position in numerous social and political contexts, he provided a case study from his own experience. The reader was presented with the case of M. J., who embodied the classic figure of the *effendi*, an employee in a respectable social station, in his mid-forties, with a high educational degree, from a good family, who was suffering from severe "compulsion neurosis" and mental anguish.[24] M. J., a bachelor, became very attached to an older woman herself married to a much older man. The patient began to have criminal thoughts of killing the husband or wishing him dead, so he could free the wife and become closer to her. He decided to kill him and tried on numerous occasions but stopped himself in the last instance out of fear of punishment or because his superego would not allow it. Eventually, the patient's illness changed for the worse; he withdrew from the world and attempted suicide. Fathi interpreted these actions as unconscious impulses leading to criminal thoughts and a criminal imagination that finally led M. J. to condemn himself to death.[25]

Analysis uncovered a classical Oedipus complex, triggered by the similarity of appearance between M. J.'s neighbor and his mother and her nearly identical marital situation, similarities that led to the identification of this woman with his mother and the identification of her husband with his father. This desire for incest and patricide was a criminal, and yet imaginary, desire of the unconscious, which pushed M. J. toward committing a real crime, in other words his guilty punishing conscience preceded any actual crime.[26] Freud referred to this as "criminality from a sense of guilt." In this instance, criminal transgressions arose after the sense of guilt, most often derived from the Oedipus complex and as a reaction to the two greatest crimes man could commit: patricide and maternal incest; the only ones the primitive horde abhorred and avenged.[27] In fact, Freud had delineated two types of criminals: those who transgressed without any sense of guilt (either without moral inhibitions or because they considered themselves justified in deed because of their conflict with society)—something later considered a hallmark of psychopathy, and those whom Friedrich Nietzsche referred to as pale criminals— motivated by a desire for punishment, thereby furnishing punishment with a new psychological basis.[28]

Fathi asked his readers to imagine a situation in which such an individual was not afforded the opportunity of analysis and ended up committing an actual crime. Nothing could then save him from execution, particularly given the grave nature of his crime: murder for the sake of adultery. There would be no place for compassion or mercy due to the exigencies of mental illness. Nor was this, Fathi was quick to point out, an isolated incident of mental illness and crime. Years of personal experience had shown him that nervous disorders, and specifically the Oedipus complex, were the cause of nervous diseases and crimes alike.[29]

The Criminal at Midcentury

Why had the criminal become the object of such intense public discourse at midcentury, the subject of vociferous debates regarding criminal intent, legal culpability, and mental illness? In order to adequately answer this question, we must first attend to the complex interconnection between legal personhood and criminality in twentieth-century Egypt, as well as its representation within a popular imaginary. In what ways was the emergence of the juridical individual linked to new legal and forensic practices in the consolidation of multiple and overlapping legal regimes?

Samah Selim has outlined the "emergence of the 'individual' and of 'personhood' as a set of ambivalent legal, rhetorical and textual concepts and practices in the 19th and early 20th centuries."[30] She rightly notes that the "genealogy of the individual in modern Europe was ... linked ... to the genesis of the criminal as both an ontological subject and an object of scientific inquiry."[31] A variety of scientific and bureaucratic practices made this possible, thereby producing the individual and the criminal alike as the subject of identity and identification.[32] Numerous scholars of colonialism have noted the extent to which foundational practices, such as fingerprinting, had their origin in colonial contexts such as British India, and one could add, Egypt.[33] In Egypt, as in Europe, the legal category of the person was bound up with political, scientific, and criminological practices that sought to secure the identity of the individual within the boundaries of the nation-state.[34]

The Egyptian case differed from the European one, however, in the vastly complex nature of legal personhood. Scholars are, for the most part, in agreement as to the extent to which Islamic law was increasingly marginalized or imploded from the late nineteenth century onward.[35] A dual and overlapping legal system in which the *shari'a* coexisted with *siyasa* (discretionary justice exercised by the head of state and executive officials) and later, the Code Napoleon; a court system that included Native Courts, Mixed Courts, and *shari'a* courts; and the presence of the capitulations that provided consular protection for foreign minorities resident in Egypt—meant "being an official 'person' in the Egypt of 1910 could be a very mysterious, complicated, even dangerous affair—and an eminently modern one at that."[36] As Khaled Fahmy has documented, people became accustomed to the mobilization and at times manipulation of multiple legal regimes.[37] Nevertheless, modern legal personhood in Egypt increasingly came to signify the self-governing autonomous subject so familiar to modern liberal theory, as Armando Salvatore and others have noted.[38] As Salvatore elaborates, the philosophical fiction of autonomous agency and the juridical fiction of legal personality became ever more significant in the redefinition of personhood, even as it allowed for the selective incorporation of usable elements of *shari'a* into positive law as a metanorm of legality and the retention of its normative kernel as a regulator of public morality and ethical behavior.[39]

One way to understand this fundamental transformation in legal regimes from Ottoman to colonial Egypt would be to take the specific example most often at hand in discussions of criminal psychology, namely, homicide. In precolonial Egypt a homicide would typically be dealt with in the first instance as a matter of *shari'a* law in which the victim's heirs constituted plaintiffs, and only subsequently as a matter of state "secular" law.[40] *Shari'a* law was exceedingly fastidious in its adherence to strict rules of evidence; for a capital punishment sentence to be meted out for a murder case, the murder would need to be both intentional and without just cause, and criminal intent would be based not only on the subjective state of mind of the perpetrator, but would also have to be clear from the choice of murder weapon used.[41] According to Rudolph Peters, *shari'a* justice appears unsatisfactory to modern liberals, since defendants who have clearly committed a crime often could not be convicted, due to reasons of formal procedure, rules of evidence, and the complexity of the substantive law of homicide.[42] To be fair, the situation was far more complex as *shari'a* and *siyasa* or state court law often worked in tandem, as they had since the beginning of Islamic law, as Khaled Fahmy has shown.[43] Thus *siyasi* evidence, such as autopsy and other forms of forensic medicine, was introduced fairly regularly by the early 1850s, particularly in homicide cases, oftentimes in order to circumvent the strict rules of *shar'i* evidence.[44]

Once Islamic criminal law was abolished and the Code Napoleon was instituted in the 1880s, however, the Parquet (*al-niyaba*), the government prosecution department of the Ministry of Justice and "an institution unknown in the *shari'a*," conducted the investigation and prosecution of criminal offenses, with the police themselves taking orders from the Parquet (prior to this in the latter half of the nineteenth century the newly established police functioned, in effect, as the prosecution).[45] Once it was clear that there was sufficient evidence for prosecution, the case would be passed on to the Judge *de renvoi* who decided if there was a prima facie case for prosecution; if so, the case would move into criminal court and back to the Parquet official who made the original inquiry for prosecution.[46] As should be clear, with the institution of the Napoleonic code an entire prosecutorial legal apparatus was now in place, replete with the presence of proxy representation and all of the modern trappings—police and prosecution—that sought to identify and incarcerate the criminal as an enemy of the common good.[47] This is not to insinuate that such attempts at criminal justice were not sought after in precolonial Egypt, but merely to note that an entirely new apparatus of lawyers and legal officials who had not heretofore existed came into being.[48]

One could argue that this modern secular legal system marked by prosecutorial zeal led to an increasing ambivalence about the relationship between the law and justice, an ambivalence that has been amply documented in the field of Egyptian literature. Stated differently, there was a tension between the functionalism of the category of the person who stood before the law and the ethical or psychological category of the criminal. This was all the more marked in a cultural and literary milieu in which criminals, bandits, and other allegedly nefarious elements often had a divergent popular life as what Samah Selim terms the criminal-hero.

Selim has analyzed the translation of Arsène Lupin into Arabic in Egypt, as an example of the French strain of detective novel in which the criminal-hero eludes detection.[49] She states:

> Far from being an enemy of "society" in the sense enshrined in liberal social theory, in the new science of criminology, and in the moral economy of the 19th-century French novel, Hamza's Arsène Lupin is a threshold figure, a hero of mediaeval romance precariously translated into the tumultuous world of automobiles and anthropometry, high finance and bureaucratic discipline, police corruption and colonial disguise.[50]

Others have also noted the ambivalent figure of the criminal, or more precisely the *futuwwa*, in interwar Egypt. Sketching out the 1936 murder of Imtithal Fawzi, a popular singer and dancer, in a Cairo nightclub by a band of assassins led by Fu'ad al-Shami, Wilson Jacob traces a historical moment "that irrevocably branded the public figure of *futuwwa* with the additional meanings of thug, mobster, and nefarious villain—*baltagi*."[51] The subsequent tale that was uncovered of extortion rackets and gangs created a media frenzy that portrayed the inability of the police to maintain law and order, and eventually led to a new police unit to deal with *futwwat* and *baltagiyya*, including a biographical register of individuals.[52] But what Jacob's careful genealogy reveals is that older precolonial meanings of the *futuwwa*, as a noble public figure who provided protection for weaker social elements, oftentimes remained and coexisted in complex ways with its new meaning as thug.

What these and other accounts also demonstrate is that a widespread popular culture of media coverage of crimes had emerged in the Arabic press. As Shaun Lopez has outlined, the sensational case of two sisters accused of mass murder, Rayya and Sakina, gripped the Egyptian press and populace, beginning from the discovery of dead bodies in Alexandria in November 1920 until the sisters' execution in December 1921, and constituted a cultural fascination that remains well into the present moment.[53] This larger public context for the reception and discussion of criminal cases meant that prosecutors and judges needed to make compelling arguments not only before the criminal court but also before the court of public opinion, a public very often inclined to see the criminal as the antihero of modernity. Is it possible that the modern secular legal system in which the criminal was ruthlessly pursued as an autonomous agent responsible for his own criminality made the emphasis on mitigating factors such as the Oedipus complex an appealing means for discussing the ambivalent status of criminality? This is, perhaps, the key to Muhammad Fathi's impassioned defense of psychoanalysis in the mainstream press. Beyond that, a high-profile licensing case, in which Fathi had intervened in 1946, had placed psychoanalysis directly before the law, a case to which we now turn.

Psychoanalysis before the Law

At midcentury psychoanalysis was seeking both public and legal legitimacy. Indeed, the question of psychoanalysis was of such pressing legal importance that Muhammad Fathi penned a full-length treatise on the topic in 1946 titled *The Problem of Psychoanalysis in Egypt*.[54] Bemoaning the absence of trained psychoanalytic professionals in Egypt, Fathi focused specifically on the question of whether or not psychoanalysis should be considered a branch of medicine as well as the legal ramifications of such a postulate. He himself was of the distinct opinion that medicine confined itself to the body and material laws while analysis dealt with the soul and the laws of meaning.[55]

The issue had been recently raised in a legal case that involved the Ministry of Health, in which Shukri Effendi Jirjis, a psychoanalyst trained abroad, had been charged with practicing without a license and ordered to close his clinic. According to the medical examiner (*tabib shar'i*) in the case, psychiatry was a subspecialization of medicine, given that many mental illnesses had an organic basis, and any individual who wished to treat mental and nervous diseases must have completed medical school. Yet, as Fathi was quick to point out, psychiatry itself was not yet an established field of study in Egyptian medicine.[56] Fathi noted that the court had been extremely hesitant in its ruling, circling around the question of whether psychoanalysis was a branch of medicine or a separate art. The court consulted solely with medical examiners, individuals he pointed out, who had no knowledge of the field.[57] Following the court ruling, Fathi published an article, "Is Psychoanalysis a Branch of Medicine or Its Own Art?" in the May 1941 issue of the prestigious and widely read *Egyptian Journal of Medicine*. Around the same time the office of the chief prosecutor issued a small booklet that argued that psychoanalysis was a branch of medicine, and that patients with mental and nervous diseases must be treated by a medical doctor.[58] Fathi took the opportunity of a personal connection with the chief prosecutor to alert him to his own article, a serendipitous encounter that would come into play in the near future.[59]

In the event, a second case was to come before the court, once again against the accused Shukri Effendi Jirjis, brought forward by other patients who had heard of the previous ruling. This time however, Shukri Effendi brought to his defense Fathi's article in the *Egyptian Journal of Medicine*. Although in November 1945 the court still ruled against Jirjis, the results were far more promising according to Fathi.[60] In the text of the ruling Jirjis was accused of practicing medicine without a license. In his own defense, Jirjis claimed that he did not perform surgery or give medication, and did no harm in accordance with the law as outlined.[61] It was this second case that was the context for Fathi's 115-page treatise in which he came to the conclusion that psychoanalysis was not a branch of medicine and that it was not in the public interest (*al-maslaha al-'amma*) for it to be so included.[62]

Beyond that, Fathi noted the dire necessity, given the vast increase in mental illness and the rarity of analysts in Egypt with proper scientific training, of establishing psychoanalysis as a practice in Egypt alongside the acknowledgment of nonmedical degrees. This would ensure the presence of psychoanalysts with proper scientific training, but more importantly with a knowledge of the language, culture, and religious practices of the nation's inhabitants. The formation of a psychoanalytic institute should be of the highest priority, as should the formation and supervision of a mental health profession employed by the state with the provision of free services to the mentally ill. In sum, Fathi noted, psychoanalysis was a branch of psychology and not medicine, and mental illness need not be conceptualized as medical illness (with an organic etiology).[63]

The court's response to Fathi's impassioned defense of psychoanalysis took many in Egypt by surprise. Ruling that psychoanalysis was not a branch of medicine, but rather a discipline with its own methods, the court nevertheless ruled that Jirjis had extended his practice by treating patients with organic illnesses, that he had misrepresented himself as a doctor when he did not possess the requisite degrees, and the court ruled against him, ordering him to close his clinic. Sadly, Jirjis died on August 23, 1945, perhaps due in part to the stress of these legal cases.[64] Significantly, however, the court stated that "it is clear that psychoanalysis is not a branch of medicine," and its practitioner need not be a doctor.[65] They noted that in Europe practitioners had the benefit of both professional societies and an enlightened public, which was not the case in Egypt. As a result, they contended, referencing Fathi's treatise, the public must be educated and laws established dictating the proper education, training, and work venues for analysts.[66] Fathi took this ruling as a historic turning point in the history of psychoanalysis in Egypt, in particular because of the extent to which the press and the public had been closely following the case, the majority of whom, he surmised wanted to ban nondoctors from the practice of analysis. All the more reason, he noted, to spread information and correct misconceptions, through the dissemination of scientific findings, much in the same way that his treatise had attempted to do.[67] In his conclusion, Fathi argued for the social responsibility of psychological treatment, viewing the analyst as a social reformer of the highest order, one who helped reconcile individuals with their conscience. It would surely be in the nation's best interest to legislate and provide an infrastructure for establishing mental health upon a sound scientific basis, and in this, Egypt could supersede many of the advanced nations of the West.[68]

Fathi's ardent attempt to distinguish psychoanalysis from the practice and field of medicine is perhaps best understood as an attempt at establishing the autonomy of psychoanalysis as a field of knowledge alongside medicine. Fathi's insistence on placing psychoanalysis before the law must, then, be situated within the longer history of the hegemony of biomedicine within the state legal apparatus, a process best illustrated by the establishment of forensic medicine in Egypt. Khaled Fahmy has noted that forensic medicine was established in Egypt in the precolonial period under Mehmed 'Ali, such that by the 1850s there was a nationwide network of forensic doctors as part of the state's larger attempts to tighten its jurisdiction over the population, monitor crime, and prevent provincial abuses of power.[69] Forensic medicine functioned as a "master of all proofs," more reliable than eyewitness testimony and confessions, and allowed for a more efficient centralized governmental control over provincial authorities.

Dispelling any notion that forensic medicine was introduced simply as a by-product of Western liberal ideas meant to displace the *shari'a*, Fahmy notes that the introduction of forensic medicine (autopsies in particular) was meant to support and supplement *shari'a* law.[70] The legal discourse of *siyasa* or state court law was not derived from *shari'a*, but was central to Ottoman governance and to medico-legal practice in nineteenth-century Egypt. *Siyasa* had newly introduced methods for criminal evidence and investigation not derived from *fiqh* (thus, for example, *shariʿa* places great weight on eye-witness testimony but with the introduction of autopsy the latter was used as a supplementary form of evidence, one that did not displace *shariʿa*).[71] By the early 1850s, then, the close connection established between law and medicine (especially criminal law and homicide) had to do with exigencies of state governance and the maintenance of law and order as well as the long-standing interconnections between the development of the medical establishment as a field of knowledge and the modernizing state. Fathi's ardent advocacy of psychoanalysis as a handmaiden to the law was meant to broaden the legal bases for the introduction of evidence in court beyond medicine and was a direct response to what he and others viewed as a crisis of mental health in Egypt.

In a critical review of Fathi's book published in *Majallat ʿIlm al-Nafs*, Sabri Jirjis, a medical doctor who specialized in mental and nervous diseases, critiqued Fathi's approach as creating an artificial barrier between medicine and psychoanalysis and posited the need for an integrative approach that viewed the body and psyche as a totality.[72] Further, Jirjis argued, Fathi had ignored recent attempts at the rapprochement of medicine and psychoanalysis, such as in the field of psychiatric medicine (*al-tibb al-ʿaqli*). So, too, did Fathi ignore figures like Franz Alexander, a physician and psychoanalyst who had published the *Medical Value of Psychoanalysis* (not to mention a treatise on psychoanalytic criminology), and Ernest Jones, who had implored the British psychoanalytic society in 1946 to foster greater connections between medicine and analysis.[73] Like the courts in Egypt, Sabri Jirjis was concerned with the increased prevalence of charlatans and tricksters (which he argued was on the rise in the late 1940s) who had given the fledging young science a bad reputation. Agreeing with Fathi that the mental health field needed to be strengthened in Egypt, Jirjis felt that Fathi's suggestion of a temporary relaxation of standards was rather misguided. Rather, a closer connection between medicine and psychology would be the most apt solution.

What, then, was the relationship of the law to these debates about the relative power of medicine and psychology? Where did the professional authority for the legal adjudication of mental states reside? Egyptian Law no. 99 of 1947 (issued one year after Fathi's treatise) stated that medical doctors and hospitals were privileged authorities in the adjudication of mental health and concomitantly retained the authority of interdiction over the insane (*majnun*).[74] Medical expertise, as Oussama Arabi argues, became correlative of the juridical function, a further extension, one might argue, of the juridical power of medical expertise begun in the mid-nineteenth century with the introduction of forensic medicine. Significantly, prior to this, under the 1875 Muhammad Qadri Pasha code of Personal Status, as well as classical Islamic law, the assertion of the state of madness and loss of legal capacity required neither a judicial verdict nor medical verification.[75] Rather, the care of the mentally ill fell within the purview of the family and community and was conceptualized in terms of a protective rather than interdictory function.[76] The expansion of state authority over the mentally ill cannot, of course, be understood outside the establishment and expansion of mental institutions. Under Mehmed 'Ali the care of the mentally ill had already been subsumed under state control through the establishment of lunatic asylums, a process further solidified with the establishment of 'Abbasiyya Mental Hospital in 1880, which fell under British administration by 1884, and al-Khanka in 1912.[77] According to Arabi the aforementioned change in the legal status of insanity was due, in part, to "the political recognition accorded to Western-trained psychiatrists" by the state as experts in mental health.[78]

Nevertheless, in the end, Fathi and others calling for the legalization of psychotherapy by qualified nonmedical professionals won their minor battle, at least in theory. The dispute surrounding licensing was resolved by Law no. 198 of May 1956, which regulated the clinical practice of psychotherapy. According to this law a license could be issued only to those with a diploma in neurology and psychiatry from a college of medicine; a certificate of specialization in psychotherapy and/or active membership in a recognized local or foreign association or organization of psychotherapy; or a graduate degree in psychology with a minimum of two years of practice in an authorized clinic, and only after having been vetted by a rigorous nine-member committee.[79] In practice, however, the number of licensed nonmedical Egyptian psychologists who practiced psychotherapy throughout the second half of the twentieth century would remain insignificant, illustrating the continued dominance of the medical profession in the mental health field.[80]

Anti-Oedipus

Fathi Bey had won his battle with the courts to include nonmedical practitioners as practicing therapists, yet there were other disputes awaiting him from within the psychological profession. In a long and detailed response to Muhammad Fathi's series of articles on the Oedipus complex and its relation to criminality in al-Misri, Mahmud al-Rawi decided to shift the discussion away from a general knowledge or lay audience to the more specialized readership of Majallat 'Ilm al-Nafs, a far more appropriate forum, he noted, for the debate.[81] Al-Rawi had himself broached the Oedipus complex several years earlier in the journal Majallat al-Riyada al-Badaniyya—a clear indication of how widely discussed Freud's ideas were at midcentury.[82] Al-Rawi was one of many thinkers for whom the criminal need not be the victim solely of his infantile sexual urges, and he felt compelled to critique this psychoanalytic reading as a reductive form of analysis that refused to see the complexity of societal factors that may have impelled individuals toward crime.

Interestingly, Freud himself might have also objected to such wide-ranging uses of the Oedipus complex, stating "precisely because it is always present, the Oedipus complex is not suited to provide a decision on the question of guilt.... 'Psychology is a knife that cuts both ways.' "[83] Reflecting on this facet of Freud's thought through a fascinating discussion of the use of psychoanalytic theory in 1930s and 1940s Mexico, Rubén Gallo details the case of a Mexican judge, Raúl Carrancá y Trujillo, who brought psychoanalysis into legal practice, most famously in the trial of Leon Trotsky's assassin. Gallo notes that while "Freud might have objected—as he did in the Halsmann case—to linking the Oedipus complex to criminality ... he certainly would have applauded Carrancá's insistence on the need to incorporate the psychoanalytic theory of the unconscious into the practice of law."[84] Would Freud have thought that Fathi had overreached in the explanatory power he had provided the Oedipus complex in the adjudication of criminal intent? While we will never know how Freud might have reacted to Fathi's particular applications of the Oedipus complex in midcentury Cairo, we may turn to the responses of the scholars who contributed to *Majallat 'Ilm al-Nafs*.

In his 1947 response to Fathi, al-Rawi framed the issue, quite simply, as whether or not the improper resolution of the Oedipus complex led to crime, and he overviewed the complex and controversies surrounding its significance in an attempt to clarify what he thought Fathi's newspaper articles had muddled for a general audience. Mahmud al-Rawi's perspective is fascinating for several reasons, not least of which is the fact the he was one of very few individuals to have incorporated a Jungian approach in his writings and was highly critical of those who unquestioningly followed Freud's theories in isolation, or any other single theorist for that matter.[85] Al-Rawi contended that Freud's well-known perspective on the resolution of the Oedipus complex by the age of four (and the concomitant formation of *das Ich* and *das Über-Ich*) should be nuanced by pointing to Melanie Klein's research. Klein had shown that prior to Oedipal resolution, between the ages of three and five, there was something akin to a conscience or censor (*damir, raqib*) encompassing knowledge of the social system that was present above the self (*ma fawq al-dhat*), after which began the libidinal stage of psychological growth. The tendency toward social comportment (*adab*, cf. *paideia, disciplina*), in other words, was also an instinct.[86] Further, all of this pertained to the resolution of the Oedipus complex at an individual level and need not translate into aggressive or criminal tendencies toward the societal collective.[87] Al-Rawi argued for a "moral substratum of subjectivity" generated through the social normativity of ethical values acquired through education and embodied in "objective social relations," here elevated to the level of an instinct.[88]

Marshaling evidence based on theorists who did not agree with Freud's basic proposition of a sexual instinct directed toward the mother, al-Rawi reviewed the theories of Otto Rank who had argued that the Oedipus complex may not be a supreme causal factor and who had reinterpreted desire for the mother as a desire for unity (as in the prenatal period); of Bronislaw

Malinowski who completely denied the existence of the Oedipus complex; as well as Trigant Burrow and Helene Deutsch.[89] Al-Rawi critiqued Freud's mechanism, his obsessive reduction of all causality to causes of a sexual nature, the omni-explanatory potential of the Oedipus complex—so capacious as to provide an explanation for everything, as well as the simplicity of its underlying idea, namely, "that which is forbidden is desired."[90] In sum, the "Oedipus complex was an imaginary construct in agreement with Freud's ideas alone."[91]

What then were the causes of a criminal personality? One possibility, according to al-Rawi, was psychopathy, characterized by a combative attitude toward society and a criminal nature, here citing Bernard Glueck's study of Sing Sing prisoners (a study well known in Egypt) that had found that 19 percent of prisoners were "constitutionally inferior or so-called psychopaths," many of whom displayed disturbances in early childhood, or at school.[92] Clearly, Fathi's examples did not conform to these psychopathic instances— since his examples were of individuals with late-onset disturbances and criminal acts. But how, then, might one explain criminals who committed crimes later in life?

Turning to Carl Jung, al-Rawi noted that he took the Freudian concept of libido and gave it a more general meaning, one he translated into Arabic as "*al-dafi' al-hayawi*," or a vital life force and general psychic energy, which need not take on sexual or narcissistic characteristics. Jung did not abide by the idea of a fundamental antagonism between the self and desire or between the self and life forces, because there was an instinct toward *adab* that could easily be directed by parents. Conflicts that existed were between aspects of the self that were easy or difficult to acclimate. Psychic struggles, then, often depended on what the individual found present or lacking in his environment, which could potentially lead to the depletion of psychic energy and other functional psychic difficulties.[93]

What then, for al-Rawi, would the difference be between a Freudian and Jungian interpretation of a psychic disturbance? For Freud the root of the problem would lay in some sort of childhood complex and once resolved would lead to a cure; whereas Jung, while not denying the presence of childhood factors, located causality in a present conflict or trauma that led to symptoms, "*the cause of a functional psychic disturbance lay not in the past but rather in the present.*"[94] Consequently, an analyst might ask, "what is it that the child has always wanted since childhood that he cannot attain until the present moment?"[95] It was possible, al-Rawi noted, that the criminal might be someone with an extreme sensitivity (*shadid al-hasasiyya*), very easily affected, an individual with extreme reactions to mild stimuli, an individual precisely such as Fathi's example of the young man who killed his neighbor's drunk and abusive husband. A normal individual in the same predicament would have simply convinced his neighbor to leave her husband, or he would have tried to save her from the abuse by sharing the information with others. Such a case provided numerous possible psychological scenarios, whereas Fathi only provided one: an unresolved Oedipus complex.[96]

Was al-Rawi's model one that allowed for more human responsibility and moral accountability in the understanding of criminal behavior than Fathi's model? In fact, both authors sought to mitigate criminal responsibility by pointing to contributing psychological factors; Fathi alluded to distant infantile and primal causes, while al-Rawi focused on the proximate causes of mental disturbances. Beyond that, al-Rawi sought to develop a psychological model of illness in which disease and environment, broadly understood to include the family but also to extend beyond it, interacted in a dynamic fashion. Such was also the view of Mustafa Isma'il Suwayf, whose thoughts on Bergson we encountered in chapter 1, and who joined al-Rawi in criticizing the Freudian conception of criminal behavior, putting forth a dynamic model of criminality.[97]

Suwayf outlined the psychoanalytic conception as one in which the criminal was either a neurotic, compelled to commit crimes because of his acute feelings of guilt and his desire to be punished, or a narcissist with a highly developed criminal superego.[98] Psychoanalytic treatment maintained therefore that punishment fulfilled a masochistic need in the criminal by relieving him of his inner conflicts—from this perspective the criminal was best not punished in order to allow for psychoanalytic treatment to relieve him of his unconscious conflicts and criminal tendencies. Suwayf acknowledged that Freudianism marked a qualitative turn in the history of psychological research, rejecting the mechanism of associationism and furnishing psychology with a foundation in dialectical philosophy, thereby allowing deeper insight into psychic activity. However, Suwayf criticized the Freudian conception for four principal reasons: psychoanalysis, he noted, was not able to proceed along the dialectical path it inaugurated and fell back into a mechanistic view in which psychic systems appeared static in nature; it overvalued childhood as a constitutive epoch in determining an individual's present and future, thereby denying the deep interaction between personality and environment; as such criminality appeared to Freudians as an individual matter of personality maladjustment whose resolution could be brought about by the analyst; and, finally, a Freudian conception of criminality fell, ultimately, into mechanical determinism, since the ego was unable to fight against the wishes of the id due to a lack of proper defense mechanisms.[99]

In juxtaposition to the orthodox Freudian view of criminality, Suwayf put forth the work of Fredric Wertham, a German American psychiatrist and advocate of psychiatric consultation in the courtroom, which he thought should play a "strong but subordinate role."[100] Suwayf outlined his book, *Dark Legend*, as an exemplar of a dynamic conception of criminality. *Dark Legend* tells the tale of young Gino, a seventeen-year-old Italian immigrant who murdered his mother in New York City. Seven years earlier the boy's father had died in Italy, at which point mother and children came to the United States, where they lived in a crowded tenement. Dr. Wertham testified to the lunacy commission that Gino had not known that his act was wrong; he was declared legally insane and committed to a state institution for the criminally insane, rather than executed.[101]

Wertham was attentive to the literary elements of this criminal psychodrama, deeply resonant with Hamlet and Orestes, describing the Orestes complex "in which the love of a son for his mother is turned to destructive hate by her unfaithfulness to the memory of her dead husband with whose image the son has identified himself."[102] But Wertham did not mobilize Gino as merely a foil for his literary allusions, rather, as Suwayf was keen to point out, Wertham situated both Gino and his crime within a social and ideological context.[103] Suwayf's interest in Wertham's interpretation lay in his focus on sociological or cultural factors that were formative in understanding the *specific* nature of the crime committed. As Wertham himself noted, "Matricide is a disease of a patriarchal society.... No emotional conflict is a duel of opposing forces in a self-contained field. It involves the social forces that underlie all human development. Gino played the social role of the father as he saw it."[104]

Social dynamics, in terms of the role of the sexes but also the social position of mothers and fathers within the family and within society, led Gino to identify with the patriarchal values that projected the image of the father as adulthood and power.[105] What then was the reason for Gino's deed? In Suwayf's rendition, the defense of family honor (as indicated by Gino's final statement to his mother: "you have defiled the family honor"), coupled with a social ideology that put forth women as a devilish source of corruption, led to a deep conflict between Gino's love of his mother (the affective) and the societal view of women as both sources of honor and enemies of society (the ideological).[106] In psychological terms, Wertham argued that Gino suffered from a catathymic crisis marked by a rigidity or loss of plasticity in thought that manifested in "the development of the idea that a violent act—against another person or against oneself—is the only solution to a profound emotional conflict whose real nature remains below the threshold of consciousness of the patient."[107]

Why was Wertham's interpretation so appealing to Suwayf? On one level Gino's case study brought to the fore cultural issues that Suwayf was surely sensitized to in the Egyptian context, namely, questions of patriarchy and family honor. Such ideological characteristics lent specificity to what would otherwise be a generic psychodynamic approach to criminality. At a methodological level, Suwayf noted, the significant aspect of the case study was not whether it was marked by an Oedipus or an Orestes complex, but how crime manifested itself in social behavior. In sum, there was little point in delineating case studies as exceptions to social laws, such as the Oedipus complex. Such a notion of social laws and exceptions would merely indicate either a lack of comprehensive study of the case or the application of the psychological facts at hand in a mechanical or deterministic way. Rather than search for predictable results (say in the application of the Oedipus complex), each unique case study should enable a revisiting of social laws. What was needed, Suwayf opined, was a dynamic dialectical interpretation, one that took seriously the interaction between an individual and his environment.[108]

Suwayf's point of view was in fact the hallmark of the integrative method developed by his mentor Yusuf Murad. Murad had outlined the integrative approach to criminality, as partially distinct from a psychoanalytic approach, in a previous issue of *Majallat 'Ilm al-Nafs*, an issue devoted exclusively to psychology and crime.[109] Murad placed criminal psychology as a branch of applied social psychology, arguing "there is no special psychology of delinquents and criminals."[110] Criminal behavior, he noted, was in fact a normal phenomenon within societies, and efforts should be devoted to understanding the circumstances under which individuals became either social animals or the criminal products of social disintegration.[111] This was in direct contrast to Lombroso. In a brief discussion of the causes of crime, Murad critiqued the once popular views of Lombroso, who had argued for the criminal as a biological individual (marked by the stigmata of degeneracy), juxtaposing the far less known theories of Prosper Despine, who had focused on the criminal mentalité as one of defective moral and affective tendencies, rather than an innate or biological attribute.[112] Despite their popularity Lombroso's views had been amply disproven.[113] An integrative approach, he noted, would look at biological, psychological, and social factors in a dynamic fashion, allowing for greater complexity in understanding.[114] Significantly, Murad here cited Muhammad Fathi's work as an example of the potential contribution psychoanalytic studies could make to criminology, indicating that Suwayf had exceeded his own mentor's critique of Freud, evidencing a far less comprehensive view of Freud's own writings, one that perhaps bordered on a simplification.

What, then, might the implications be for the treatment and rehabilitation of criminals? Previous efforts at fighting crime, Murad noted, were conceptualized in an entirely defensive or reactive fashion, with a focus on punishment as a fear-inducing deterrent to crime that served to mollify public opinion.[115] Yet the psychological basis behind such notions was based on a calculus of pleasure and pain apropos, perhaps, to animals and small children, but not adults. Punishment only further reinforced the sense that the criminal was the enemy of society, further inculcating this feeling in him. Reform, Murad argued, could only be accomplished through scientific studies on the etiology of crime and the correction of social circumstances as part of a larger total social reform project, a process that would need to rally public opinion and support.[116] Murad noted that in the past few years (presumably from the mid-

1940s) a very palpable change could be felt in the courts, one in which there was a concern for reform and treatment. In the past the court had sentenced the criminal based solely on the nature of the crime, whereas now psychological and social circumstances were brought to bear on the facts of the case through the interventions of psychiatrists, psychologists, and social workers.[117] This was partly the result of Muhammad Fathi's indefatigable efforts to establish criminal psychology as an indispensable part of the Egyptian criminal court system.

What was at stake in these debates, of course, was the question of criminal culpability a question that had received much attention, but little resolution, at midcentury.[118] For many the complexity of the legal subject meant that the prosecution of the "criminal" was no easy matter. For some, such as criminal psychologist and lawyer Muhammad Fathi, a recourse to the language of psychoanalysis meant that criminal culpability was attenuated to account for individual psychological disturbances that were the product of unresolved infantile psychosexual conflicts. Others, such as Yusuf Murad and those who followed the integrative method, sought recourse to what they argued was a more complex model in which criminal psychology could not be divorced from wider societal issues and maladies. In both cases, however, an emphasis was placed on prevention and treatment in which an interventionist model of social welfare or individual psychotherapy would address the social and psychological anomie that had led to crime in the first place. This was in keeping with larger efforts in the late 1930s and 1940s aimed at the palliative amelioration of social conditions for the working classes in order to stave off social anomie and political upheaval, efforts that would culminate in the social welfare mode of regulation of the Nasserist regime.[119]

The Political Unconscious

The significance of a social welfare framework for understanding criminality inflected debates on the etiology of crime and cast a long shadow on criminological research, up to and including the formation of the National Institute for Criminology in 1955 (later renamed the National Center for Social and Criminological Research) under the new Nasserist regime.[120] Traditional psychoanalytic approaches were marred by what critics termed Freud's ahistorical universalism. Instead, they argued for an emphasis on the political and social elements of the unconscious, rather than the nuclear familial unit, in understanding criminality. Mahmud al-Rawi, who had critiqued the Oedipus complex as an explanatory framework for homicide, took a similar approach in a series of articles that explicitly addressed the political dimensions of crime.

In a discussion of political assassination, al-Rawi once again targeted Muhammad Fathi and accused him of a simplified and omnipresent use of

Freudian insights in order to understand political crime.[121] One could, he jested, explain civil wars, political party antagonisms, individual political differences, and even socialism and communism as an Oedipal revolt against the father.[122] Rather, he asserted, the economic, political, and religious conditions, which in the primitive horde had led individuals to kill their father, had certainly transformed over time. Leadership had moved from notions of divinity, to monarchy, to law, and new historical conditions, such as capitalism, had come into existence. Economic and political domains were the new terrain of social conflict, whether of party politics, conflicts between nations, or leaders' desire for domination.[123] Further, the psychology of groups surely differed from the psychology of individuals, as recent social psychology had amply demonstrated. One need only think of the French and Russian revolutions, German fascism, or even Egypt's 1919 revolution to acknowledge the existence and strength of collective psychology.[124]

Turning to political assassination, al-Rawi laid out the factors that would need to be addressed in any psychological study: the conditions of international conflict; individual conceptions of war and peace; individual and partisan competition (party politics); and above all, popular attitudes toward, and conceptions of, the leader. Any exploration of political assassination would have to distinguish between a premeditated murder committed for social reasons in order to benefit a political group, protect them from harm, or create a counterleader; from those committed by individuals without a vision, often at the behest of a political mastermind.[125] Further, there was the possibility that an unbalanced individual previously filled with love and admiration for a leader could transform into a paranoid obsessive and subsequently attempt a political assassination.[126] In sum, the motives of political crimes were to be found in actual conflicts present in consciousness and not solely in conflicts of an infantile origin, and were also related to the desire for ascendance and domination. Much would be learned if psychologists were afforded the opportunity to speak with prisoners who had committed political crimes.

Al-Rawi's emphasis on political assassination must be placed within the context of the numerous waves of political assassination that took place in the first half of the twentieth century in colonial Egypt, between 1919 and 1924, 1945 and 1949, with smaller waves between 1910 and 1915 and in the 1930s.[127] Clustered around the aftermath of the world wars and in moments of anti-colonial nationalist agitation, assassinations targeted prominent individuals such as Sir Lee Stack, the sirdar and governor general of the Sudan in 1924, as well as numerous attempts on Egyptians, such as prime ministers Ahmad Mahir and Mustafa al-Nahhas. Mahir was assassinated in February 1945, while then heading a coalition cabinet, and had served briefly as education minister under Saʿd Zaghlul, briefly as finance minister in 1938, twice as speaker of the Wafdist parliament in 1936 and again in 1940, and had even previously led the secret apparatus and been unsuccessfully tried for the assassination of Stack. Mahir had been killed by a young nationalist, Mahmud 'Issawi, who belonged to a wing of the Watanists that had seceded from Young Egypt. 'Issawi had shot him down as he crossed from the chamber of deputies to the senate in order to prepare a call for war against Germany and Japan so that Egypt might take part in the United Nations. According to Donald Reid, for 'Issawi, this represented "treasonable truckling to the British."[128] Prior to his execution 'Issawi confessed only to his affiliation with the Watanists, although some later claimed his involvement with the Muslim Brotherhood.

Additional assassination attempts included the unsuccessful car bombing and attempt on Mustafa al-Nahhas's life (judge, cabinet minister, five-time premier, and Wafd party leader) in December 1945, which was almost immediately followed by the assassination of Amin 'Uthman, who was the main link between Nahhas and the British embassy in January 1946, by assailant Husayn Tawfiq, a known political criminal who had earlier targeted British officers.[129] The sheer political complexity of these cases helps us understand al-Rawi's insistence on a focus on contemporary political circumstances and conflicts and the ways in which they might affect political psychology. Al-Rawi was prescient, in fact astonishingly so. Almost immediately after the publication of his article (published in October 1947), between March 1948 and February 1949, escalating violence centered on the Muslim Brotherhood, including the notorious assassination of Supreme Leader Hasan al-Banna in February 1949 by the secret police. Two months prior, Prime Minister al-Nuqrashi was killed in December 1948 by a student attached to the Brotherhood, a mere twenty days after issuing a ban on their organization. These incidents had been preceded by intense violence, including the March 1948 assassination of a judge who had sentenced a Brother for a bombing attack on a British officers' club and the December 1948 assassination of the hated Cairo police chief Salim Zaki, also by Muslim Brothers.[130]

Al-Rawi continuously emphasized the significance of the political present over the distant psychic past, preferring proximate to primal causes in his attempt to subvert what he termed a Freudian psychological logic. Writing a decade and a half later, Frantz Fanon argued that political violence was inherent to the colonial context, namely, in the creation of a Manichaean world in which the colonizer arrogated unto himself the privileges of the wealth and well-being of the colonized.[131] Like al-Rawi, Fanon surmised that distant or universal unconscious forces retained a less powerful effect than the accumulated or genealogical accretions of the Jungian collective unconscious. In his 1952 *Black Skin, White Masks*, Fanon refashioned the Jungian collective unconscious (which al-Rawi translated as *al-la-shu'ur al-mushtariq*) as materially embodied in cultural artifacts and repositories of memory, while historically constituted by the colonial encounter.[132]

Yet there was a crucial difference between the two. In an important sense, for Fanon, violence constituted the antithesis of nationalist politics (understood as reformist, mollifying, and palliative). It "break[s] the lull introduced by colonialism and make[s] History."[133] It therefore ushered in the temporality of revolution and established what one might call the revolutionary anticolonial sublime: a violence of mythic yet perfectly symmetrical proportions.[134] By contrast, al-Rawi's refutation of Freudian models that reached back into the distant or primal past was premised on developing a political psychology that secured the consent of the governed. Political violence, whether individual or collective, for al-Rawi, was the antithesis of a reformist palliative political program that could harness the insurrectionary potential of individuals and the masses.[135] Political psychology could provide a workable model for dealing with Egypt's most pressing political problems of the tumultuous 1940s—namely, resistance to British imperialism and political oppression at the hands of a political elite beholden to colonial interests, and the increasingly unequal distribution of wealth and political resources. Political psychology, in short, was the cure for the political anomie that had beleaguered Egypt in the late 1930s and 1940s.

Psychopathy

Political crime was a topic that attracted great attention in the 1940s, even in instances where one least expected to find it. While al-Rawi had focused his attention on assassinations and strikes, Sabri Jirjis devoted much of his early career to an exploration of psychopathy, publishing the first full-length Arabic treatise on psychopathy in 1946 *Mushkilat al-Suluk al-Sikubati*.[136] The psychopath had emerged as a new social type in the middle of the twentieth century with the 1941 publication of Hervey Cleckley's *The Mask of Sanity*. Almost half of Jirjis's third edition text was devoted to the description, analysis, and discussion of case studies based predominantly on his work at the ʿAbbasiyya Mental Hospital and later as a director of a psychological clinic at the Ministry of Education.[137] By and large a concern for "the singular, the general, and the normative" marked his case studies.[138] In Jirjis's account "the case" became an illustration of the integrative method established by his mentor Yusuf Murad. The integrative method was useful not in ascertaining the etiology of psychopathy, a process still quite poorly understood at midcentury, but in the description and diagnosis of psychopathy as constituting the disintegration of personality. In Jirjis's rendering:

> By the integrative method is meant that . . . approach which deals with man as a socio-psychobiological unit. Personality, normal or abnormal, is the outcome of the interplay of a multitude of factors, hereditary, constitutional, and environmental, in the broadest sense of these terms.

It is not the summation of its constituent traits, nor is it a synthesis of these traits. It is a dynamic concept in which the biological constitution of the individual, his acquired psychic experience, the social situations to which he is subjected and his future potentialities are all integrated into [a] unitary whole.[139]

Jirjis mobilized a methodology that combined a genetic method with a focus on the past; a cross-sectional method, which focused on the present; and a future-oriented approach that focused on patterns and potentialities.[140] Drawing on Murad, Jirjis argued that integration took place on three levels: biologically speaking integration occurred through the nervous system; psychically, integration took place through memory as a primary register of experience; and at the social level, language, and in particular the stability of meaning, allowed for integration. Thus, language, memory, and the nervous system were the main axes of integration and unity, and conversely of psychic disintegration.[141]

Psychopathy, then, represented disintegration in the sense of an inability to assimilate temporal experience, or, put differently, a psychotic disintegration that prevented the individual from experiencing objective reality and assimilating social values. For example, at the level of language, signs were divorced from their meaning, a process Jirjis, following Cleckley, referred to as semantic dementia. The psychopath, as a result, "lies because he is incapable of experiencing the meaning of truth."[142] Egocentricity, shallow affect, emotional immaturity and instability, impulsiveness, ruthlessness, lack of insight, faulty judgment, unevenness, and absurdity, the principal characteristics, in other words, of psychopathy, were best understood as the absence of the integrating mechanisms of language, memory, and the nervous system.

Empirically, Jirjis's study was based on the analysis of numerous cases of patients at the 'Abbasiyya Mental Hospital observed over a prolonged period of one to three years. Patients were chosen on the basis of gross asocial or antisocial behavior, from all social classes and of all educational levels.[143] Many of the cases appear, in historical hindsight, formulaic. But it is important to remember that at midcentury psychopathy was a fairly new diagnosis. So much so that publication of Cleckley's 1941 magnum opus, *The Mask of Sanity*, electrified specialists and the general public alike. Jirjis's case studies were clearly chosen with an eye toward differential diagnoses. In his case study of M., a twenty-five-year-old, slightly withdrawn male, Jirjis detailed a normal family background beset by early heterosexual experiences with a household servant and later homosexual desires that culminated in a severe breakdown characterized by psychopathic behavior such as arson. In his interpretation Jirjis concluded that the patient was in fact a schizophrenic who was experiencing an extreme dissonance between his strict military-style upbringing and household, with its high standard of moral values, and his own sexual encounters and desires.[144] Somewhat similar was the case of B., a twenty-one-year-old male from a broken family who lacked familial stability and love, who harbored sexual feelings for his stepmother.[145] Although his be-havior included some psychopathic features, such as chronic lying, car theft, and acting out at home and school, Jirjis concluded that this was not a case of psychopathy due to the very clear psychological struggles that had worked themselves through in psychopathic behavior. The aforementioned cases only *appeared* as psychopathy, but were in reality manifestations of clearly delin-eated psychosexual complexes. Such cases were juxtaposed to "textbook" cases, such as the case of L., a twenty-two-year-old male whose entire life was char-acterized by the sole pursuit of immediate pleasure, often of a sexual nature. A narcissist in need of constant attention who had been antagonistic since childhood, L. was completely indulged by his family, exhibited very little con-cern for others except to further his own needs, and bore no signs of psycho-logical struggles.[146] Clearly, then, for Jirjis the presence or absence of psycho-logical complexes and struggles functioned as the ultimate diagnostic indicator for psychopathy.

The case study most relevant to our purposes, because of its highly politi-cal content, was the case of Z., a twenty-two-year-old male arrested and ac-cused of assassinating an Egyptian political figure with ties to the British.[147] Due to clear psychological disturbances, Z. was eventually transferred from prison to ʿAbbasiyya Mental Hospital where Jirjis was able to observe him. Z. hailed from a normal family but exhibited signs of extreme violence and cruelty in childhood; wanted total freedom from his family, and in particular from paternal authority; and was a compulsive liar, thief, and masturbator who was subject to emotional outbursts. Marked by what one would now term delusions of grandeur, and what Jirjis referred to as a hero complex, Z. thought of himself as the greatest leader of Egypt and the world, of the ilk of Napoleon Bonaparte, Mustafa Kamil, and Saʿd Zaghlul; he was Egypt's savior who would free the East, spanning the Maghreb to the Indian Ocean, from colonial rule. His intense hatred of the English colonizers was as marked as his derision of Egyptian rulers. After three initial days of denying his crime, Z. confessed, noting his goal of ridding the country of the English and their Egyptian handmaidens. In the process Z. confessed to other violent attacks on the English, crimes reaching back to when he was sixteen years old.

Of central, almost obsessive interest to Jirjis was the status of Z.'s political beliefs and opinions. Was Z. truly a nationalist intent on freeing Egypt from the British and their lackeys? Or was he merely conniving to garner the bene-fit of public sentiment in order to be set free? According to Jirjis, a careful reading of his confessions and other legal documents made it quite clear that Z. lied continuously and frequently modified or altered his confession story, particularly regarding the causes of the assassination. Bewilderingly, the court records also made clear that Z. lied even when it was not to his personal benefit. His political "beliefs," Jirjis opined, were merely explosive utterances; descriptions of, never the reasons for, his crimes were provided.[148] In fact, Jirjis went out of his way to prove that both Z. and his political crime were not nationalist. Nationalist sentiment (*wataniyya*), he noted, was the apex of social emotions and affect in humans. To be nationalist one needed, quite simply, the capacity for love and sacrifice, sentiments that were not possible in a man ruled by hatred and resentment. Z.'s *nafs* was not capable of *wataniyya*; the self capable of nationalism was a self that was moved by love and the social good.[149]

Z.'s political opinions, Jirjis concluded, were merely a forgery; his aggression had simply shifted from animals and young children toward politicians and colonizers; his desire to free the East was merely a means to satisfy his childish pride and self-aggrandizement. In sum, all of his high-minded attitudes were merely a front for his primal aggression. His nationalist words were signs emptied of meaning, signifiers detached from what they signified, the imitation of sentiment, rather than genuine sentiment. Yet perhaps Jirjis's obsessive desire to draw a clear distinction between an "authentic" nationalism and the affectation of nationalism induced by psychopathy betrayed a deeper anxiety regarding the boundaries between mental health and illness, the normal and the pathological, and between pure psychopathy and the latent potential for a colonial psychosis. As Fanon noted with respect to Algeria's war of liberation, the alleged "criminality" of the Algerian was not a product of an organic disturbance, but, rather, the direct product of the colonial situation.[150]

Undeterred by doubts as to the political undercurrents of Z.'s actions, Jirjis argued that it was the lack of fit between words and their meanings, or between speech and action, that was most indicative of Z.'s illness. Marked by impulsiveness, lack of purpose or objective, grandiosity and primal pride, narcissism, explosiveness, an inability to love, a poverty of affect, a lack of remorse, and an antagonistic relationship to the external world, his confession was merely a childhood hero fantasy.[151] These characteristics coupled with the absence of congenital illness or defect, a solid home environment, and multiple attempts at rehabilitation led Jirjis to conclude that this was a textbook case of psychopathy.[152] A man who could not distinguish imagination from reality, truth from lies, who did not learn from experience, who did not respond to punishment, who lived in a narcissistic and self-focused world devoid of meaning and purpose, and whose total lack of insight, presented us with a rare glimpse of pure psychopathy.[153]

The psychopath, marked by the total absence of affective ties—to other individuals, to the family, and to society—signaled the complete disintegration of personality. How would criminal culpability be adjudicated in this extreme instance? For Jirjis, society had unjustly treated the psychopath as a criminal, when in reality he was in need of mental treatment and supervision in a facility. In the case of the criminal or neurotic, deep-seated emotional conflicts were often causally related, but for the psychopath there was no known cause of illness. Psychopathy was a form of madness, and society, he argued, must come to terms with mental illness.[154] Rather than punitive legal actions, Jirjis suggested a plan that included patient isolation in a special hospital; experimental medical, social, and psychological treatments; and attempts at reeducation.[155] Elsewhere in *Majallat 'Ilm al-Nafs* authors had lobbied vehemently for increased attention to mental health and mental illnesses, which many had argued increased dramatically in the postwar period, in some cases accounting for a higher portion of violent crimes.[156] Although many, such as Mustafa Suwayf, noted that a concern for psychology had developed and could be seen in the increase in the number of books, articles, specialized journals, not to mention films and novels, all bemoaned the absence of psychological clinics, suggesting the need for social workers to function as a liaison between doctors and patients.[157]

Conclusion

At midcentury debates surrounding psychoanalysis and criminology were intensely interconnected. Prominent lawyer and advocate Muhammad Fathi argued for psychoanalysis as a supplement to the law through a secret affinity for hermeneutics, deep causality, and enchanted evidence. The *nahdawi* model of erudition enabled the figure of the lawyer to function as a mediatory personage of modernity, reconciling the new sciences of psychology with the exigencies of the criminal court system, and mediating between a public inclined to see the criminal as the antihero of modernity, and a zealous prosecutorial legal system that was, in part, the complex legacy of European colonialism and the attendant marginalization of Islamic law. Descriptions of the criminal as the besieged victim of an unresolved Oedipus complex served simultaneously to attenuate criminal culpability and appeal to the court of public opinion.

The attempt to introduce psychoanalysis as a new and supplementary form of evidence in the courtroom was met, however, by numerous challenges. Psychoanalysis came directly before the law in a prominent legal case regarding the proper licensing of practicing psychotherapists. Muhammad Fathi passionately argued that psychoanalysis was not a branch of medicine and that licensing laws should be modified to reflect this reality, a view that would ultimately triumph by 1956. Yet Fathi's views faced other challenges from within the psychological profession. Many argued that a psychoanalytic framework for understanding criminality was reductive, and some, following Jung, argued for locating causality in present unconscious conflicts, while others argued for an integrative framework that took into consideration social, psychological, and political factors at one and the same time. Nevertheless, thoroughgoing Freudians and anti-Freudians alike emphasized mitigating factors and the need for rehabilitation and reform, rather than punishment, in the prosecution of criminals. This was part and parcel of a larger social welfare orientation that characterized Egypt in the 1940s and 1950s and was embodied in the establishment of the 1955 National Institute for Criminology, which situated crime and criminality within its larger social and ideological contours. This framework was most apparent in the discussions of political crime, many of which focused on political assassinations, a marked feature of Egypt's political landscape in the second half of the 1940s. Political psychology was posited by some as the cure for the political anomie—the rash of political assassinations, strikes, and student revolts—that had rocked Egypt in the late 1930s and 1940s. Ultimately, theorists and practitioners opted for a view of the transparency of the human subject, one in which criminal intent could be rendered visible, and the criminal could be further subject to the technocratic gaze of the postcolonial state.

Epilogue

Between two subjects, there is only speech or death, salutation or stone.

—MOUSTAPHA SAFOUAN, *SPEECH OR DEATH?*

I WOULD LIKE to reiterate a question with which I began but with an added urgency, what does it mean, *now*, to think through psychoanalysis and Islam together, not as a "problem," but as a creative encounter of ethical engagement? If we take psychoanalysis, at its most fundamental level, to be a practice that allows itself to be transformed by the discourse of the other, we can begin to see the ethical imperative involved in the coupling of these two terms.

Speaking to the Women's Forum organized by *Lacan Quotidien* and *l'École de la cause freudienne* in October 2011, Julia Kristeva attempts to breathe life into Jacques Lacan by examining "the collision, torn from the headlines, as it were, among psychoanalysis, politics, and women."[1] Focusing on the case of Rafah Nashed, a Syrian psychoanalyst imprisoned by Bashar al-Assad from September to November 2011, Kristeva meditates on the singularity and intersubjectivity of psychoanalytic thought and experience, which, she notes, should respond to the central preoccupation of the current millennium, namely, "*happiness* through *freedom*." Indeed, a "psychoanalytic approach, to what is human is opposed as much to a pseudohumanism, ready to constrain sick people in the straitjacket of risk management, as it is to the terror that fundamentalist systems of religion and politics spew out."[2] This is very much in keeping with Kristeva's identification elsewhere of the twin evils of our times, namely, religious fundamentalism and "the management via technology of the human species."[3]

Within this normative framework, Kristeva presents Nashed's work in Syria as disruptive to a tyrannical regime, but also as a response to the "backwardness of psychiatry in Syria, with the fear of saying 'I' and 'no' in a land where tradition does not encourage personal speech, and under a violent and physically repressive regime."[4] Her assessment of Nashed's work is most clearly laden by an overarching concern: "Let's be serious. Nobody knows what will follow the current regime. Many of us fear that the revolution may lead to the empowerment of a fundamentalism that will be insidious early on, but disastrous in the long run."[5] And it is on the basis of that fear that she positively evaluates Nashed's program of translating psychoanalytic texts, and of her "efforts to interpret, in the light of psychoanalysis, Islamic religious experience."[6]

It is not my intent here to parse Nashed's writings on psychoanalysis and Islam, her juxtaposition of the interior experience of Sufism with the "psychic apparatus" of Freud and the "topologies" of Lacan, or her assertion "that psychoanalysis is a work of civilization, that is to say, a work of life ... which is almost impossible to communicate directly in Arabic.... Arab society has not entered post-modernism."[7] That would be a task appropriate to another time and another place. Rather, what intrigues me is Kristeva's reduction of Nashed's psychoanalytic program to a bulwark against

> the fundamentalist threat that politics cannot resolve purely with laws, economic measures, or even military campaigns.... Yet Rafah Nashed does not attack this head on. She does not target scarves or burkas, the imprisonment of women or the calls to jihad. Faced with the religious practices of Islam, Rafah and her colleagues take an interest in Sufism, because of the psychical link, in that practice, between "Me [*Moi*]" and "THEE [*TOI*]."[8]

Such a framing of Nashed's work is part of the "civilizing mission" that international (and particularly French) psychoanalytic associations have been engaged in, conceptualized as a battle that pits psychoanalysis against fundamentalism and theocracy.[9] A reliance on a civilizational paradigm, which has, perhaps, always bedeviled Freud, leads Kristeva to recapitulate the alleged "distinctive features of Islam," features that "make an Islamic theo-*logy* improbable if not impossible, and, similarly, any 'discussion' between Sunnis and Shiites, not to mention with the other two monotheisms. These distinctive features also handicap a possible opening of Islam toward the ethical and political problems raised by the freedoms, full of risks, of the men and women of the third millennium and by the different ways of thinking in confrontation on these subjects."[10] Islam is, once again, contrasted with the "genius of Christianity," Catholicism's brilliance, or the "deepening produced, in the case of Judaism, by the murder perpetrated against the religion's founding figure."[11]

It would be inaccurate to portray this civilizing mission of psychoanalysis as solely a European endeavor, and contemporary Arab analysts, such as Fethi Benslama, have forayed into this debate. For Benslama, psychoanalysis can provide the basis of an inquiry into "the rise of Islamist movements and the historical conditions of their discourse" as well as a bulwark against contemporary Islamist movements.[12] Joseph Massad has critiqued such writings as bearing the mark of their liberal location, emanating from authors in the margins of the Arab diaspora in Paris. Such writings are constitutively stained, he notes, by their "unwavering commitment to the liberal values of individualism, freedom, tolerance, and separation of the theological from the political," indicative, to use his terms, of a conversion to liberalism.[13] To Benslama, Stefania Pandolfo juxtaposes the writings of Egyptian Lacanian Moustapha Safouan whose discussion of political Islamic movements, such as the Muslim Brotherhood, rejects an understanding of them as simply antidemocratic formations, but sees them, rather, as having the power to interrupt the tyranny of the state while moving against the subjugation of the subject.[14]

Safouan's more generous reading, as it were, of political Islam may relate, in part, to his lack of a presumption of a secularized subject of analysis. In *Speech or Death?*, a book that grew out of political discussions of the Iranian revolution, even as it bears no outward traces of that kernel of thought, Safouan returns to the necessity of the transcendental.[15] Safouan, it must be recalled, was trained in Alexandria by Abu al-ʿAlaʾ al-Afifi, one of the foremost scholars of the medieval mystic Ibn ʿArabi, before joining Lacan's circle in Paris in 1949 and translating Freud's *Interpretation of Dreams* into Arabic in 1958.

"Belief," he notes, "gives a name to the law, but a name which is borrowed from death, the sole kingdom to lend us the transcendental, namely, God, beyond his prophets, ancestors, totems or even dreams. The giving of a name to the law, the creating of the sovereign in beliefs, is the necessary and at the same time pointless detour by means of which the law of the name, operating . . . from behind, is guaranteed in the eyes of consciousness by the name of the law."[16] In other words, religion is "what gives the symbolic a real efficacy, albeit by way of the imaginary."[17] Thus he asks whether "the prohibition upon lying and that upon murder, together with the obligation associated with the gift, might not constitute, with the incest prohibition, a set of four laws for which no subject, however lofty his social status, could assume the paternity."[18] The "secret," then, shared between psychoanalysis and religion is in the belief in this third location, beyond I and thou, a place from which the law emanates; the "transcendental is the only mechanism by which you can imagine law or even give effectiveness to law. That is the necessity of the imaginary to grasp the symbolic."[19] Both religion and psychoanalysis, then, attempt to grasp how the subject becomes the addressee of a divine or transcendental discourse.[20]

Let us return to the question of the relationship between Islam and politics. In *Why Are the Arabs Not Free?*, a text beset by Orientalist notions of civilizational lethargy, but nonetheless intriguing, Safouan argues that Arab political culture has been marked by a "'con-fusion' between theology and political coercion."[21] According to Safouan, political legitimacy in the Middle East has been derived from the power of "the Monarch or the One who governs" on the basis of a divine or religious character. This system of government is based on a complete abyss between the One and the masses—the subjects he governs. Subjectivity, and intersubjective relations, within this system are impossible—as the place of the monarch "is outside the realm of individuals who resemble each other and of the equality of egos."[22] This figure of the Third occupied by a person, rather than a signifier, leads to the absolute and unlimited power of the political monarch and the patriarch—the "unhappy lot [of] Arabs."[23] This political theology that marks the Arab world forecloses, for Safouan, proper political subjectivity, which for him is only possible in democracy.

But perhaps the most interesting and provocative thesis that Safouan develops is that political theology in the Arab world is intimately linked to the hegemony of language, and in particular to the elevation of classical Arabic over demotic languages.[24] The antagonism is not between religion as such and (political) subjectivity. It is not, in other words, the case that in Islam ipso facto the monarch occupies the place of the transcendent. Rather, it is the ancient legacy of writing in what he terms the "archaic state," which has imbued the monarch with a role as transcendent lawgiver, and in which the main purpose of writing was to maintain social differences between rulers and ruled.[25] Thus neither the Qur'an nor Islam have led to the culture of political coercion, but rather, "Islam was the victim of the nations it invaded, because they themselves were the victims of political regimes and administrative apparatuses whose sole purpose was to ensure the state's domination over all aspects of life."[26]

In his concluding chapter, presciently titled "The Fraud of the Islamic State," Safouan argues that

> except for the Prophet, God did not ascribe the knowledge of the final meaning or of truth to any particular individual, whatever might be his or her status, or to any institution, whatever might be its authority.... Indeed, to claim to share God's knowledge is as blasphemous as to claim that there are other gods that share God's divinity.
>
> It is precisely on such a blasphemous lie that the Islamic state was built. It was built on the claim that God delegated to it not only His power, but also His knowledge of the "truth."[27]

The Prophet, properly speaking, Safouan argues, should have no successor, and the institution of an Islamic state, or caliphate, after his death is the fraud Safouan refers to in his title. Although the distinctive feature of Islam is its lack of institutionalization in the form of a Church, he argues that it is the Islamic state that usurped this role, arrogating itself as the highest religious and political authority.[28] "The Prophet's relation to God was unique, and he can have no successor."[29] The implication of this argument, as Colin MacCabe notes, is that "the question of what Islam means politically in the modern era is an open one."[30] Safouan's position, therefore, differs decidedly from that of

Julia Kristeva and Fethi Benslama, whose discussions, as we have seen, rest on the normative assumptions of a great divergence between politics and theology and of a secular subject of psychoanalysis.

The arguments of one of Safouan's Egyptian colleagues and advocates, psychoanalyst Husayn ʿAbd al-Qadir, are instructive in this regard. Distinguishing his quest from what he terms the chauvinistic and illusory search for the past, he expounds upon the sources of the self within the Arabic tradition while offering pages from a history of science that recognizes the universal nature of all scientific knowledge.[31] Documenting an unexplored terrain, namely, that of the notions of the psyche embedded within the Arabic tradition, and beginning from the ʿAbbasid era, he details a rich heritage not limited to the mere translation and transmission of Greek texts but inclusive of the array of Arabo-Islamic sciences, and in particular, philosophy, medicine, and the religious sciences.[32]

Thus, for instance, ʿAbd al-Qadir notes that Freud's 1923 discussion of the tripartite distinction of the self, the id, ego, and superego, could be found in Abu Hamid al-Ghazali's *Ihya' ʿUlum al-Din*, which was translated into German in 1913; that Avicenna's view of the self and of fantasy was similar to that of Freud's, and that some of Avicenna's methods foreshadowed those of the group psychodrama techniques established by Jacob Moreno in the 1920s; and that Abu Bakr Muhammad Bin Zakariyya al-Razi's *Spiritual Physick* heavily theorized the relationship between the psyche and the body, arguably the main concern of psychoanalysis.[33] In demonstrating the innovations and depth of thought of the Arabic tradition on the psyche or *nafs*, ʿAbd al-Qadir departs from Rafah Nashed's assertion "that psychoanalysis is a work of civilization ... which is almost impossible to communicate directly in Arabic." In this he recollects the work of the midcentury psychologists on which this book has centered.

Yusuf Murad and his coterie of students likewise traversed literatures premodern and modern and plumbed the depths of the classical Islamic tradition on selfhood to register epistemological resonances between prepsychoanalytic (Aristotelian and Islamic) and analytic traditions. Not seen as the purview of a singular civilization, psychoanalysis was opened up as a discourse that engaged the collective ends of man, rather than the phantasmatic lure of the "I."[34] Such collective ends were not to be realized through the extirpation of a past allegedly hostile to the secular ends of analysis. Writing in the middle of the twentieth century, psychoanalysis had not yet been reduced to a political and ideological signifier emptied of all meaning, a mere weapon in a Manichaean struggle between secularism and civilization on the one hand and nonsecular forms of reason and ethics on the other.[35]

And yet psychoanalysis may continue to offer, one, although not the only possible, outlet to the maladies of our time, an ethical stance in which we not only subject ourselves and our drives to radical critique but simultaneously open ourselves up to an ethical encounter with the Other. What might it mean to take personal responsibility, in the words of Henry Corbin, for the connection between the modalities of the inner self and the appearance of the outer world?[36] What types of encounters might then be possible?

Introduction: Psychoanalysis and Islam

1. Yusuf Murad, "Bab al-Taʿrifat: Niwa li-Qamus ʿIlm al-Nafs," *Majallat ʿIlm al-Nafs* 1, no. 1 (1945): 106.

2. Yusuf Murad, *Shifaʾ al-Nafs* (Cairo: Dar al-Maʿarif, 1943); Muhammad Fathi, *Mushkilat al-Tahlil al-Nafsi fi Misr* (Cairo: Matbaʿat Misr, 1946).

3. See *Tafsir al-Ahlam*, trans. Mustafa Safwan, rev. Mustafa Ziywar (Cairo: Dar al-Maʿarif, 2004). For a partial catalog of Arabic translations of Freud, see Josette Zoueïn, "Freud en arabe: Notice bibliographique," *Che vuoi?* 21 (2004): 100–104. https://www.cairn .info/revue-che-vuoi-2004-1-page-101.htm. It is important to note that English and French translations of Freud and Arabic synopses were available and widely read prior to formal translation efforts.

4. Jacques Lacan, *The Seminar of Jacques Lacan, Book VII: The Ethics of Psychoanalysis, 1959–1960*, ed. Jacques-Alain Miller, trans. Dennis Porter (New York: Norton, 1992), 37.

5. Very few studies have addressed the grammar and vocabulary of modern selfhood within Middle Eastern societies. Anthropologists and literary scholars, however, have paved the way in this regard. See, for example, Stefania Pandolfo, *Impasse of the Angels* (Chicago: University of Chicago Press, 1997); Pandolfo, "The Thin Line of Modernity: Some Moroccan Debates on Subjectivity," in *Questions of Modernity*, ed. Timothy Mitchell (Minneapolis: University of Minnesota Press, 2000), 115–47; Pandolfo, "'Soul Choking': Maladies of the Soul, Islam, and the Ethics of Psychoanalysis," *Umbr(a): Islam* (2009): 71–103; Pandolfo, *Knot of the Soul: Madness, Psychoanalysis, Islam* (Chicago: University of Chicago Press, 2017); Suad Joseph, ed., *Intimate Selving in Arab Families: Gender, Self, and Identity* (Syracuse, NY: Syracuse University Press, 1999); Joseph, "Learning Desire: Relational Pedagogies and the Desiring Female Subject in Lebanon," *Journal of Middle East Women's Studies* 1, no. 1 (2005): 79–109; Joseph, "Thinking Intentionality: Arab Women's Subjectivity and Its Discontents," *Journal of Middle East Women's Studies* 8, no. 2 (2012): 1–25; Amira Mittermaier, *Dreams That Matter: An Anthropology of the Imagination in Modern Egypt* (Berkeley: University of California Press, 2011); Stephen Sheehi, *Foundations of Modern Arab Identity* (Gainesville: University Press of Florida, 2004); Sheehi, "Inscribing the Arab Self: Butrus al-Bustani and Paradigms of Subjective Reform," *British Journal of Middle Eastern Studies* 27, no. 1 (2000): 7–24.

6. I am drawing on Talal Asad's idea of "Islam as a discursive tradition," in "The Idea of an Anthropology of Islam," *Occasional Papers, Center for Contemporary Arab Studies* (Washington, DC: Georgetown University, 1986) and Samira Haj, *Reconfiguring Islamic Tradition: Reform, Rationality, and Modernity* (Stanford, CA: Stanford University Press, 2009).

7. Tawfiq al-Hakim, "Introduction to King Oedipus," in *The Arab Oedipus: Four Plays from Egypt and Syria*, ed. Marvin Carlson (New York: Martin E. Segal Theatre Center Publications, 2005), 16–40, see especially 22, 27, 32.

8. Salama Musa, *al-ʿAql al-Batin, aw Maknunat al-Nafs* (Cairo: al-Hilal, 1928).

9. On Salama Musa's psychoanalytic forays, see Joseph Massad, *Desiring Arabs* (Chicago: University of Chicago Press, 2007), 128–41.

10. Musa, *al-ʿAql al-Batin*, 7.

11. Ibrahim Naji, "al-Shabab al-Misri wa-l-Mushkila al-Jinsiyya," *al-Hilal* 47 (1938): 57–60. Naji noted that students were reading Freud outside of their university curriculum and in a rather haphazard and at times refracted fashion.

12. 'Ali Adham, "Fruyd wa-l-Harb," *al-Thaqafa* 3, no. 153 (December 2, 1941): 1564–69; Sigmund Freud, "Thoughts for the Times of War and Death" (1915), in vol. 14 of *The Standard Edition of the Complete Psychological Works of Sigmund Freud*, trans. and ed. James Strachey et al. (London: Hogarth Press, 1981; cited hereafter as *SE*), 273–302; Freud, *Beyond the Pleasure Principle* (1920), *SE* 18: 1–64. I am grateful to Israel Gershoni for bringing 'Ali Adham's article to my attention and providing me with a copy.

13. See, for example, Mustafa Ziywar's book review of *'Ilm al-Nafs al-'Amali*, *Majallat 'Ilm al-Nafs* 1, no. 1 (1945): 75–78.

14. Kamal al-Din 'Abd al-Hamid Nayal, "Athar 'Alaqat al-Tifl bi-Walidayhi fi Zawajuhu," *Majallat 'Ilm al-Nafs* 7, no. 1 (1951): 25–33.

15. Marvin Carlson, "Editor's Introduction," in Carlson, *Arab Oedipus*, 1–13. According to Carlson, "the first exposure of the Arab world to the Sophoclean legend" was to Voltaire's neoclassical version, translated as *Udib, aw al-Sirr al-Ha'il* by Najib al-Hadad in 1905. I thank Ellen McLarney for drawing my attention to this literature.

16. Carlson, "Editor's Introduction," 5–6; Tawfiq al-Hakim, *King Oedipus*, in Carlson, *Arab Oedipus*, 41–119, especially act 3, scene 1. See also William M. Hutchins, *Tawfiq al-Hakim: A Reader's Guide* (Boulder, CO: Lynne Rienner, 2003), 102–3.

17. Naguib Mahfouz, *The Mirage*, trans. Nancy Roberts (New York: Anchor Books, 2012), 23. On the Oedipus complex in Arabic literature, see Jurj Tarabishi, *'Uqdat Udib fi al-Riwaya al-'Arabiyya* (Beirut: Dar al-Tali'a, 1982); for a discussion of Arabic literature's hospitality to psychoanalysis, see Julia Borossa, "The Extensibility of Psychoanalysis in Ahmed Alaidy's *Being Abbas el Abd* and Bahaa Taher's *Love in Exile*," *Journal of Postcolonial Writing* 47, no. 4 (2011): 404–15.

18. Sayyid Qutb, *al-Naqd al-Adabi, Usuluh wa-Manhajihu* (Beirut: Dar al-Shuruq, 1970), 182.

19. Ibid., 182–89; Sigmund Freud, *Leonardo da Vinci and a Memory of His Childhood* (1910), *SE* 11: 57–137.

20. Qutb, *al-Naqd al-Adabi*, 184–85. Qutb bases his discussion of Leonardo da Vinci on Mustafa Isma'il Suwayf, "al-Tahlil al-Nafsi wa-l-Fannan," *Majallat 'Ilm al-Nafs* 2, no. 2 (1946): 282–302; cf. Massad, *Desiring Arabs*, 124–26. There is no evidence of Qutb's direct familiarity with Freud.

21. Massad, *Desiring Arabs*, 84–90; Muhammad al-Nuwayhi, *Nafsiyyat Abi Nuwas* (Cairo: Maktabat al-Khanji, 1970); 'Abbas Mahmud al-'Aqqad, *Abu Nuwas al-Hasan ibn Hani', Dirasa fi al-Tahlil al-Nafsani wa-l-Naqd al-Tarihki* (Cairo: Dar al-Hilal, 1960). In 1965 Husayn Muruwa criticized the bourgeois orientation of psychoanalysis, with its focus on the individual self rather than social conditions, through a discussion of Abu Nuwas, see Massad, *Desiring Arabs*, 90–92; Muruwa, *Dirasa Naqdiyya fi daw' al-Manhaj al-Waqi'i* (Beirut: Makatabat al-Ma'arif, 1965). Interestingly, al-'Aqqad had also included a quasi-Freudian analysis of Adolf Hitler's personality in his 1940 book *Hitler in the Balance*, see Israel Gershoni, "The Demise of the 'Liberal Age'?: 'Abbas Mahmud al-'Aqqad and Egyptian Responses to Fascism during World War II," in *Arabic Thought beyond the Liberal Age: Towards an Intellectual History of the Nahda*, ed. Jens Hanssen and Max Weiss (Cambridge: Cambridge University Press, 2016), 298–322.

22. Sara Pursley, "The Stage of Adolescence, Anticolonial Time, Youth Insurgency, and the Marriage Crisis in Hashimite Iraq," *History of the Present* 3, no. 2 (2013): 160–97, quotation 185; see also Massad, *Desiring Arabs*, 142–44.

23. Charles Taylor, *Sources of the Self: The Making of the Modern Identity* (Cambridge, MA: Harvard University Press, 1989).

24. Jerrold Seigel, *The Idea of the Self: Thought and Experience in Western Europe since the Seventeenth Century* (Cambridge: Cambridge University Press, 2005), 43.

25. Ibid.

26. Ibid., 25.

27. See Ranjana Khanna, *Dark Continents: Psychoanalysis and Colonialism* (Durham, NC: Duke University Press, 2003), 5, 10–11. Similarly, the edited volume *Unconscious Dominions* asks, "How, indeed, did the modern psychoanalytic subject—a distinctive style of imagining one's subjectivity or psychic makeup—go global?" and explores the "conflicted cosmopolitan figure of the universalized, psychoanalyzable subject" as a constitutively "colonial creature." Warwick Anderson, Deborah Jenson, and Richard Keller, eds., *Unconscious Dominions: Psychoanalysis, Colonial Trauma, and Global Sovereignties* (Durham, NC: Duke University Press, 2011), 1.

28. Shruti Kapila, "The 'Godless' Freud and His Indian Friends: An Indian Agenda for Psychoanalysis," in *Psychiatry and Empire*, ed. Sloan Mahone and Megan Vaughan (Basingstoke, UK: Palgrave Macmillan, 2007), 124–52; see also Kris Manjapra, *Age of Entanglement: German and Indian Intellectuals across Empire* (Cambridge, MA: Harvard University Press, 2014), chap. 9; Ashis Nandy, *The Savage Freud and Other Essays on Possible and Retrievable Selves* (Princeton: Princeton University Press, 1995), 81–144. For a contemporary consideration of these issues, see "Psychoanalysis and India," in special issue, *Psychoanalytic Review* 102, no. 6 (2015), especially Salman Akhtar's thought-provoking, "Where Is India in My Psychoanalytic Work?" 873–911; see also Ahmed Fayek, "Islam and Its Effect on My Practice of Psychoanalysis," *Psychoanalytic Psychology* 21, no. 3 (2004): 452–57.

29. Christiane Hartnack, "Colonial Dominions and the Psychoanalytic Couch: Synergies of Freudian Theory with Bengali Hindu Thought and Practices in British India," in Anderson, Jenson, and Keller, *Unconscious Dominions*, 97–111; Mariano Ben Plotkin, *Freud in the Pampas: The Emergence and Development of Psychoanalytic Culture in Argentina* (Stanford, CA: Stanford University Press, 2001); Rubén Gallo, *Freud's Mexico: Into the Wilds of Psychoanalysis* (Cambridge, MA: MIT Press, 2010), 2. Within Middle East studies, for a brief discussion of the Iranian reception of Freud, see Afsaneh Najmabadi, "Genus of Sex: Or the Sexing of *Jins*," *International Journal of Middle East Studies* 45, no. 2 (2013): 211–31; for an exploration of the relationship between psychiatry, psychology, and "medicalized modernity" in Iran, see Cyrus Schayegh, *Who Is Knowledgeable Is Strong: Science, Class, and the Formation of Modern Iranian Society, 1900–1950* (Berkeley: University of California Press, 2009); Schayegh, "'A Sound Mind Lives in a Healthy Body': Texts and Contexts in the Iranian Modernists' Scientific Discourse of Health, 1910s–40s," *International Journal of Middle East Studies* 37, no. 2 (2005): 167–88; Orkideh Behrouzan, *Prozak Diaries: Psychiatry and Generational Memory in Iran* (Stanford, CA: Stanford University Press, 2016); and for a discussion of the relation between the psychoanalytic theory of the unconscious and pedagogy in Iraq, see Pursley, "Stage of Adolescence." In the East Asian context, on early psychoanalysis in Japan and its relationship to Buddhism, see Geoffrey H. Blowers and Serena Yang Hsueh Chi, "Freud's *Deshi*: The Coming of Psychoanalysis to Japan," *Journal of the History of the Behavioral Sciences* 33, no. 2 (1997): 115–26; Christopher Harding, "The Therapeutic Method of Kosawa Heisaku: 'Religion' and the 'Psy Disciplines,'" in *Japanese Contributions to Psychoanalysis*, vol. 4, ed. Toyoaki Ogawa (Tokyo: Japan Psychoanalytic Society, 2014), 151–68. Li Zhang has explored the fusion of Western psychotherapeutic approaches with Buddhism and Daoism in postsocialist China, see "Cultivating Happiness: Psychotherapy, Spirituality, and Well-Being in a Transforming Urban China," in *Handbook of Religion and the Asian City: Aspiration and Urbanization in the Twenty-First Century*, ed. Peter van der Veer (Oakland: University of California Press, 2015): 315–32; "Bentuhua: Culturing

Psychotherapy in Postsocialist China," *Culture, Medicine, and Psychiatry* 38, no. 2 (2014): 283–305.

30. Khanna, *Dark Continents*, 6.

31. Nathan Gorelick, "Translating the Islamicate Symptom: A Review Essay of *Doing Psychoanalysis in Tehran* and *Lacan and Religion*," *SCTIW Review: Journal of the Society for Contemporary Thought and the Islamicate World*, June 9, 2015, quotation 12; Sigmund Freud, *Moses and Monotheism: Three Essays* (1939), *SE* 23: 7–137; "Obsessive Actions and Religious Practices" (1907), *SE* 9: 115–27; *The Future of an Illusion* (1927), *SE* 21: 1–56; *Civilization and Its Discontents* (1930), *SE* 21: 57–145; see also Donald Capps, introduction to Donald Capps, ed., *Freud and Freudians on Religion: A Reader* (New Haven, CT: Yale University Press, 2001).

32. Sudhir Kakar, *The Analyst and the Mystic: Psychoanalytic Reflections on Religion and Mysticism* (New Delhi: Penguin, 2007), chap. 3.

33. Bruno Bettelheim, *Freud and Man's Soul: An Important Re-Interpretation of Freudian Theory* (London: Flamingo, 1985), 35; Kakar, *The Analyst and the Mystic*, 66–67.

34. Peter Gay emphasizes Freud's atheism in *A Godless Jew: Freud, Atheism, and the Making of Psychoanalysis* (New Haven, CT: Yale University Press, 1989). For discussions of the significance of the Jewish context of Freud's life and work, see Emmanuel Rice, *Freud and Moses: The Long Journey Home* (Albany: State University of New York Press, 1990); Yosef Hayim Yerushalmi, *Freud's Moses: Judaism Terminable and Interminable* (New Haven, CT: Yale University Press, 1991); Richard J. Bernstein, *Freud and the Legacy of Moses* (Cambridge: Cambridge University Press, 1998); Eliza Slavet, *Racial Fever: Freud and the Jewish Question* (New York: Fordham University Press, 2009); Adam Phillips, *Becoming Freud: The Making of a Psychoanalyst* (New Haven, CT: Yale University Press, 2014); Ruth Ginsburg and Ilana Pardes, eds., *New Perspectives on Freud's Moses and Monotheism* (Berlin: Walter de Gruyter, 2006); Michael Mack, "The Savage Science: Sigmund Freud, Psychoanalysis, and the History of Religion," *Journal of Religious History* 30, no. 3 (2006): 331–53; Stephen Frosh, "Hauntings: Psychoanalysis and Ghostly Transmission," *American Imago* 69, no. 2 (2012): 241–64. For a discussion of the relationship of Moses, and Freud's rethinking of him, to the distinction between true and false religion, see Jan Assmann, *Moses the Egyptian: The Memory of Egypt in Western Monotheism* (Cambridge, MA: Harvard University Press, 1998). For what remains the best discussion of Freud's historical context, see John Toews, "Historicizing Psychoanalysis: Freud in His Time and for Our Time," *Journal of Modern History* (1991): 504–45.

35. David Bakan, *Sigmund Freud and the Jewish Mystical Tradition* (New York: Schocken Books, 1965).

36. Edward W. Said, *Freud and the Non-European* (London: Verso, 2003), 44. Interestingly, the reception of *Moses and Monotheism* in Egypt in 1939 was fairly hostile, and scholars argued against Moses's Egyptian origin, passionately upholding his Jewish ancestry, which, Fethi Benslama claims, "shows that there was little sympathy for the anti-Semitic spirit shown in Europe," Fethi Benslama, *Psychoanalysis and the Challenge of Islam*, trans. Robert Bononno (Minneapolis: University of Minnesota Press, 2009), 185. Indeed, any negative associations with Freud's Jewishness, for example by linking it to Zionism, occur only much later, starting in 1970 according to Joseph Massad, "Psychoanalysis, Islam, and the Other of Liberalism," *Umbr(a)*: Islam (2009): 43–68, 66–67n68.

37. Said, *Freud and the Non-European*, 54. See Jacqueline Rose's nuanced "Response to Edward Said," in Said, *Freud and the Non-European*, 65–79.

38. James J. DiCenso, *The Other Freud: Religion, Culture, and Psychoanalysis* (New York: Routledge, 1999), 2, 3; Kenneth Reinhard, "Freud, My Neighbor," *American Imago* 54, no. 2 (1997): 165–95, quotation 190.

39. James W. Jones, *Contemporary Psychoanalysis and Religion: Transference and Transcendence* (New Haven, CT: Yale University Press, 1993). For a rethinking of the relationship between Freud and religious studies, see Gregory Kaplan and William B. Parsons, eds., *Disciplining Freud on Religion: Perspectives from the Humanities and Social Sciences* (Lanham, MD: Lexington Books, 2010).

40. Eric L. Santner, *On the Psychotheology of Everyday Life: Reflections on Freud and Rosenzweig* (Chicago: University of Chicago Press, 2001).

41. DiCenso, *Other Freud*, 6–7, 35; William H. Wahl, "Pathologies of Desire and Duty: Freud, Ricoeur, and Castoriadis on Transforming Religious Culture," *Journal of Religion and Health* 47 (2008): 398–414, quotation 399; Paul Marcus, "Religion without Promises: The Philosophy of Emmanuel Levinas and Psychoanalysis," *Psychoanalytic Review* 93, no. 6 (2006): 923–51.

42. DiCenso, *Other Freud*, 4.

43. Lacan, *Ethics of Psychoanalysis*, 171; Reinhard, "Freud, My Neighbor," 180.

44. Kenneth Reinhard and Julia Reinhard Lupton, "The Subject of Religion: Lacan and the Ten Commandments," *Diacritics* 33, no. 2 (2003): 71–97, quotation 71. They conclude: "it is not the temptation but rather the opportunity and even responsibility of psychoanalysis to come to be in the place vacated by monotheism in modernity—not in order to fill that place but, lovingly, to probe it" (96).

45. James J. DiCenso, "Symbolism and Subjectivity: A Lacanian Approach to Religion," *Journal of Religion* 74, no. 1 (1994): 45–64, quotation 47; Reinhard and Lupton, "Subject of Religion"; Clayton Crockett, "On Sublimation: The Significance of Psychoanalysis for the Study of Religion," *Journal of the American Academy of Religion* 68, no. 4 (2000): 837–55; Marcus Pound, "Towards a Lacanian Theology of Religion," *New Blackfriars* 84, no. 993 (2003): 510–20. See the special issue of *American Imago*, 54, no. 2 (Summer 1997), especially: Richard R. Glejzer, "Lacan with Scholasticism: Agencies of the Letter," *American Imago* 54, no. 2 (1997): 105–22; Marcia Ian, "Freud, Lacan, and Imaginary Secularity," *American Imago* 54, no. 2 (1997): 123–47; Reinhard, "Freud, My Neighbor."

46. Reinhard, "Freud, My Neighbor," 185; DiCenso, "Symbolism and Subjectivity," 64.

47. Marion Milner, *The Suppressed Madness of Sane Men* (London: Routledge, 1988), 265.

48. Ibid., 265–66.

49. Freud, *Civilization and Its Discontents, SE* 21: 64.

50. Ibid., 68.

51. Ibid., 68–73.

52. Khanna, *Dark Continents*, 95. On the racial and colonial subtext of Freud's work on religion in relation to the concept of primitivity, see Celia Brickman, "Primitivity, Race, and Religion in Psychoanalysis," *Journal of Religion* 82, no. 1 (2002): 53–74.

53. Freud, *Civilization and Its Discontents*, 65. William James, a contemporary of Freud, lectured on the varieties of religious experience at the turn of the twentieth century. Like Freud, he noted for his audience that he had never himself experienced a mystical state, "for my own constitution shuts me out from their enjoyment almost entirely." James, *The Varieties of Religious Experience: A Study in Human Nature* (New York: Penguin Books, 1982), 379.

54. William Parsons, *The Enigma of the Oceanic Feeling: Revisioning the Psychoanalytic Theory of Mysticism* (Oxford: Oxford University Press, 1999), 14; Parsons, "The Oceanic Feeling Revisited," *Journal of Religion* 78, no. 4 (1998): 501–23.

55. Jeffrey J. Kripal, "*The Enigma of the Oceanic Feeling: Revisioning the Psychoanalytic Theory of Mysticism* by William B. Parsons," *Journal of Religion* 80, no. 2 (2000): 372–74, quotation 374.

56. Marc De Kesel, *Eros and Ethics: Reading Jacques Lacan's Seminar VII*, trans. Sigi Jöttkandt (Albany: State University of New York Press, 2009), 65–66.

57. Ibid., 50–51.

58. Lacan, *Ethics of Psychoanalysis*, 145–51; Jacques Lacan, "God and the *Jouissance* of The Woman. A Love Letter," in *Feminine Sexuality: Jacques Lacan and the école freudienne*, ed. Juliet Mitchell and Jacqueline Rose, trans. Jacqueline Rose (New York: W. W. Norton, 1985), 137–61; 140–41.

59. The discussion of *das Ding* permeates Lacan, *Ethics of Psychoanalysis*, the reference to "religion in all its forms" is on 130; Freud discusses *das Ding* in the *Project for a Scientific Psychology* (1895), *SE* 1: 281–397. For an elaboration see Kesel, *Eros and Ethics*, chap. 4; Bruce Fink, *The Lacanian Subject: Between Language and Jouissance* (Princeton, NJ: Princeton University Press, 1995), 95–96.

60. Kesel, *Eros and Ethics*, 102–3.

61. Lacan, *Ethics of Psychoanalysis*, 130, 118; Stephen J. Costello, "The Real of Religion and Its Relation to Truth as Cause," *The Letter* 13 (Summer 1998): 69–81, quotation 80. As Lacan notes, "Freud left us with the problem of a gap once again at the level of *das Ding*, which is that of religious men and mystics, at a time when we could no longer rely on the father's guarantee," *Ethics of Psychoanalysis*, 100; and sublimation raises the object to the dignity of the Thing, *Ethics of Psychoanalysis*, 117–18.

62. Lacan as cited by Kesel, *Eros and Ethics*, 164.

63. Michel de Certeau, *The Mystic Fable*, vol. 1, *The Sixteenth and Seventeenth Centuries*, trans. Michael B. Smith (Chicago: University of Chicago Press, 1992), 7–8, 11, 13, quotation 8. In other words, mysticism "had for its place an *elsewhere* and for its sign an *anti-society* which would nevertheless represent the initial ground [*fonds*] of man," ibid., 12. Richard E. Webb and Michael Sells likewise place mysticism and psychoanalysis in conversation in "Lacan and Bion: Psychoanalysis and the Mystical Language of 'Unsaying,'" *Theory and Psychology* 5, no. 2 (1995): 195–215.

64. Benslama, *Psychoanalysis and the Challenge of Islam*, 220n34.

65. Tunisian analyst Raja Ben Slama comments that "the first translators rendered it [the unconscious] by an old term evident in the great Andalusian mystic Ibn Arabi (1165–1240): *lâshu'ur* which is a negation of knowledge and feeling," "The Tree That Reveals the Forest: Arabic Translations of Freudian Terminology," *Transeuropéennes*, November 5, 2009, 7. http://www.transeuropeennes.eu/en/articles/106/The_Tree_that_Reveals_the_Forest. Here she is not referencing Yusuf Murad, of whom she seems unaware, but later translators.

66. Ibn 'Arabi as cited by Jean-Michel Hirt, "To Believe or to Interpret," trans. Kristina Valendinova, in *S, Journal of the Jan van Eyck Circle for Lacanian Ideology Critique* 2 (2009): 10–13, quotation 13; for a different translation, see Ibn al-'Arabi, *The Bezels of Wisdom*, trans. R.W.J. Austin (New York: Paulist Press, 1980), 99.

67. Hirt, "To Believe or to Interpret," 12, 13. See also Toshihiko Izutsu's discussion of the significance of Ibn 'Arabi's interpretation of Abraham's dream in *Sufism and Taoism: A Comparative Study of Key Philosophical Concepts* (Berkeley: University of California Press, 1983), 3–15.

68. Benslama, *Psychoanalysis and the Challenge of Islam*, 182.

69. Ibid., 182; Benslama, "Of a Renunciation of the Father," trans. Roland Végsö, *Umbr(a): Islam* (2009): 25–33, quotation 29. I retain Benslama's transliterations.

70. Benslama, "Of a Renunciation of the Father," 31.

71. Ibid., 31; Hirt, "To Believe or to Interpret," provides a poetic reading of Ibn 'Arabi's reading of Abraham's dream as one in which belief in the dream is juxtaposed to interpretation, as manifest content is to latent content.

72. Benslama, "Of a Renunciation of the Father," 31.

73. On Ibn 'Arabi's influence on Lacan, see Benslama, *Psychoanalysis and the Challenge of Islam*, 220n34, and my discussion in chapter 2.

74. Benslama, "Of a Renunciation of the Father," 25. For a wide-ranging exploration of psychoanalysis in the Arab and Islamic world, see Chawki Azouri and Elisabeth Roudinesco, eds., *La psychoanalyse dans le monde arabe et islamique* (Beirut: Presses de l'Université Saint-Joseph, 2005).

75. Abdelkebir Khatibi, "Frontiers: Between Psychoanalysis and Islam," trans. P. Burcu Yalim, *Third Text* 23, no. 6 (2009): 689–96, quotation 691.

76. Benslama, *Psychoanalysis and the Challenge of Islam*, vii; Benslama, "Of a Renunciation of the Father," 30–31; see also the special issue "Islam and Psychoanalysis," eds. Sigi Jöttkandt and Joan Copjec, of *S, Journal of the Jan van Eyck Circle for Lacanian Ideology Critique* 2 (2009), for example, Fethi Benslama and Jean-Luc Nancy, "Translations of Monotheisms," trans. Ed Pluth, 74–89; Keith Al-Hasani, "The Qur'an and the Name-of-the-Father," 90–95; Slavoj Žižek, "A Glance into the Archives of Islam," *Lacan.com* (2006), http://www.lacan.com/zizarchives.htm.

77. Nathan Gorelick, "Fethi Benslama and the Translation of the Impossible in Islam and Psychoanalysis," *Umbr(a)*: Islam (2009): 188–92, quotation 191; Benslama, *Psychoanalysis and the Challenge of Islam*; Benslama, "Dying for Justice," trans. Roland Végsö, in *Umbr(a)*: Islam (2009): 13–23; Benslama, "Of a Renunciation of the Father."

78. Benslama, *Psychoanalysis and the Challenge of Islam*, 9, viii. In contrast, Andrea Mura has sought to mobilize psychoanalysis to further the exploration of contemporary Islamist discourses, criticizing Benslama's reading of Islamism for its essentialism. While "Benslama asserts that Islamism constitutes a 'delusional' and 'melancholic' attempt to 'restore' the shield of religious illusion against the crisis of the traditional authoritative system," Mura argues instead for "the way in which a number of Islamist discourses, creatively, assertively or in a non-melancholic way, re-organize symbolic economy around the master signifier Islam, thereby reflecting the complexity of the Islamist discursive universe." Andrea Mura, "Islamism Revisited: A Lacanian Discourse Critique," *European Journal of Psychoanalysis* 1 (2014): 107–26, quotation 108. See also Bobby S. Sayyid, *A Fundamental Fear: Eurocentrism and the Emergence of Islamism* (London: Zed Books, 1997).

79. For the clearest statement of this position, see "Islam and Psychoanalysis: A Tale of Mutual Ignorance," interview by Gabriela M. Keller with Fethi Benslama, Qantara.de, 2006. http://en.qantara.de/content/islam-and-psychoanalysis-a-tale-of-mutual-ignorance. For a critique of this literature, see Massad, "Psychoanalysis, Islam, and the Other of Liberalism."

80. Raja Ben Slama, "La psychanalyse en Égypte: Un problème de non-advenue," *Topique* 110 (2010/11): 83–96. See also Moustapha Safouan, *Why Are the Arabs Not Free? The Politics of Writing* (Malden, MA: Blackwell Publishing, 2007).

81. Massad, "Psychoanalysis, Islam, and the Other of Liberalism," 46, 58.

82. Ibid., 60; Massad is here citing Abdelkabir Khatibi.

83. Alberto Toscano, *Fanaticism: On the Uses of an Idea* (London: Verso, 2010), 165–66. Toscano notes, "is there a psychic *Sonderweg* (special path) which accompanies the secular *Sonderweg* of the Christian West, such that psychoanalysis would be compelled both to recognize its interiority to such a path and its differential (or even normative) relationship to the 'Islamic subject'? If so, psychoanalysis could find itself as a midwife of secularism.... What are the pitfalls of 'secularizing' the psychoanalytic subject, and of turning psychoanalysis into a secular clinic, a move whose political payoff would be to welcome recalcitrant cultures into a disenchanted West?" 162–63. I address these issues in the epilogue.

84. For example, she notes that "Islam means submission, and demands absolute obe-dience to God the father," Gohar Homayounpour, *Doing Psychoanalysis in Tehran* (Cambridge, MA: MIT Press, 2012), 55. Significantly, this interpretation goes against Benslama's astute observation that "in Islam one never speaks of 'god-the-father,' and any comparison of the divine with the paternal is proscribed." Benslama, *Psychoanalysis and the Challenge of Islam*, 87.

85. Cf. Benslama, *Psychoanalysis and the Challenge of Islam*; Žižek, "A Glance into the Archives of Islam"; Julia Kristeva, *This Incredible Need to Believe*, trans. Beverly Bie Brahic (New York: Columbia University Press, 2009).

86. Pandolfo, "Soul Choking," 77.

87. Sigi Jöttkandt and Joan Copjec, "Editorial," *S, Journal of the Jan van Eyck Circle for Lacanian Ideology Critique* 2 (2009): 2–4, quotation 4.

88. Pandolfo, "Soul Choking," 78; Ebrahim Moosa, *Ghazālī and the Poetics of Imagi-nation* (Chapel Hill: University of North Carolina Press, 2005), 229–32.

89. Joan Copjec, "Introduction: Islam and the Exotic Science," *Umbr(a)*: Islam (2009): 5–11; see also Julia Borossa's thoughtful discussion of "The Extensibility of Psychoanalsyis."

90. Thus the instantiation of the global subject of analysis was always already medi-ated by its coauthors, whether by Jacques Lacan or the Egyptian analyst Moustapha Safaoun.

91. Spivak as cited by Kalpana Seshadri-Crooks, "The Primitive as Analyst: Postcolo-nial Feminism's Access to Psychoanalysis," *Cultural Critique*, no. 28 (Autumn 1994): 175–218, quotation 176; Jacques Derrida, "Geopsychoanalysis: '. . . and the Rest of the World,'" *American Imago* 48, no. 2 (1991): 199–231, quotation 199.

92. Derrida, "Geopsychoanalysis," 204.

93. Khanna, *Dark Continents*, 100.

94. Ibid., 103.

95. Seshadri-Crooks, "The Primitive as Analyst," 177.

96. Ibid., 177.

97. Ibid., 200–201.

98. For example, Timothy Mitchell, *Colonising Egypt* (Cambridge: Cambridge Uni-verity Press, 1988); Dipesh Chakrabarty, *Provincializing Europe: Postcolonial Thought and Historical Difference* (Princeton, NJ: Princeton University Press, 2000); Talal Asad, *Formations of the Secular: Christianity, Islam, Modernity* (Stanford, CA: Stanford Uni-versity Press, 2003); Ranjana Khanna, *Algeria Cuts: Women and Representation, 1830 to the Present* (Stanford, CA: Stanford University Press, 2008).

99. Abdallah Laroui, *The Crisis of the Arab Intellectual: Traditionalism or Histori-cism?*, trans. Diarmid Cammell (Berkeley: University of California Press, 1976). Other iterations of this argument can be found in Anouar Abdel-Malek, ed., *Contemporary Arab Political Thought*, trans. Michael Pallis (London: Zed Books, 1983), and Mahmud Amin al-'Alim, *al-Fikr al-'Arabi bayn al-Khususiyya wa-l-Kawniyya* (Cairo: Dar al-Mustaqbal al-'Arabi, 1996). In the case of Egypt its status as simultaneously colonizer and colonized must be borne in mind, see Eve Troutt Powell, *A Different Shade of Colonialism: Egypt, Great Britain, and the Mastery of the Sudan* (Berkeley: University of California Press, 2003); Omnia El Shakry, *The Great Social Laboratory: Subjects of Knowledge in Colonial and Postcolonial Egypt* (Stanford, CA: Stanford University Press, 2007).

100. Deeply intertwined with this narrative was a lingering concern for the autonomy of decolonized cultural and intellectual formations, whether from European colonial for-mations or allegedly moribund religious traditions. For a critique of Laroui, see Pandolfo, "Thin Line of Modernity." For a sophisticated rethinking of the history of Arab intellectual thought, see Jens Hanssen and Max Weiss, eds., *Arabic Thought beyond the Liberal Age*.

101. Pandolfo, "Soul Choking," 77.

102. Discussing Moroccan novelist Driss Chraibi, Stefania Pandolfo focuses on a "narrative of encounter," which "stages the multidimensional present where in spite of the 'cut,' and in fact precisely in its place, an encounter becomes possible. A visionary materialization of the rift, the Thin Line is a space of subjectivity." "Thin Line of Modernity," 142–43.

103. Katherine Pratt Ewing, *Arguing Sainthood: Modernity, Psychoanalysis, and Islam* (Durham, NC: Duke University Press, 1997); Mittermaier, *Dreams That Matter*; Paola Abenante, "Inner and Outer Ways: Sufism and Subjectivity in Egypt and Beyond," *Ethnos: A Journal of Anthropology* 78, no. 4 (2013): 490–514.

104. Javed Majeed, *Muhammad Iqbal: Islam, Aesthetics, and Postcolonialism* (London: Routledge, 2009), xxvi.

105. Naveeda Khan, *Muslim Becoming: Aspiration and Skepticism in Pakistan* (Durham, NC: Duke University Press, 2012), 9–10.

106. Mahmud Amin al-ʿAlim, "Quli Lahum ini Ahabuhum Jamiʿan," *al-Musawwar*, no. 2190 (September 30, 1966): 32–33.

107. Frederick Cooper, "Conflict and Connection: Rethinking Colonial African History," *American Historical Review* 99, no. 5 (1994): 1516–45, quotation 1539.

108. Yoav Di-Capua, *No Exit: Arab Existentialism, Jean-Paul Sartre, and Decolonization* (Chicago: University of Chicago Press, 2018). For more on the significance of the postwar period for Arab intellectual history, see Max Weiss and Jens Hanssen, eds., *Arabic Thought against the Authoritarian Age: Towards an Intellectual History of the Present* (Cambridge: Cambridge University Press, 2017); Omnia El Shakry, "'History without Documents': The Vexed Archives of Decolonization in the Middle East," *American Historical Review* 120, no. 3 (2015): 920–34; Elizabeth Suzanne Kassab, *Contemporary Arab Thought: Cultural Critique in Comparative Perspective* (New York: Columbia University Press, 2010); Ibrahim M. Abu Rabiʿ, *Contemporary Arab Thought: Studies in Post-1967 Arab Intellectual History* (London: Pluto Press, 2004); Roel Meijer, *The Quest for Modernity. Secular Liberal and Left-Wing Political Thought in Egypt, 1945–1958* (London: RoutledgeCurzon, 2002).

109. Derrida, "Geopsychoanalysis," 215. In fact, in *Cold War Freud: Psychoanalysis in an Age of Catastrophes* (Cambridge: Cambridge University Press, 2017), Dagmar Herzog has demonstrated the ethical and political entanglements of postwar psychoanalysis with sexual politics, Nazism's legacies, and decolonization.

110. Dominique Scarfone, *The Unpast: The Actual Unconscious*, trans. Dorothée Bonnigal-Katz (New York: Unconscious in Translation, 2015), 92; DiCenso, *Other Freud*, 35. On the vicissitudes of melding psychoanalysis with attempts to create a "new man" and its attendant relationship to the will to power in Russia in the 1910s to 1930s, see Alexander Etkind, *Eros of the Impossible: The History of Psychoanalysis in Russia*, trans. Noah and Maria Rubins (Boulder, CO: Westview Press, 1997).

111. Antonio Viego, *Dead Subjects: Towards a Politics of Loss in Latino Studies* (Durham, NC: Duke University Press, 2007); Joan Copjec, *Read My Desire: Lacan against the Historicists* (London: Verso, 2015), 209.

112. Viego, *Dead Subjects*.

113. For studies that move in this direction, see Hosam Aboul-Ela, "The World Republic of Theories," unpublished manuscript; Fadi Bardawil, "When All This Revolution Melts into Air: The Disenchantment of Levantine Marxist Intellectuals" (PhD diss., Columbia University, 2010); Samer Frangie, "Theorizing from the Periphery: The Intellectual Project of Mahdi ʿAmil," *International Journal of Middle East Studies* 44, no. 3 (2012): 465–82.

114. Edward Baring, *The Young Derrida and French Philosophy, 1945–1968* (Cambridge: Cambridge University Press, 2011), 12.

Chapter One: Psychoanalysis and the Psyche

1. This chapter is adapted from "The Arabic Freud: The Unconscious and the Modern Subject," *Modern Intellectual History* 11, no. 1 (2014): 89–118.

2. Mustafa Suwayf, "Yusuf Murad: Ra'id al-Manhaj al-Takamuli," *al-Fikr al-Mu'asir* 21 (1966): 62–68.

3. Although earlier usages of *"al-la-shu'ur"* exist, Murad formalized its entry into the Arabic language. For an extended discussion of *"al-la-shu'ur"* and a critique of the popular usage of *"al-'aql al-batin,"* see Ishaq Ramzi, *'Ilm al-Nafs al-Fardi: Usulu wa-Tatbiqu,* 2nd ed. (Cairo: Dar al-Ma'arif bi-Misr, 1961), 17–26. Murad was Ramzi's supervising dissertation advisor. Interestingly, by the 1970s, the unconscious is translated as *"al-la-wa'y,"* a term that connotes "the negation of consciousness, with a reference to the idea of a container," see Ben Slama, "The Tree That Reveals the Forest."

4. For more on this generation, see Yoav Di-Capua, "Arab Existentialism: An Invisible Chapter in the Intellectual History of Decolonization," *American Historical Review* 117, no. 4 (2012): 1061–91; Di-Capua, "The Intellectual Revolt of the 1950s and the 'Fall of the Udabā,'" in *Reflections on/of the Political in Arabic Literature since the 1940s,* ed. Friederike Pannewick, Georges Khalil, and Yvonne Albers (Wiesbaden: Ludwig Reichert Verlag, 2015): 89–104; Di-Capua, *No Exit.*

5. Attendance at the salon was gleaned from obituaries and confirmed with Samir Mourad, personal communication with the author, January 15, 2012, and September 29, 2012. Obituaries include: Mahmud Amin al-'Alim, "Quli Lahum," *al-Musawwar*; Yusuf al-Sharuni, "Yusuf Murad: Ra'idan wa-Ustadhan," *al-Majalla* 10, no. 119 (1966): 21–28; Suwayf, "Yusuf Murad"; Murad Wahba, "Yusuf Murad Kama 'Ariftuhu," in *Yusuf Murad wa-l-Madhhab al-Takamuli,* ed. Murad Wahba (Cairo: al-Haya' al-Misriyya al-'Amma li-l-Kitab, 1974), 3–9.

6. In an erudite and moving obituary Mahmud Amin al-'Alim placed Murad among the luminaries of twentieth-century Egyptian literature, such as Tawfiq al-Hakim, Najib Mahfuz, and the doyen of Arabic letters, Taha Husayn; al-'Alim, "Quli Lahum."

7. Yusuf Murad, *Mabadi' 'Ilm al-Nafs al-'Amm,* 7th ed. (1948; Cairo: Dar al-Ma'arif, 1978). Murad's other key publications include *Shifa' al-Nafs* (Cairo: Dar al-Ma'arif, 1943); *Sikulujiyyat al-Jins* (Cairo: Dar al-Ma'arif, 1954); *Dirasat fi al-Takamul al-Nafsi* (Cairo: Mu'assasat al-Khanji bi-l-Qahira, 1958); *'Ilm al-Nafs fi al-Fann wa-l-Haya* (Cairo: Dar al-Hilal, 1966). His collected articles are published in Wahba, *Yusuf Murad wa-l-Madhhab al-Takamuli* and in a newer collection of both published and unpublished work, in Wahba, ed., *Yusuf Murad Faylasufan* (Cairo: al-Haya' al-Misriyya al-'Amma li-l-Kitab, 2012). Biographical information on Murad is from Farag 'Abd al-Qadir Taha, *Mawsuw'at 'Ilm al-Nafs wa-l-Tahlil al-Nafsi* (Cairo: Dar Sa'd al-Sabah, 1993), 702–4 and the obituaries cited above.

8. Murad's dissertation, "L'eveil de l'intelligence," in the words of his thesis supervisor, Paul Guillaume, "presented to French scientists experimental truths and results that they themselves, unfortunately, had ignored." Taha, *Mawsuw'at 'Ilm al-Nafs,* 702.

9. Psychology had been taught at the philosophy department of the Egyptian (now Cairo) University as early as the university's founding in 1908. By midcentury there were academic psychologists in all of the major universities and institutes in Cairo and Alexandria, such as Cairo University, Alexandria University, 'Ayn Shams University, and the Higher Institute of Education. For surveys of psychology in Egypt, see E. Terry Prothro and H. Levon Melikian, "Psychology in the Arab Near East," *Psychological Bulletin* 52, no. 4 (1955): 303–10; S. E. Farag, "Egypt," in *International Handbook of Psychology,* ed. A. R. Gilgen and C. K. Gilgen (New York: Greenwood Press, 1987), 174–83; Fouad Abou-

Hatab, "Egypt," in *International Psychology: Views from around the World*, ed. Virginia Sexton and John Hogan (Lincoln: University of Nebraska Press, 1992), chap. 12; Ramadan Ahmed, "Psychology in Egypt," in *Handbook of International Psychology*, ed. Michael J. Stevens and Danny Wedding (New York: Brunner-Routledge, 2004), chap. 23; Moustafa I. Soueif and Ramadan A. Ahmed, "Psychology in the Arab World: Past, Present, and Future," *International Journal of Group Tensions* 30, no. 3 (2001): 211–40.

10. Mustafa Radwan Ziywar (1907–1990) was the first Arab member of the Paris Institute for Psychoanalysis. Upon his return to Cairo, he taught at Faruq (now Alexandria) University and later established a Psychology Department (jointly with Sociology) at Ibrahim Pasha (now ʿAyn Shams) University in 1950. Ziywar specialized in psychosomatics and combined medical knowledge, psychology, psychoanalysis, and philosophy. In addition, he supervised translations of Sigmund and Anna Freud, as well as other critical publications in psychoanalysis. After *Majallat ʿIlm al-Nafs* ceased publication, Ziywar edited and published *Majallat al-Sihha al-Nafsiyya (Journal of Mental Health)* in 1958 and hosted a series of popular radio talk shows on psychology in the 1950s, where he covered topics like gambling and depression. See Taha, *Mawsuwʿat ʿIlm al-Nafs*, 372–77. For a brief history of psychoanalysis in Egypt that forefronts Ziywar as the "father" of psychoanalysis, see Hussein Abdel Kader, "La psychanalyse en Égypte entre un passé ambitieux et un futur incertain," *La célibataire—La psychanalyse et le monde arabe* 8 (2004): 61–73.

11. Yusuf Murad and Mustafa Ziywar, "Tasdir," *Majallat ʿIlm al-Nafs* 1, no. 1 (1945): 10–12.

12. Yusuf Murad, "Bab al-Taʿrifat: Niwa li-Qamus ʿIlm al-Nafs," *Majallat ʿIlm al-Nafs* 1, no. 1 (1945): 100–106. The remaining installments were published as Murad, "Bab al-Taʿrifat: al-Majmuʿa al-Thaniyya," *Majallat ʿIlm al-Nafs* 1, no. 2 (1945): 243–48; "Bab al-Taʿrifat: al-Majmuʿa al-Thalitha min Mustalahat ʿIlm al-Nafs," *Majallat ʿIlm al-Nafs* 1, no. 3 (1946): 382–84; "Bab al-Taʿrifat: al-Majmuʿa al-Rabiʿa min Mustalahat ʿIlm al-Nafs," *Majallat ʿIlm al-Nafs* 2, no. 2 (1946): 362–69; "Bab al-Taʿrifat: al-Majmuʿa al-Khamisa," *Majallat ʿIlm al-Nafs* 3, no. 3 (1948): 467–70.

13. Murad, "Bab al-Taʿrifat: Niwa li-Qamus ʿIlm al-Nafs," 100–101. Murad quoted Freud at length: "Clear basic concepts and sharply drawn definitions are only possible in the mental sciences in so far as the latter seek to fit a department of facts into the frame of a logical system. In the natural sciences, of which psychology is one, such clear-cut general concepts are superfluous and indeed impossible.... The basic ideas or most general concepts in any of the disciplines of science are always left indeterminate at first and are only explained to begin with by reference to the realm of phenomena from which they were derived; it is only by means of a progressive analysis of the material of observation that they can be made clear and can find a significant and consistent meaning." Sigmund Freud, *An Autobiographical Study* (1925), *SE* 20: 1–74, quotation 57–58. Murad cited the complete passage, which he had translated into Arabic, whereas I have abridged it.

14. André Lalande, *Vocabulaire technique et critique de la philosophie* (Paris: Presses Universitaires de France, 1951). The dictionary was exceedingly popular and went through numerous editions beginning from 1926, and it continues to be cited until today. Lalande, a French philosopher, had taught at Cairo University in the 1920s and 1930s.

15. Murad, "Bab al-Taʿrifat: Niwa li-Qamus ʿIlm al-Nafs," 101. His students often commented on his intense concern for creating an eloquent Arabic lexicon of psychology, Suwayf, "Yusuf Murad," 62; al-Sharuni, "Yusuf Murad," 24. For a thoughtful discussion of the politics of science translations in modern Arabic, see Marwa Elshakry, "Knowledge in Motion: The Cultural Politics of Modern Science Translations in Arabic," *Isis* 99, no. 4 (2008): 701–730 and Elshakry, *Reading Darwin in Arabic, 1860–1950* (Chicago: University of Chicago Press, 2013).

16. Crucially, Murad defined the psyche or *nafs* in his psychological dictionary as: *soul, spirit, âme*; an essential substance in the body, yet distinct from it, "Bab al-Ta'rifat: Niwa li-Qamus 'Ilm al-Nafs," 106. See Bruno Bettelheim's discussion of psyche and *die Seele* in *Freud and Man's Soul* (London: Flamingo, 1985), 70–78. Murad translated *das ich* as *al-ana* and *das Über-ich* as *al-ana al-a'la*, "Bab al-Ta'rifat: al-Majmu'a al-Thaniyya," 245–46. Bettelheim discusses the problematic nature of the English translation as "super-ego" and the more suitable "above-I" in *Freud and Man's Soul*, 49–64.

17. Kapila, "The 'Godless' Freud," 145; Mittermaier, *Dreams That Matter*, chap. 6.

18. "Whether it be a sacred text, a novel, a play, a monologue, or any conversation whatsoever, allow me to represent the function of the signifier by a spatializing device, which we have no reason to deprive ourselves of. This point around which all concrete analyses of discourse must operate I shall call a quilting point.... Everything radiates out from and is organized around this signifier, similar to these little lines of force that an upholstery button forms on the surface of material. It's the point of convergence that enables everything that happens in this discourse to be situated retroactively and prospectively." Jacques Lacan, *The Seminar of Jacques Lacan, Book III: The Psychoses, 1955–1956*, ed. Jacques-Alain Miller, trans. Russell Grigg (New York: W. W. Norton, 1993), 267–68.

19. Murad and Ziywar, "Tasdir."

20. Jan Goldstein, *The Post-Revolutionary Self: Politics and Psyche in France, 1750–1850* (Cambridge, MA: Harvard University Press, 2005).

21. Lacan was not widely engaged in *Majallat 'Ilm al-Nafs*. There was, however, one prominent Egyptian member of Lacan's circle, Moustapha Safouan.

22. Murad, "Bab al-Ta'rifat: Niwa li-Qamus 'Ilm al-Nafs," 106. I discuss the *nafs* in depth in chapter 2.

23. Ranjana Khanna has argued that diverse notions of selfhood emerged in postwar Europe, as for instance with Jean-Paul Sartre's critique of the idea of the unconscious, which he viewed as an example of bad faith and an abdication of political responsibility for historical ills such as colonialism, thereby signaling a loss of the ideal of national affiliation embodied by Freud. See *Dark Continents*, 99–144.

24. Frantz Fanon, *The Wretched of the Earth*, trans. Richard Philcox (New York: Grove Press, 2004). Murad's student Sami al-Durubi cotranslated this text into Arabic, *Mu'adhdhabu al-Ard*, trans. Sami al-Durubi and Jamal al-Atasi (Damascus: al-Matba'a al-Ta'awuniyya, 1968).

25. As Carolyn Dean outlines, "whereas elsewhere psychoanalysis rescued the rational subject, the self, from the domination of the unconscious, in France it was tied in with the dissolution of the self," most notably in the writings of Jacques Lacan, who rejected Freud's post-1920 conceptualization of the ego as an agent of adaptation, integration, and synthesis. Carolyn Dean, *The Self and Its Pleasures: Bataille, Lacan, and the History of the Decentered Subject* (Ithaca, NY: Cornell University Press, 1992), 13–14. As noted, Murad's emphasis was on the *nafs* (self, soul) and not the ego. Further, as I discuss below, he disagreed with Freud's foreclosure of the possibility of social integration. For a contemporary attempt to integrate Freudian metapsychology with the notion of psychic unity and integration, see Jonathan Lear, *Freud*, 2nd ed. (London: Routledge, 2015).

26. Pandolfo, "Thin Line of Modernity," 121, 127.

27. Yusuf Murad, "al-Usus al-Nafsiyya li-l-Takamul al-Ijtima'i," *Majallat 'Ilm al-Nafs* 2, no. 3 (1947): 425–42.

28. Ibid., 441.

29. Yusuf Murad, "al-Manhaj al-Takamuli wa-Tasnif Waqa'i' al-Nafsiyya," *Majallat 'Ilm al-Nafs* 1, no. 3 (1946): 273–304.

30. This element of Murad's thought was highlighted in almost all of the academic obituaries, see, for example, Suwayf, "Yusuf Murad," 62; al-Sharuni, "Yusuf Murad," 25; al-'Alim, "Quli Lahum."

31. Murad, "al-Manhaj al-Takamuli," 303.

32. See, for example, Mustafa Isma'il Suwayf, "Ma'na al-Takamul al-Ijtima'i 'ind Birjsun," *Majallat 'Ilm al-Nafs* 5, no. 2 (1949–50): 203–36; Soueif, "Bergson's Theory of Social Integration," *Majallat 'Ilm al-Nafs* 5, no. 2 (1949–50): 326–32; Murad Wahba, "al-La-Shu'ur 'ind Birjsun," *Majallat 'Ilm al-Nafs* 8, no. 2 (1952–53): 213–22; Henri Bergson, *al-Taqa al-Ruhiyya (L'energie spirituelle)*, trans. Sami al-Durubi (Cairo: Dar al-Fikr al-'Arabi, 1946), reviewed by Yusuf al-Sharuni in *Majallat 'Ilm al-Nafs* 2, no. 3 (1947): 527–30; Bergson, *al-Dahik: Bahth fi Dallalat al-Mudhik (Laughter)*, trans. Sami al-Durubi (Cairo: Dar al-Katib al-Misri, 1947). For a discussion of Bergson's postcolonial relevance, see Souleymane Bachir Diagne, *Bergson postcolonial: L'élan vital dans la pensée de Léopold Sédar Senghor et de Mohamed Iqbal* (Paris: CNRS Editions, 2011).

33. Suzanne Guerlac, *Thinking in Time: An Introduction to Henri Bergson* (Ithaca, NY: Cornell University Press, 2006), 19.

34. Ibid., 47n2, 90–91.

35. Or as Bergson states, "turning backwards is meaningless," *Time and Free Will: An Essay on the Immediate Data of Consciousness*, trans. F. Pogson (New York: Harper Torchbooks, 1960), 153; Murad, "al-Manhaj al-Takamuli," 287–90.

36. Murad used the Arabic phrase "*bi-fadl ... wa-'ala al-raghm minu.*" Thus, for example, unity exists, because of, and in spite of, multiplicity. Ibid., 290.

37. Derrida poses the *après coup* in contradistinction to Hegelian teleology. Jacques Derrida, *Margins of Philosophy*, trans. Alan Bass (Chicago: University of Chicago Press, 1985), 21.

38. Murad, "al-Manhaj al-Takamuli," 304; cf. Bergson, *Time and Free Will*, 128, 183, 221.

39. Murad, "al-Usus al-Nafsiyya."

40. On the pastoral, see Lacan, *Ethics of Psychoanalysis*, 88–100.

41. Murad cited Ian Suttie, *Origins of Love and Hate* (London: Regan Paul, 1935); Karen Horney, *New Ways in Psychoanalysis* (New York: Norton, 1939); and Ranyard West, *Conscience and Society* (London: Methuen, 1942); Murad, "al-Usus al-Nafsiyya," 436–41.

42. Suttie, *Origins of Love and Hate*, 30, 35–37, quotation 35–36. For more on Suttie, see Gabriele Cassullo, "Back to the Roots: The Influence of Ian D. Suttie on British Psychoanalysis," trans. Francesco Capello, *American Imago* 67, no. 1 (2010): 5–22.

43. Suttie, *Origins of Love and Hate*, 228–230; see also Jonathan Lear's thoughtful comments on the death drive, *Freud*, 162–63; Lear, *Open Minded: Working Out the Logic of the Soul* (Cambridge, MA: Harvard University Press, 1999), 178–81.

44. Ibn 'Arabi, *Divine Governance of the Human Kingdom*, trans. Shaikh Tosun Bayrak al-Jerrahi al-Halveti (Louisville, KY: Fons Vitae, 1997), 8.

45. Ibid., 49, see also 154–55, 260–61. Murad had consulted Ibn 'Arabi's *al-Tadbirat al-Ilahiyya fi Islah al-Mamlaka al-Insaniyya* and *Kabs al-Anwar wa-Bahjat al-Asrar* in manuscript form and *al-Futuhat al-Makkiyya* in print form, see Youssef Mourad, *La physiognomonie arabe et le kitāb al-firāsa de Fakhr al-Dīn al-Rāzī* (Paris: Librairie Orientaliste Paul Geuthner, 1939), 145–47.

46. Ibn 'Arabi, *Divine Governance*, 154–55.

47. Al-Halveti, afterword to Ibn 'Arabi, *Divine Governance*, 260. William Chittick is careful to point out that the term "*wahdat al-wujud*" or Oneness of Essence is never actually used by Ibn 'Arabi, although the doctrine is widely attributed to him by later commentators.

Chittick, "Waḥdat al-S̲h̲uhūd," in *Encyclopaedia of Islam*, 2nd ed., edited by P. Bearman, Th. Bianquis, C. E. Bosworth, E. van Donzel, and W. P. Heinrichs. http://dx.doi.org /10.1163/1573-3912_islam_SIM_7819. See also Michel Chodkiewicz, introduction to Ibn al-ʿArabi, *The Meccan Revelations*, vol. 2, *Selected Texts of al-Futûhât al-Makkiya*, ed. Michel Chodkiewicz, trans. Cyrille Chodkiewicz and Denis Gril (New York: Pir Press, 2004), 18, 48–49n81.

48. "Hence he asserts both the oneness of God's *wudjūd* and the manyness of His knowledge, the unity of His Essence and the multiplicity of His names." William C. Chittick, "Taṣawwuf, 2. Ibn al-ʿArabī and after in the Arabic and Persian Lands and Beyond," in *Encyclopaedia of Islam*, 2nd ed., edited by P. Bearman, Th. Bianquis, C. E. Bosworth, E. van Donzel, and W. P. Heinrichs. http://dx.doi.org/10.1163/1573-3912_islam_COM _1188. For a useful introduction to Ibn ʿArabi's thought, and in particular the dialectic between oneness and manyness, see William C. Chittick, *The Sufi Path of Knowledge: Ibn al-ʿArabi's Metaphysics of Imagination* (Albany: State University of New York Press, 1989), especially chapter 1; see also Chittick, *The Self-Disclosure of God: Principles of Ibn al-ʿArabi's Cosmology* (Albany: State University of New York Press, 1998), 72–76, 167–78; Chittick, "Towards Sainthood: Saints and Stations," in Ibn al-ʿArabi, *The Meccan Revelations*, vol. 1, *Selected Texts of al-Futûhât al-Makkiya*, ed. Michel Chodkiewicz, trans. William C. Chittick and James W. Morris (New York: Pir Press, 2002), 127–39, 181–88, 248n87; Izutsu, *Sufism and Taoism*, 77–108.

49. Samir Mourad, personal communication with the author, January 15, 2012, and September 29, 2012. On Ibn ʿArabi's view of the multiplicity of historical religions and beliefs among mankind, see Izutsu, *Sufism and Taoism*, 83–85.

50. On the significance of the experimental approach to psychology in France and the eventual dominance of *Gestalttheorie* or *psychologie de la forme*, see Daniel Andler, "Cognitive Science," in *The Columbia History of Twentieth Century French Thought*, ed. Lawrence D. Kritzman, Brian J. Reilly, M. B. DeBevois (New York: Columbia University Press, 2007), 175–81. Much of the imprint of this training can be traced in *Majallat ʿIlm al-Nafs*. See, for example, Youssef Mourad, "La conduite de l'effort d'après Pierre Janet," *Majallat ʿIlm al-Nafs* 5, no. 3 (1950): 478–90; see the translated selections from Paul Guillaume, *Psychologie* (1931), Henri Piéron, *Psychologie experimentale* (1927), and Th. Ribot, *Les maladies de la personalité* (1881), in "Nusus Mukhtara fi ʿIlm al-Nafs," *Majallat ʿIlm al-Nafs* 1, no. 2 (1945): 233–42; and the review of Henri Wallon, *L'evolution psychologique de l'enfant* (1941), ibid., 209–10. Wallon's *De l'acte à la pensée, essays de psychologie comparée* (1942) and *Les origines de la pensée chez l'enfant* (1945) were also reviewed in *Majallat ʿIlm al-Nafs* 2, no. 1 (1946): 176–80; and Piéron's *La psychologie différentielle* (1949), volume 1 of Piéron's *Traité de psychologie appliquée* in *Majallat ʿIlm al-Nafs* 5, no. 2 (1949–50): 315–18.

51. Andler, "Cognitive Science," 177.

52. Alden O. Weber, "*Gestalttheorie* and the Theory of Relations," *Journal of Philosophy* 35, no. 22 (1938): 589–606, quotation 590.

53. Mitchell Ash, *Gestalt Psychology in German Culture, 1890–1967: Holism and the Quest for Objectivity* (Cambridge: Cambridge University Press, 1998).

54. According to Weber part of the difficulty was *Gestalttheorie*'s vacillation between absolute idealist rationalism and empiricism, "*Gestalttheorie*," 605–6.

55. Furthermore, psychoanalysis like *Gestalttheorie*, as Paul Ricoeur noted, was organismic in its belief that "all behavior is integrated and indivisible," Ricoeur, *Freud and Philosophy: An Essay on Interpretation* (New Haven, CT: Yale University Press, 1970), 348.

56. John I. Brooks III, *The Eclectic Legacy: Academic Philosophy and the Human Sciences in Nineteenth-Century France* (Newark: University of Delaware Press, 1998). On Cousin see Goldstein's masterful study, *The Post-Revolutionary Self*.

57. See Brooks, *Eclectic Legacy*; Jan Goldstein, "Foucault and the Post-Revolutionary Self: The Uses of Cousinian Pedagogy in Nineteenth-Century France," in *Foucault and the Writing of History*, ed. Jan Goldstein (London: Wiley-Blackwell, 1994), 99–115, 276–80; Goldstein, "The Advent of Psychological Modernism in France: An Alternate Narrative," in *Modernist Impulses in the Human Sciences*, ed. Dorothy Ross (Baltimore: Johns Hopkins University Press, 1994), 190–209, 342–46; and J. Carroy and R. Plas, "How Pierre Janet Used Pathological Psychology to Save the Philosophical Self," *Journal of the History of the Behavioral Sciences* 36, no. 3 (2000): 231–40.

58. In some respects, Murad's interest in the unity of the self also resonated with many of Janet's writings; see Carroy and Plas, "How Pierre Janet Used Pathological Psychology."

59. Yusuf Murad, "Min al-Istibtan ila al-Tahlil al-Nafsi," in Wahba, *Yusuf Murad wa-l-Madhhab al-Takamuli*, 113–22, 113–14. This was originally published in *Majallat 'Ilm al-Nafs* 7, no. 3 (1952): 301–10.

60. Murad, "Min al-Istibtan ila al-Tahlil al-Nafsi," 115–18.

61. Ibid., 118–19.

62. Ibid., 120–21.

63. Ibid., 121–22.

64. Jacques Lacan, *The Seminar of Jacques Lacan, Book I: Freud's Papers on Technique, 1953–1954*, ed. Jacques-Alain Miller, trans. John Forrester (New York: W. W. Norton, 1991), 2.

65. Ibid., 11–12.

66. Yusuf Murad, "Min al-Istibtan ila al-Tahlil al-Nafsi (2): Manhaj al-Tahlil al-Nafsi wa-Tabiya'tu al-Takamuliyya," *Majallat 'Ilm al-Nafs* 8, no. 1 (1952): 15–32. This piece was based in part on an exhaustive review of Freud's major texts: *The Interpretation of Dreams* (1900), *SE* 4–5; *Introductory Lectures on Psychoanalysis* (1915–17), *SE* 15–16; *Beyond the Pleasure Principle* (1920), *SE* 18: 1–64; *Group Psychology and the Analysis of the Ego* (1921), *SE* 18: 65–143; *The Ego and the Id* (1923), *SE* 19: 1–66; "Postscript to a *Question of Lay Analysis*" (1927), *SE* 20: 251–58; *New Introductory Lectures on Psychoanalysis* (1933), *SE* 22: 1–182; and his *Collected Papers*: "The Dynamics of Transference" (1912), *SE* 12: 99–108; "On the History of the Psychoanalytic Movement" (1914), *SE* 14: 1–66; "Observations on Transference Love" (1915), *SE* 12: 157–71; "Preface to Reik's Ritual Psycho-Analytic Studies" (1919), *SE* 17: 257–63; "Analysis Terminable and Interminable" (1937) *SE* 23: 210–53, among others. The article included references to Theodore Reik, Charles Odier, Franz Alexander, Daniel Lagache, and Anna Freud, demonstrating the depth of Murad's familiarity with the analytic tradition.

67. Murad, "Min al-Istibtan ila al-Tahlil al-Nafsi (2)," 15.

68. Ibid., 18–22.

69. Ibid., 16, 22–23.

70. Ibid., 23–27.

71. Ibid., 28–29.

72. Ibid., 29n2.

73. Ibid., 30.

74. Ibid.

75. Lacan, *Ethics of Psychoanalysis*, 73.

76. Ricoeur, *Freud and Philosophy*, 366–67. For the similarities between Murad and Ricoeur, see Ricoeur, "Epistemology: Between Psychology and Phenomenology," in Ricoeur, *Freud and Philosophy*, 344–418.

77. Murad, "Min al-Istibtan ila al-Tahlil al-Nafsi (2)," 30–31, cf. Ricoeur, *Freud and Philosophy*, 386–87, 406–18.

78. Murad, "Min al-Istibtan ila al-Tahlil al-Nafsi (2)," 31.

79. Ibid., 32. Murad here emphasized Freud's insistence on the analyst's polymath training, encompassing psychology, the history of civilizations, sociology, biology, and the study of the unconscious roots of human behavior (24). As Ricoeur commented, it has been argued that the whole of Freud's discovery lay in the following: "the psychical is defined as meaning, and this meaning is dynamic and historical," *Freud and Philosophy*, 379.

80. Fink, *Lacanian Subject*, 46.

81. *Firasa* refers to keen observation, perspicacity, acumen, discernment, and an intuitive knowledge of human nature. It was originally referred to as *qiyafa*, referring to the ability to deduce the interior of a thing from its exterior. Hans Wehr, *A Dictionary of Modern Written Arabic*, ed. Milton Cowan, 3rd ed. (Ithaca, NY: Spoken Language Services, 1976), 704.

82. Mourad, *La physiognomonie arabe*.

83. Ibid., 7–21. See also Davide Stimilli, *The Face of Immortality: Physiognomy and Criticism* (Albany: State University of New York University Press, 2005).

84. Mourad, *La physiognomonie arabe*, 46–52. See also George Sarton, "Review of Youssef Mourad, *La physiognomonie arabe*," *Isis* 33, no. 2 (1941): 248–49.

85. See Mahmoud Manzalaoui, "The Pseudo-Aristotelian 'Kitab Sirr al-Asrar': Facts and Problems," *Oriens* 23/24 (1974): 147–257. For more on Badawi, see Di-Capua, "Arab Existentialism"; Di-Capua, *No Exit*.

86. Mourad, *La physiognomonie arabe*, 1–3, 57–61.

87. Ibid., 61–63. Ibn 'Arabi discusses *firasa* in *Divine Governance*, chap. 8. Murad also notes his lengthier discussion in *al-Futuhat al-Makkiyya* (Cairo, 1207), in Mourad, *La physiognomonie arabe*, 61.

88. Mourad, *La physiognomonie arabe*, 34.

89. Ibid., 61–63.

90. Abu'l-Qasim al-Qushayri, *al-Qushayri's Epistle on Sufism: Al-Risalah al-qushayriyya fi 'ilm al-tasawwuf*, trans. Alexander Knysh (Reading, UK: Garnet Publishing, 2007), 242–52.

91. Ibn 'Arabi, *Divine Governance*, 95.

92. Ibid., 96.

93. Mourad, *La physiognomonie arabe*, 17.

94. Ibid., 17–18.

95. "Man is to God, what the pupil is to the eye," Ibn 'Arabi, quoted in Benslama, *Psychoanalysis and the Challenge of Islam*, 133.

96. Guerlac, *Thinking in Time*, 21.

97. Ibid., 2–4, 63–64; and Gilles Deleuze, *Bergsonism*, trans. Hugh Tomlinson and Barbara Habberjam (New York: Zone Books, 1991).

98. Guerlac, *Thinking in Time*, 63–64.

99. Bergson, *Time and Free Will*, 164; Guerlac, *Thinking in Time*, 5, 43, 92. See my discussion of al-Taftazani's conception of intuition in chapter 2.

100. Wahba, "al-La-Shu'ur 'ind Birjsun." He noted that Bergson provided a critique of associationism, and a critique of the moments in which science tried to touch the soul, cf. Guerlac, *Thinking in Time*, 24.

101. Wahba cited Bergson's *al-Taqa al-Ruhiyya*, a translation of *L'energie spirituelle*. See *Mind-Energy*, trans. H. Wildon Carr (London: Macmillan, 1920).

102. Wahba, "al-La-Shu'ur 'ind Birjsun," 214–15.

103. Ibid., 216–19. Wahba discussed Bergson's notion of the fundamental or deeper self that represented human interiority (the *batin*) and that would give new meaning to the Delphic injunction to "know thyself."

104. Suwayf, "Ma'na al-Takamul al-Ijtima'i 'ind Birjsun"; Soueif, "Bergson's Theory of Social Integration." For a critique of Suwayf, see Muhammad Ja'far, "Naqd Maqal 'Ma'na al-Takamul al-Ijtima'i 'ind Birjsun,'" *Majallat 'Ilm al-Nafs* 5, no. 3 (1950): 454–56.

105. On the "textual concealment" and repression of Henri Wallon within intellectual history, see Yannis Stavrakakis, "Wallon, Lacan, and the Lacanians: Citation Practices and Repression," *Theory, Culture, and Society* 24 (2007): 131–38; Elisabeth Roudinesco, "The Mirror Stage: An Obliterated Archive," in *The Cambridge Companion to Lacan*, ed. Jean-Michel Rabaté (Cambridge: Cambridge University Press, 2003), 25–34. Roudinesco situates Wallon within the wider milieu of French intellectual thought in *Jacques Lacan and Co.: A History of Psychoanalysis in France, 1925–1985* (Chicago: University of Chicago Press, 1990).

106. Henri Wallon, "The Role of the Other in the Consciousness of the Ego," in *The World of Henri Wallon*, ed. Gilbert Voyat (New York: Jason Aronson, 1984), 91–103, 91. Wallon's writings appeared as "Le Role de 'l'autre' dans le conscience du 'moi,'" *Majallat 'Ilm al-Nafs* 2, no. 1 (1946): 215–26, and "Athar 'al-Akhir' fi Takwin al-Shu'ur bi-l-Dhat," *Majallat 'Ilm al-Nafs* 2, no. 2 (1946): 252–67, translated and annotated by Yusuf Murad.

107. Wallon, "Role of the Other in the Consciousness of the Ego," 94.

108. Ibid., 100, 103. See Murad's extensive discussion of the *socius* in "Athar 'al-Akhir' fi Takwin al-Shu'ur bi-l-Dhat," 264n3. As he points out, Janet uses the Latin term *socius* to indicate the social aspect introjected into the self since childhood in an unconscious fashion.

109. Georg Wilhelm Friedrich Hegel, *Phenomenology of Spirit*, trans. A. V. Miller (Oxford: Oxford University Press, 1977), 111–19; see also Alexandre Kojève, *Introduction to the Reading of Hegel*, trans. James H. Nichols Jr. (Ithaca, NY: Cornell University Press, 1980). Kojève may well have influenced the Egyptian reading of Hegel via his colleague and friend Alexandre Koyré, who taught on and off at Cairo University from 1932 to 1941.

110. Buqtur was a teacher at the Suez secondary school. Zakariyya Ibrahim Buqtur, "Mushkilat al-Shu'ur," *Majallat 'Ilm al-Nafs* 3, no. 2 (1947): 259–62. In another exposition on existentialist readings of absence (*al-ghiyab*), Buqtur drew on Gabriel Marcel's *Creative Fidelity*, arguing for the interconnected nonbinary nature of absence and presence; "every absence indicates an expression of another presence." See Zakariyya Ibrahim Buqtur, "Sikulujiyyat al-Ghiyab," *Majallat 'Ilm al-Nafs* 6, no. 1 (1950): 3–12.

111. Zakariyya Ibrahim Buqtur, "al-Dallala al-Siykulujiyya li-l-Nazra," *Majallat 'Ilm al-Nafs* 6, no. 2 (1950–51): 225–32.

112. Ibid., 227. Jean-Paul Sartre, *Being and Nothingness: An Essay in Phenomenological Ontology*, trans. Hazel E. Barnes (New York: Washington Square Press, 1966), 243.

113. Buqtur, "al-Dallala al-Siykulujiyya li-l-Nazra," 232.

114. One could even argue that it constitutes a differential economy of vision. For a discussion of the alternative Sufi economy of vision within a contemporary context, see Mittermaier, *Dreams That Matter*, chap. 3. As Mittermaier notes, the possibility and prevalence of a "blessing gaze" among Egyptian Sufis stands contrary to Lacan's claim that "it is striking, when one thinks of the universality of the function of the evil eye, that there is no trace anywhere of a good eye, of an eye that blesses," 88.

115. Eric Ormsby, "The Poor Man's Prophecy: Al-Ghazālī on Dreams," in *Dreaming across Boundaries: The Interpretation of Dreams in Islamic Lands*, ed. Louise Marlow (Boston: Ilex Foundation, 2008), 142–52, quotation 150.

116. Martin Jay, *Downcast Eyes: The Denigration of Vision in Twentieth Century French Thought* (Berkeley: University of California Press, 1993), 291.

117. Wahba, *Yusuf Murad wa-l-Madhhab al-Takamuli*, 17.

118. Goldstein, *Post-Revolutionary Self*, 100.

119. Yusuf Murad, "'Ilm al-Nafs al-Sina'i," *Majallat 'Ilm al-Nafs* 3, no. 3 (1948): 329–42; Murad, "'Ilm al-Nafs fi Khidmat al-Intaj al-Qawmi," *Majallat 'Ilm al-Nafs* 8, no. 2 (1952–53): 145–52. Even when discussing the role of applied psychology for national production, Murad was keen to point out that it should never aim merely at maximizing production at the expense of spiritual principles.

120. I term this a social welfare mode of regulation, see El Shakry, *Great Social Laboratory*, chap. 7.

121. Scarfone, *The Unpast*, 92.

122. Ibid.

123. Khanna, *Dark Continents*, 103.

124. Di-Capua, "Intellectual Revolt of the 1950s"; Di-Capua, "Arab Existentialism," 1076–78.

125. On the juxtaposition of Sartre and Guevara, see Di-Capua, *No Exit*.

126. Samah Selim, *The Novel and the Rural Imaginary in Egypt, 1885–1985* (London: Routledge, 2004), 140–41. To be fair, as Selim outlines, al-'Alim and Anis represented one segment of a highly complex literary field that included more multifaceted and less dogmatic positions. On Hegelian murder, see Jacques Lacan, "The Mirror Stage," in *Écrits*, trans. Alan Sheridan (New York: Norton, 1977), 6; Khanna, *Dark Continents*, 103.

127. Najib Baladi, "al-Huriyya wa-l Madi," *Majallat 'Ilm al-Nafs* 4, no. 3 (1949): 393–406.

Chapter Two: The Self and the Soul

1. Ibn al-'Arabi, *Bezels of Wisdom*, 172–86; 47–59. See Qur'an 4:1 "Mankind, fear your Lord, who created you of a single soul (*nafs*)," or more metaphorically from a single breath.

2. Ibn al-'Arabi, *Bezels of Wisdom*, 172. R.W.J. Austin notes that the two key terms Ibn 'Arabi uses "are *ruh* [spirit] and *nafakha* [to blow]. In relation to the primordial Breath [*nafas*], the former is its content, while the latter describes its mode of operation. The Spirit, the root meaning of which, in Arabic, is closely related in meaning to the root *nafasa*." Ibid., 172. See Qur'an 15:28–29; 21:91; 32:9; 38:72; 66:12 (*nafakha*); and 4:1; 6:98; 41:53; 91:7–10 (*nafs*). On the *nafs* and the *ruh*, see E. E. Calverley and I. R. Netton, "Nafs," in *Encyclopaedia of Islam*, 2nd ed., edited by P. Bearman, Th. Bianquis, C. E. Bosworth, E. van Donzel, and W. P. Heinrichs. Brill online, 2012. http://dx.doi.org/10.1163/1573-3912_islam_COM_0833. As they note, "*rūḥ* equates with *rīḥ* and means the 'breath of life' (cf. Gen. ii, 7), the creation of which belongs to Allāh." The analogy here is between the *Pneuma*—a movement of air; the spirit, the vital principle by which the body is animated; a spirit, a simple essence, possessed of the power of knowing, desiring, deciding, and acting; God's power and agency; the disposition or influence which fills and governs the soul of any one—and the *Nafas Rahmani*; see Joseph Henry Thayer, *A Greek-English Lexicon of the New Testament* (New York: American Book, 1889), 520–23. For a contemporary philosophical genealogy of breath, see Lenart Škof, *Breath of Proximity: Intersubjectivity, Ethics, and Peace* (Dordrecht: Springer, 2015).

3. Henry Corbin, *Alone with the Alone: Creative Imagination in the Sufism of Ibn 'Arabi* (Princeton, NJ: Princeton University Press, 1998), 185; on the Divine Breath, or the *Nafas Rahmani*, the Breath or Sigh of Divine Compassion, see also 115–17, 159, 161, 184–85, 297–300. William Chittick translates it as the "Breath of the All-merciful," which as Ibn 'Arabi states, "bestows existence upon the possible things"; Chittick, "Divine Names and Theophanies," in Ibn al-'Arabi, *Meccan Revelations*, vol. 1: 50–56; see also Chittick, *Self-Disclosure of God*, 69–70; Izutsu, *Sufism and Taoism*, 131–40; Michael Sells, "Ibn 'Arabī's Garden among the Flames: A Reevaluation," *History of Religions* 23, no. 4 (1984):

287–315. On the relation between the *Nafas al-Rahmani* and the Arabic letters that take shape in human breath, see Chittick, *Sufi Path of Knowledge*, 127–30; and Denis Gril, "The Science of Letters," in Ibn al-ʿArabi, *Meccan Revelations*, vol. 2: 120–21.

4. Corbin, *Alone with the Alone*, 117.

5. Pandolfo, "Soul Choking," 78; Pandolfo, *Knot of the Soul*.

6. "It is only by sustaining the non-religious, radically atheistic, anti-metaphysical foundations of psychoanalysis that the question of its applicability among Islamicate cultures can unfold. These symbolic orders—their theologies and mythologies, laws and practices, languages and histories—are human inventions. This is why psychoanalysis takes them seriously. Religion in Tehran, as in the West, is a symptom." Gorelick, "Translating the Islamicate Symptom," 12.

7. Christian Jambet, "Four Discourses on Authority in Islam," trans. Sigi Jöttkandt, *S, Journal of the Jan van Eyck Circle for Lacanian Ideology Critique* 2 (2009): 44–61, quotations 44, 45.

8. Ibid.

9. Ewing, *Arguing Sainthood*, 35.

10. DiCenso, "Symbolism and Subjectivity," 64.

11. Dr. Abu al-Wafa al-Ghunaymi al-Taftazani (1930–1994), was an expansive Islamic thinker who held the post of deputy dean and professor of Islamic philosophy at Cairo University and was eventually appointed head of the Supreme Council of Sufi Orders in Egypt in 1983. At various points in his career he was a member of the Higher Institute of Culture, the Higher Council of Islamic Affairs, and the head of the Philosophy Association in Egypt. Mustafa Najib, "Dr. Abu al-Wafa al-Taftazani," *Aʿlam Misr fi al-Qarn al-ʿIshrin* (Qalyub, Egypt: al-Ahram, 1996), 83; Muhammad ʿAtif al-ʿIraqi, ed., *al-Duktur Abu al-Wafa al-Ghunaymi al-Taftazani: Ustadhan li-l-Tasawwuf wa-Mufakkiran Islamiyyan, 1930–1994* (Cairo: Dar al-Hidaya li-l-Tibaʿa wa-l-Nashr wa-l-Tawziʿ, 1995). His theses were published as *Ibn ʿAtaʾ Allah al-Sakandari wa-Tasawwufu*, 2nd ed. (Cairo: Maktabat al-Anjlu al-Misriyya, 1969), and *Ibn Sabʿin wa-Falsafat al-Sufiyya* (Beirut: Dar al-Kitab al-Libnani, 1973). In addition, he was the author of two popular introductory texts on Sufism and theology: *Madhkhal ila al-Tasawwuf al-Islami*, 3rd ed. (Cairo: Dar al-Thaqafa li-l-Nashr wa-l-Tawziʿ, 1979), and *ʿIlm al-Kalam wa-Baʿd Mushkilatih* (Cairo: Maktabat al-Qahira al-Haditha, 1966).

12. As Ebrahim Moosa has shown with respect to the thought of medieval theologian al-Ghazali (d. 1111), this enables us to explore "how a knowledge tradition coheres while also generating subjects with divergent and overlapping subjectivities," *Ghazālī*, 29.

13. On the idea of a clash of discourses, see Ewing, *Arguing Sainthood*, 103–7. As Ewing notes, both Frantz Fanon and Ashis Nandy posited the presence of Westernized public selves and "secret" traditional private selves under the pressures of colonial modernization, 126–27, 228; Fanon, *Black Skin, White Masks*; Nandy, *Savage Freud*.

14. For an exploration of mysticism (of all types) and psychoanalysis, see Webb and Sells, "Lacan and Bion," where they emphasize the role of healing, the viability of truth, and the status of the unconscious, all in relation to the mystical language of unsaying, or *apophasis*.

15. Reinhard, "Freud, My Neighbor," 191.

16. Indeed, he goes so far as to refer to psychoanalysis as a secularized form of Jewish mysticism. See Bakan, *Sigmund Freud and the Jewish Mystical Tradition*. See also the discussion of and selections from David Bakan in Capps, *Freud and Freudians on Religion*, 85–120. On the Jewish mystical tradition, see Elliot Wolfson, *Language, Eros, Being: Kabbalistic Hermeneutics and Poetic Imagination* (New York: Fordham University Press, 2005).

17. Toews, "Historicizing Psychoanalysis," 525.

18. On the bilateral influence of Jewish and Islamic mysticism, see Paul B. Fenton, "Judaism and Sufism," in *History of Islamic Philosophy*, ed. Seyyed Hossein Nasr and Oliver Leaman (Abingdon, UK: Routledge, 2007), 755–68.

19. In part because of this connection between Lacan and Corbin, I draw extensively on Corbin's reading of Ibn 'Arabi in what follows. As William Chittick, the foremost Western scholar of Ibn 'Arabi, notes, Corbin's own reading of Ibn 'Arabi was somewhat idiosyncratic and tended to overemphasize the *mundus imaginalis* at the expense of the concept of *tawhid* or divine unity. Chittick, introduction to *Sufi Path of Knowledge*. While I acknowledge this imbalance, Corbin nevertheless remains central to the analytic tradition's understanding of mysticism. On the influence of Corbin on Lacan, see Elisabeth Roudinesco, *Jacques Lacan*, trans. Barbara Bray (New York: Columbia University Press, 1997).

20. Lacan references Corbin in the context of "Courtly Love and Anamorphosis," in *Ethics of Psychoanalysis*, 139–54; Benslama notes that Lacan returned to Ibn 'Arabi at a 1960 conference in Brussels. Benslama, *Psychoanalysis and the Challenge of Islam*, 220n34. For the encounter between Averroës and Ibn 'Arabi, see Corbin, *Alone with the Alone*, 41–43, and Chittick, "*Sufi Path of Knowledge*, xiii–xiv.

21. Lacan, "God and the *Jouissance* of Woman," 147.

22. Safouan had studied psychoanalysis with Mustafa Ziywar and Islamic philosophy with Abu al-'Ala' al-Afifi (who had written extensively on Ibn 'Arabi) at Faruq I University in Alexandria. Safouan began training in Paris with Lacan in 1949 and was one of his first students after the war. After returning to Egypt in the 1950s and translating Freud's *Interpretation of Dreams* into Arabic, Safouan returned to Paris where he wrote widely in French on psychoanalysis, speech, and language and is considered an eminent Lacanian psychoanalyst. See Moustapha Safouan, "Interview with Colin MacCabe," *Zamyn*, http://www.zamyn.org/interviews/maccabe-safouan/interview.html. On his brief psychoanalytic pratice in Cairo, see also Safouan, "Five Years of Psychoanalysis in Cairo," trans. Juliet Flower MacCannell, *Umbr(a)*: Islam (2009): 35–42.

23. Ibrahim Abu Rabi', "Al-Azhar and Islamic Rationalism in Modern Egypt: The Philosophical Contributions of Muṣṭafā 'Abd āl-Raziq and 'Abd al-Ḥalim Maḥmūd," *Islamic Studies* 27, no. 2 (1988): 129–50, 130; Arthur Goldschmidt Jr., "'Abd al-Raziq, Shaykh Mustafa," *Biographical Dictionary of Modern Egypt* (Cairo: American University in Cairo Press, 2000), 8–9.

24. 'Abd al-Raziq emphasized the significance of critical reasoning (*'aql naqdi*) as a method in Islamic thinking, but unlike many of his predecessors was sympathetic to Sufism, viewing it as an integral component of the Islamic tradition. Abu Rabi', "Al-Azhar and Islamic Rationalism," 136. On 'Abd al-Raziq and his students as exemplars of "Sufi philosophers," see Andreas Christmann, "Reconciling Sufism with Theology: Abū l-Wafā al-Taftāzānī and the Construct of 'al-Taṣawwuf al-Islāmī' in Modern Egypt," in *Sufism and Theology*, ed. Ayman Shihadeh (Edinburgh: Edinburgh University Press, 2007), 177–98, 181, 195n17.

25. For historical overviews, see Frederick de Jong, "Opposition to Sufism in Twentieth Century Egypt (1900–1970): A Preliminary Survey," in *Islamic Mysticism Contested: Thirteen Centuries of Controversies and Polemics*, ed. Frederick de Jong and Bernd Radtke (Leiden: Brill, 1999), 310–23; Julian Johansen, *Sufism and Islamic Reform in Modern Egypt: The Battle for Islamic Tradition* (Oxford: Clarendon Press, 1996). Although al-Azhar, the oldest religious institution of learning in Egypt, had no official position toward Sufism, many of its affiliates did. Turn-of-the-century Islamic reformers of al-Azhar, such as Muhammad 'Abduh (d. 1905), represented one strand of anti-Sufism. On this relation-

ship, see Ibrahim Abu Rabiʿ, "Al-Azhar Sufism in Modern Egypt: The Sufi Thought," *Islamic Quarterly* 32, no. 4 (1989): 208–35. Aptly referred to as both Sufi and anti-Sufi by Elizabeth Sirriyeh, ʿAbduh was personally inclined toward Sufism, particularly in his early years, but viewed its antirationalist idealist tendencies as detrimental to Egyptian modernity and railed against the "corrupt" practices of the Sufi orders such as saint worship. ʿAbduh's student, Rashid Rida (d. 1935), embodied a more thoroughgoing anti-Sufism that criticized many of its core components, such as the doctrine of *fana*ʾ or the annihilation of the self, and the shaykh-disciple relation, which he viewed as harmful to independent critical thinking. Elizabeth Sirriyeh, *Sufis and Anti-Sufis: The Defence, Rethinking, and Rejection of Sufism in the Modern World* (Richmond, UK: Curzon, 1999); Abu Rabiʿ, "Al-Azhar Sufism"; Haj, *Reconfiguring Islamic Tradition*.

26. Jong, "Opposition to Sufism," 312.

27. Abu Rabiʿ, "Al-Azhar Sufism," 211–12; Jong, "Opposition to Sufism."

28. Jong, "Opposition to Sufism," 319; al-Banna himself was not unsympathetic to Sufism, but the organization was, see Abu Rabiʿ, "Al-Azhar Sufism," 210.

29. Jong, "Opposition to Sufism," 319–21; Sirriyeh, *Sufis and Anti-Sufis*; Abu Rabiʿ, "Al-Azhar Sufism."

30. Andreas Christmann, "Reclaiming Mysticism: Anti-Orientalism and ʿIslamic Mysticism' in Postcolonial Egypt," in *Religion, Language, and Power*, ed. Nile Green and Mary Searle-Chatterjee (New York: Routledge 2008), 57–79. In an otherwise erudite account, Christmann instrumentalizes al-Taftazani's use of "the modern science of human psychology as a convenient exegetical tool to harmonise the mystical and theological traditions of Islam." Christmann, "Reconciling Sufism with Theology," 177.

31. Christmann, "Reconciling Sufism with Theology," 183–89. For example, al-Taftazani cautioned that if one were to take Sufi utterances out of context and read them literally, one might come to the conclusion that the individual suffered from psychosis. Abu al-Wafa al-Ghunaymi al-Taftazani, "Sikulujiyyat al-Tasawwuf (1)," *Majallat ʿIlm al-Nafs* 5, no. 2 (1949): 291–96, 292. On the distinct genre of "ecstatic utterances" or *shathiyat*, see Carl W. Ernst, *Words of Ecstasy in Sufism* (Albany: State University of New York, 1985).

32. Abu Rabiʿ, "Al-Azhar and Islamic Rationalism," 147n47.

33. Muhammad Mustafa Hilmi, *Ibn al-Farid wa-l-Hubb al-Ilahi*, 2nd ed. (Cairo: Dar al-Maʿarif, 1985). Hilmi's book was based on his thesis, defended in 1940, on the Islamic mystic Ibn al-Farid (d. 1235) and his conception of divine love. His doctoral committee included the intellectual luminaries Taha Husayn, the doyen of Arabic letters; Arabic scholar Ahmad Amin; and was supervised by Mustafa ʿAbd al-Raziq. Ibn al-Farid is also central to contemporary Egyptian Sufi understandings of God, see, for example, Michael Frishkopf's discussion of Shaykh Yasin al-Tuhami, the southern Egyptian musician and *munshid* (panegyrist) whose extensive poetic repertoire relies heavily on Ibn Farid (as well as Ibn ʿArabi), "Shaykh Yasin al-Tuhami: A Typical Layla Performance," *Garland Encyclopedia of World Music*, vol. 6 (2002); Frishkopf, "Thus Spake the Reed Flute," *al-Ahram Weekly* (864), September 27–October 3, 2007.

34. Ibrahim Abu Ghurra, "Fi al-Tasawwuf wa-ʿIlm al-Nafs: Ibn al-Farid wa-l-Hubb al-Ilahi li-l-Duktur Mustafa Muhammad Hilmi," *Majallat ʿIlm al-Nafs* 1, no. 2 (1945): 220–22. Hilmi had also written a general introduction to spiritual life in Islam, *al-Haya al-Ruhiyya fi al-Islam* (Cairo: Dar Ihyaʾ al-Kutub al-ʿArabiyya, 1945).

35. Abu al-Wafa al-Ghunaymi al-Taftazani, "Sikulujiyyat al-Tasawwuf (2)," *Majallat ʿIlm al-Nafs* 5, no. 3 (1950): 377–84. Al-Taftazani draws heavily on al-Ghazali's discussion of the soul as: heart (*qalb*), spirit (*ruh*), soul (*nafs*), and intelligence (*ʿaql*), see al-Ghazālī, *The Marvels of the Heart, Kitāb sharḥ ʿajāʾib al-qalb, Book 21 of The Revival of the Religious*

Sciences, Iḥyā' 'ulūm al-dīn, translated with an introduction and notes by Walter James Skellie (Louisville, KY: Fons Vitae, 2010), especially chap. 1.

36. Moosa, *Ghazālī*, 224.

37. Sigmund Freud, "The Unconscious" (1915), *SE* 14: 159–204, 172–76.

38. Lacan, "God and the *Jouissance* of Woman," 155.

39. William C. Chittick, "On Sufi Psychology: A Debate between the Soul and the Spirit," in *Consciousness and Reality: Studies in Memory of Toshihiko Izutsu*, ed. Sayyid Jalal al-Din Ashtiyani, Hideichi Matsubara, Takashi Iwami, and Akiro Matsumoto (Leiden: Brill, 2000), 341–66, 344–46, 364–365n14. Adding to this heterogeneity is the fact that some authors define the *nafs* as what others refer to as the *ruh*, 344.

40. Moosa, *Ghazālī*, 224; see also Calverley and Netton, "Nafs."

41. Al-Ghazali as translated and cited by Sara Sviri, "The Self and Its Transformation in Sufism: With Special Reference to Early Literature," in *Self and Self-Transformation in the History of Religions*, ed. David Shulman and Guy G. Stroumsa (Oxford: Oxford University Press, 2002), 195–215, quotation 195. The quote is from *Rawdat al-Talibin wa-'Umdat al-Salikin*. On al-Ghazali's conception of the self and soul, see al-Ghazālī, *Marvels of the Heart*; Taneli Kukkonen, "The Self as Enemy, the Self as Divine: A Cross-roads in the Development of Islamic Anthropology," in *Ancient Philosophy of the Self*, ed. Paulina Remes and Juha Sihvola (Dordrecht: Springer Science + Business Media BV, 2008), 205–24.

42. Certain Sufi ontologies have mapped out the various levels of the soul as stages of purification through which it must transform itself; see Sviri's discussion on the transformation and training of the self in "The Self and Its Transformation," 199–207; and Chittick, "On Sufi Psychology," 344–46.

43. Al-Taftazani, "Sikulujiyyat al-Tasawwuf (2)," 379–80. Al-Taftazani referenced al-Qushayri's *Risalah* and al-Ghazali's *Ihya' 'Ulum al-Din*. See, for example, al-Qushayri, *al-Qushayri's Epistle on Sufism*, 109–10.

44. Sviri, "The Self and Its Transformation," 196–97.

45. Al-Qushayri, *al-Qushayri's Epistle on Sufism*, 121.

46. Al-Taftazani, "Sikulujiyyat al-Tasawwuf (2)," 380. On Ibn 'Arabi's conception of the self and the soul, see Chittick, *Self-Disclosure of God*, 269–73. Chittick cites the following from Ibn 'Arabi's *al-Futuhat al-Makkiyya*: "The *nafs* is those attributes of the servant that are infirm (II 568.1)," 270. On the prevalence of the negative conception of selfhood (*nafs*) in Ibn 'Arabi's time, see Jari Kaukua, "I in the Eye of God: Ibn 'Arabī on the Divine Human Self," *Journal of the Muhyiddin Ibn 'Arabi Society* 47 (2010): 1–22, 17.

47. Chittick, "On Sufi Psychology," 347–50, quotation 350; Chittick, *Sufi Path of Knowledge*, 16–17.

48. On Ibn 'Ata' Allah al-Sakandari (al-Iskandari), including his dispute with Ibn Tay-miyya, see G. Makdisi, "Ibn 'Aṭā' Allāh al-Iskandari," in *Encyclopaedia of Islam*, 2nd ed., edited by P. Bearman, Th. Bianquis, C. E. Bosworth, E. van Donzel, and W. P. Heinrichs. Brill online, 2012, http://dx.doi.org/10.1163/1573-3912_islam_SIM_3092; for a general introduction, including the connections between Ibn 'Ata' Allah and Ibn 'Arabi's controversial oeuvre, see Mohamed Mosaad Abdelaziz Mohamed, "Ibn 'Aṭā' Allāh al-Sakandarī: A Sufi, 'Alim and Faqīh," *Comparative Islamic Studies* 9, no. 1 (2013): 41–65. There are numerous translations available of his work: al-Iskandari, *The Key to Salvation: A Sufi Manual of Invocation*, trans. Mary Ann Koury Danner (Cambridge: Islamic Texts Society, 1996); *The Book of Illumination*, trans. Scott Alan Kugle (Louisville, KY: Fons Vitae, 2005); *The Subtle Blessings in the Saintly Lives of Abū al-'Abbās al-Mursī and His Master Abū al-Ḥasan al-Shādhilī, the Founders of the Shādhilī Order*, trans. Nancy Roberts (Louisville, KY: Fons Vitae, 2005); *The Book of Wisdom, Ibn 'Ata'illah and Intimate Conversa-*

tions, Kwaja Abdullah Ansari, trans. Victor Danner and Wheeler M. Thackston (New York: Paulist Press, 1978); Sherman Jackson, *Sufism for Non-Sufis? Ibn ʿAṭaʾAllāh al-Sakandarī's Taj al-ʿArūs* (Oxford: Oxford University Press, 2012).

49. Al-Taftazani, *Ibn ʿAtaʾAllah al-Sakandari wa-Tasawwufu*, 156–158; see Ibn ʿAtaʾ Allah's sustained meditation on darkness and luminosity in *The Book of Wisdom, Ibn ʿAtaʾillah*; Mohamed ("Ibn ʿAṭāʾ Allāh al-Sakandarī," 50–51) notes that this is an elaboration of al-Ghazali's *Mishkat al-Anwar*. On this "metaphysics of light," see al-Ghazālī, *The Niche of Lights: A Parallel English-Arabic Text*, translated, introduced, and annotated by David Buchman (Provo, UT: Brigham Young University Press, 1998).

50. Al-Taftazani, *Ibn ʿAtaʾAllah al-Sakandari*, 157.

51. Ibid., 157–59. In addition to al-Sakandari, al-Taftazani cited al-Qushayri, *al-Risala*; al-Ghazali, *ʿIhya ʿUlum al-Din*; Ibn ʿArabi, *al-Futuhat al-Makkiyya*; al-Jurjani, *Taʿrifat*; and Suhrawardi, *ʿAwarif al-Maʿarif*. For al-Sakandari's view on the *nafs* as an obstruction of the path to God, see Jackson, *Sufism for Non-Sufis?*

52. *Nafs* was the essence (*jawhar bukhari*) that carried the life force, sense, movement, and will, equivalent to Aristotle's *âme sensitive*, in contrast to the vegetative and rational souls. Al-Taftazani, *Ibn ʿAtaʾAllah al-Sakandari*, 150. On Muslim tripartite divisions of the soul, see also, Mourad, *La physiognomonie arabe*, 70–71; Calverley and Netton, "Nafs"; and Edward William Lane, *An Arabic-English Lexicon in Eight Parts, Part 8* (Beirut: Librairie du Liban, 1968), 2826–29.

53. Al-Taftazani, *Ibn ʿAtaʾAllah al-Sakandari*, 152. On *al-nafs al-ammara bi-l-suʾ*, the commanding self, controlled by passions and impulses, that commands evil, see Qurʾan 12:53; on *al-nafs al-lawwama*, the reproaching or upbraiding self, torn between good and evil, see Qurʾan 75:2; on *al-nafs al-mutmaʾinna*, the tranquil self, see Qurʾan 89:27. See Calverley and Netton, "Nafs." For a discussion of the malleable nature of the human soul, and on the evil-commanding and self-assured selves and their relationship to the soul, see Ibn ʿArabi, *Divine Governance*, 23–59.

54. Al-Taftazani, *Ibn ʿAtaʾAllah al-Sakandari*, 163–64. Sufis could further be characterized in modern psychological language as introverts, beset by *monoïdéisme*. In the words of psychologist James Leuba, the mystic attained a "ʿpsychic homogeneity' from which all distinctions have disappeared and in which nothing remains but a general awareness of existence: his own life and that of the universe seem merged together." Al-Taftazani, *Ibn ʿAtaʾAllah al-Sakandari*, 188, 197; James Leuba, *The Psychology of Religious Mysticism* (Abingdon, Oxon: Routledge, 1925), 170. On *monoïdéisme* al-Taftazani cited André Lalande's *Vocabulaire technique et critique de la Philosophie*.

55. Al-Taftazani, *Ibn ʿAtaʾAllah al-Sakandari*, 162–63. To be more precise, the *nafs* was placed in a liminal position between the body and the heart, ibid., 151.

56. Ibid., 163. Al-Taftazani cited Yusuf Murad, *Mabadiʾ ʿIlm al-Nafs al-ʿAmm*.

57. Al-Taftazani, *Ibn ʿAtaʾAllah al-Sakandari*, 163–64.

58. Ibid., 164.

59. Al-Taftazani, "Sikulujiyyat al-Tasawwuf (2)," 381.

60. Chittick, "On Sufi Psychology," 357–59.

61. He noted, in passing, that some Sufis add reason or *ʿaql* as another faculty capable of empirical, rather than intuitive, perception, but then he quickly added, "perception is only available to those who are pure and free of passions," the *qalb* was the seat of Godly knowledge and intuitive sciences. Al-Taftazani, "Sikulujiyyat al-Tasawwuf (2)," 381.

62. Ebrahim Moosa refers to it as conscience, *Ghazālī*, 221; Marshall Hodgson refers to it as the inner "secret" of the heart, *The Venture of Islam: Conscience and History in a World Civilization*, vol. 1, *The Classical Age of Islam* (Chicago: University of Chicago Press, 1974), 406; Chittick refers to it as the "divine mystery," "On Sufi Psychology," 346.

63. "*Sirr al-sirr ma infarad bihi al-haqq 'an al-'abd*," al-Taftazani, "Sikulujiyyat al-Tasawwuf (2)," 381. Compare al-Qushayri, "If the bone next to my heart learns the secret of my heart, I will surely cast it away," *al-Qushayri's Epistle on Sufism*, 110; and see Ewing's discussion of "the secret" in al-Ghazali as an esoteric-exoteric split, *Arguing Sainthood*, 239–43.

64. Chittick, "On Sufi Psychology," 346. On " 'mystical' as the adjective of a secret" see Certeau, *Mystic Fable*, 94–101.

65. Al-Taftazani, "Sikulujiyyat al-Tasawwuf (2)," 381.

66. Ormsby, "Poor Man's Prophecy," 144.

67. See also Abu Rabi'’s discussion of 'Abd al-Halim Mahmud in "Al-Azhar Sufism," 221–23.

68. Lacan, "God and the *Jouissance* of Woman," 155.

69. Chittick, "On Sufi Psychology," 344–45.

70. Certeau, *Mystic Fable*, 14.

71. Chittick, "On Sufi Psychology," 345.

72. Ibn 'Arabi, *Divine Governance*, 16.

73. Chittick, "On Sufi Psychology," 345.

74. Al-Taftazani, "Sikulujiyyat al-Tasawwuf (2)," 382.

75. Chittick, "On Sufi Psychology," 344–46; Sviri notes that "transformation of the self from its lowly instinctual nature to the ultimate state of subsistence in God" can be considered a definition of Sufism itself; "The Self and Its Transformation," 196.

76. On the significance of alchemy for Ibn 'Arabi, see Jari Kaukua, "I in the Eye of God," 12. This conception differs from the eschatological pietistic view in which the apotheosis of the *nafs* is attained in the afterlife, see Sviri, "The Self and Its Transformation," 196–97.

77. Al-Taftazani, "Sikulujiyyat al-Tasawwuf (1)."

78. On the significance of *wijdaniyya* or affect in the Islamic *sahwa* or revival, see Ellen McLarney, *Soft Force: Women in Egypt's Islamic Awakening* (Princeton, NJ: Princeton University Press, 2015), especially the epilogue.

79. Hodgson, *Venture of Islam*, 1: 406; see also *al-Qushayri's Epistle*, 78–79; and 'Ali Ibn Muhammad al-Jurjani, *al-Ta'rifat* (Beirut: 'Alam al-Kutub, 1987), 114.

80. Al-Taftazani, "Sikulujiyyat al-Tasawwuf (1)," 292; cf. al-Taftazani, "al-Ma'rifa al-Sufiyya: Adatuha wa-Manhajuha wa-Mawdu'iha 'ind Sufiyyat al-Muslimin (2)," *al-Risala* 19, no. 933 (1951): 576–78, 576.

81. Al-Taftazani, "Sikulujiyyat al-Tasawwuf (1)"; see also al-Taftazani, "al-Idrak al-Mubashir 'ind al-Sufiyya," *Majallat 'Ilm al-Nafs* 4, no. 3 (1949): 369–72, 369.

82. Al-Taftazani, "Sikulujiyyat al-Tasawwuf (1)," 293.

83. Ibid., 294.

84. According to Christmann, al-Taftazani "defines *al-fana'* not as the entire extinction of a Sufi's will to exist and act in this world but only as the total disappearance of bad character traits" ("Reconciling Sufism with Theology," 183). This is in keeping with Qushayri's view, but I elaborate below on al-Taftazani's somewhat different discussion of *fana'* in his earlier writings.

85. Lacan, "God and the *Jouissance* of Woman," 155.

86. "These levels were commonly ordered in set sequences, one achievement laying the groundwork for the next; different analysts differed in describing the sequence." Hodgson, *Venture of Islam*, 1: 406; see also *al-Qushayri's Epistle*, 77–79 on mystical stations and states. Yet, as Michel Chodkiewicz points out, the notion of a ladder of stations is inappropriate insofar as stations are distributed "in line with the predispositions of each individual being; this is why we see so many differences from one author to the next in the

hierarchy and number of stations." Further, according to Ibn 'Arabi, "*traveling through the* mâqâmat *does not consist in leaving one* mâqam *behind* [in order to reach the next one], *but rather in obtaining something that is higher than it, without leaving the station you have already been in. It consists in 'going toward' not 'leaving behind.'*" Chodkiewicz, introduction to Ibn al-'Arabi, *Meccan Revelations*, vol. 2: 11.

87. Muhammad Mustafa Hilmi, "al-Khasa'is al-Nafsiyya li-l-Riyadat wa-l-Adhwaq al-Sufiyya," *Majallat 'Ilm al-Nafs* 6, no. 3 (1951): 329–45.

88. Al-Qushayri, *al-Qushayri's Epistle*, 194.

89. Al-Taftazani, "al-Ma'rifa al-Sufiyya: Adatuha wa-Manhajuha wa-Mawdu'iha 'ind Sufiyyat al-Muslimin (1)," *al-Risala* 19, no. 932 (1951): 550–54, 550–51. In a different but analogous context, Sudhir Kakar discusses the stages of ascetic mysticism as one of degrees of intensity rather than qualitative difference. Kakar, *The Analyst and the Mystic*, 20.

90. Lacan, "God and the *Jouissance* of Woman," 140.

91. Al-Taftazani, "Sikulujiyyat al-Tasawwuf (1)," 295.

92. Al-Taftazani, "Sikulujiyyat al-Tasawwuf (1)," 294–95; Michael Sells, "The Infinity of Desire: Love, Mystical Union, and Ethics in Sufism" in *Crossing Boundaries: Essays on the Ethical Status of Mysticism*, ed. G. William Barnard and Jeffrey J. Kripal (New York: Seven Bridges Press, 2002), 184–229. Sells traces the significance of love within Islamic discourse, in part, to the centrality of lyrical poetic traditions. See also, Sells, "Bewildered Tongue: The Semantics of Mystical Union in Islam," in *Mystical Union and Monotheistic Faith: An Ecumenical Dialogue*, ed. Moshe Idel and Bernard McGinn (New York: Macmillan, 1989), 87–124. For an ethnographic discussion of mystical eros, see J. Andrew Bush, "How 'God Becomes a Lover': Sufi Poetry and the Finitude of Desire in Kurdistan," *Journal of Middle East Women's Studies* 12, no. 1 (2016): 68–87.

93. Corbin, *Alone with the Alone*, 155.

94. "They [mystics] sense that there must be a *jouissance* which goes beyond. That is what we call a mystic." Lacan, "God and the *Jouissance* of Woman," 147.

95. Ibid., 142.

96. *Man 'arafa nafsahu 'arafa rabbahu.* Ibn 'Arabi elaborates extensively on this hadith in *Kitab al-ahadiyyah: A Treatise on the One Alone*, in *Divine Governance*, 231–53, especially pages 237–39; see also Ibn al-'Arabi, *Bezels of Wisdom*, 92; Corbin, *Alone with the Alone*, 95; Izutsu, *Sufism and Taoism*, 39–47; Chittick, *Sufi Path of Knowledge*, 344–46; A. E. Affifi, *The Mystical Philosophy of Muhyid dín-Ibnul 'Arabí* (Cambridge: Cambridge University Press, 1939), 119; and the discussions in Kaukua, "I in the Eye of God," and Kukkonen, "The Self as Enemy, the Self as Divine."

97. Corbin, *Alone with the Alone*, 207.

98. Ibid., 95.

99. "'When you have entered into my Paradise, you have entered into yourself (into your "soul," *nafs*) and you know yourself with another knowledge, different from that which you had when you knew *your* Lord by the knowledge you had of yourself,' for now you know Him and it is through Him that you know yourself," Ibn 'Arabi as cited by Corbin, *Alone with the Alone*, 133.

100. Freud, *The Psychopathology of Everyday Life* (1901), *SE* 6: 258.

101. Corbin, *Alone with the Alone*, 80.

102. Ibid., 133.

103. Ibid., 125–26, 160. "The Godhead is in mankind as an Image is in a mirror. The *place* of this Presence is the consciousness of the individual believer, or more exactly, the theophanic Imagination invested in him. His *time* is *lived psychic* time." Ibid., 275.

104. Referred to as "*akhir maqamat al-wusul*," al-Taftazani, "Sikulujiyyat al-Tasawwuf (1)," 296; cf. *al-Qushayri's Epistle*, 89–91; al-Jurjani, *al-Ta'rifat*, 282.

105. Stated as "*ina 'dam shu 'ur al-shakhs bi-l-ana,*" "*'adam shu 'ur al-shakhs bi-nafsu,*" al-Taftazani, "Sikulujiyyat al-Tasawwuf (1)," 295–96; cf. al-Jurjani, *al-Ta 'rifat,* 217. Michael Sells discusses this as the ego-self, which is to be annihilated, in much the same way that for Lacan the ego is a symptom, a fiction of selfhood; Webb and Sells, "Lacan and Bion," 200–209.

106. Corbin, *Alone with the Alone,* 202. On unveiling or *kashf* as composed of *fana'* (annihilation) and *baqā'* (subsistence) in Ibn 'Arabi's thought, see Izutsu, *Sufism and Taoism,* 44–45.

107. Lacan, "God and the *Jouissance* of Woman," 147.

108. Al-Taftazani, *Ibn 'Ata' Allah al-Sakandari wa-Tasawwufu,* 169–74.

109. Al-Taftazani, "Sikulujiyyat al-Tasawwuf (2)," 378.

110. Hilmi, "al-Khasa'is al-Nafsiyya." He also referenced the exoteric-esoteric divide, but as *'ilm al-zahir* and *'ilm al-qulub* or *'ilm al-sirr.*

111. Hilmi, "al-Khasa'is al-Nafsiyya," 332.

112. Al-Taftazani, "Sikulujiyyat al-Tasawwuf (2)," 378; al-Taftazani, *Ibn 'Ata' Allah al-Sakandari wa-Tasawwufu,* 172–73. See al-Qushayri, *al-Qushayri's Epistle,* 213–17, for an elaboration of *irada* (desire) and the *murid.*

113. Al-Taftazani, "Sikulujiyyat al-Tasawwuf (2)," 379; al-Taftazani, "al-Ma'rifa al-Sufiyya (1)," 550.

114. Ibn 'Arabi, *Divine Governance,* 20.

115. See Michael Sells, "Ibn 'Arabi's Polished Mirror: Perspective Shift and Meaning Event," *Studia Islamica* 67 (1988): 121–49; Kaukua, "The I in the Eye of God," 19–22; Corbin, *Alone with the Alone,* 275.

116. Al-Taftazani, *Ibn 'Ata' Allah al-Sakandari wa-Tasawwufu,* 194.

117. Al-Taftazani, *Ibn 'Ata' Allah al-Sakandari wa-Tasawwufu,* 194–96. Ibn 'Ata' Allah wrote an entire treatise on *dhikr,* among the first of its kind, elaborating on the spiritual and technical aspects of the Sufi practice. See al-Iskandari, *Key to Salvation;* Victor Danner, introduction to *Book of Wisdom,* 29–30.

118. Ewing, *Arguing Sainthood,* 197.

119. Hodgson, *Venture of Islam,* 1: 407. Elsewhere Hodgson critiqued Freud's conceptualization of "oceanic feeling" as strangely detached and de-contextualized from actual mystical practices, since "the subjective transformation need not be oceanic, this is but one subjective manifestation"; Hodgson, *Venture of Islam,* 1: 396–97. For a discussion of Freud and oceanic feeling, see my introduction.

120. Rifa'at Abou-El-Haj, "The Ottoman Dervish Orders as Acculturating Institutions," unpublished manuscript; and Kakar, *The Analyst and the Mystic.*

121. Kakar, *The Analyst and the Mystic,* 50–51.

122. Al-Taftazani, "Sikulujiyyat al-Tasawwuf (2)," 384. Here he quoted from Yusuf Murad's *Mabada' 'Ilm al-Nafs al-'Amm* (*General Principles of Psychology*).

123. For Freud, sublimation entails a de-sexualization, "a 'positive' vicissitude through which the drive chooses a different, nonsexual aim in order to gain pleasure"; Kesel, *Eros and Ethics,* 167.

124. Abu Ghurra, "Fi al-Tasawwuf wa-'Ilm al-Nafs," 220–21.

125. Abu Rabi', "Al-Azhar Sufism," 218; see also Abu Rabi', "Al-Azhar and Islamic Rationalism," on 'Abd al-Halim Mahmud as a direct continuation of 'Abd al-Raziq's thought.

126. Hilmi, "al-Khasa'is al-Nafsiyya."

127. Al-Taftazani, "Sikulujiyyat al-Tasawwuf (2)," 382; al-Taftazani, *Ibn 'Ata' Allah al-Sakandari wa-Tasawwufu,* 165–202.

128. Al-Taftazani, *Ibn 'Ata' Allah al-Sakandari wa-Tasawwufu,* 167.

129. Al-Taftazani, "Sikulujiyyat al-Tasawwuf (2)," 382–83; al-Taftazani, *Ibn 'Ata'Allah al-Sakandari wa-Tasawwufu*, 174–75.

130. Pandolfo, "Soul Choking," 90; Pandolfo, *Knot of the Soul*; Pandolfo, "'The Burning': Finitude and the Politico-Theological Imagination of Illegal Migration," *Anthropological Theory* 7, no. 3 (2007): 329–63.

131. Pandolfo, "Soul Choking," 80–90; Pandolfo, *Knot of the Soul*.

132. Pandolfo, "Soul Choking," 85–86.

133. Corbin, *Alone with the Alone*, 204. As Christian Jambet states, "The perfect identity of the one with itself does not contradict the multiple epiphany, rather it enevelopes it and unfolds itself in it," "The Stranger and Theophany," trans. Roland Végsö, in *Umbr(a): The Dark God* (2005): 27–41, quotation 36.

134. Jambet, "Four Discourses on Authority," 44. In fact, Hegel critiqued Islam for "making the abstract One the absolute object of attention and devotion, and to the same extent, pure subjective consciousness—the Knowledge of this One alone—the only aim of reality; making the *Unconditioned* the *condition* of *existence*"; Hegel as cited by Toscano, *Fanaticism*, 152.

135. Julien Maucade, "Cogito and the Subject of Arab Culture," trans. Sigi Jöttkandt and Ed Pluth, *S, Journal of the Jan van Eyck Circle for Lacanian Ideology Critique* 2 (2009): 6–9, quotation 9.

136. To clarify, from a Lacanian perspective, concepts of unity and oneness belong to the domain of the Imaginary (the domain of psychic reality) and provide the Symbolic order (the structure of signifiers, discourse, and society) with its efficacy. Yet the mystic, in assuming that they partake of a divine and transcendental unity (for example through a mystical union with the Beloved), mistakes the Symbolic order for the Real (that which never becomes available for subjectivation). As Alberto Toscano states, "the unrepresentable Real comes to colonize and to undermine the Symbolic order" (Toscano, *Fanaticism*, 153). Thus, while it is true that Lacanian psychoanalysis perceives a category error on the part of religious belief (it mistakes the Symbolic for the Real), both religion and psychoanalysis strive to understand the subject as the addressee of divine or transcendental discourse, of something which goes *beyond* symbolization, a point I elaborate on with reference to *das Ding*. For a brief and lucid introduction to Lacanian register theory, see Adrian Johnston, "Jacques Lacan," *Stanford Encyclopedia of Philosophy* (summer 2014 edition), Edward N. Zalta, ed., http://plato.stanford.edu/archives/sum2014/entries/lacan/.

137. Al-Taftazani, "al-Ma'rifa al-Sufiyya (2)," 576–77.

138. R. Arnaldez, "Ma'rifa," *Encyclopaedia of Islam*, 2nd ed., edited by P. Bearman, Th. Bianquis, C. E. Bosworth, E. van Donzel, and W. P. Heinrichs, Brill online, 2012, http://referenceworks.brillonline.com/entries/encyclopaedia-of-islam-2/marifa-COM_0686; Chittick, *Sufi Path of Knowledge*, 145–89.

139. Al-Taftazani, "al-Idrak al-Mubashir," 369.

140. Hans Wehr, *A Dictionary of Modern Written Arabic*, ed. Milton Cowan, 3rd ed. (Ithaca, NY: Spoken Language Services, 1976), 863; al-Taftazani, "al-Ma'rifa al-Sufiyya (1)," 552–53. In his two lectures on mysticism, William James noted two principal characteristics that defined mystical states of consciousness, ineffability and a noetic quality. Noetic referred to "inner knowing," a kind of intuitive consciousness, providing direct and immediate access to knowledge beyond what was available to normal senses and the power of reason, from the Greek *nous*. James, *Varieties of Religious Experience*, 380–81.

141. Al-Taftazani, "al-Idrak al-Mubashir," 370.

142. Quoting Ahmad Zarruq, he stated, "the use of symbolism is caused by a lack of patience in expressing an inner power that refuses to be silenced." Al-Taftazani, "Sikulujiyyat

al-Tasawwuf (1)," 291; cf. Ahmad Bin Muhammad Zarruq, *Qawaʿid al-Tasawwuf* (Cairo: Maktabat al-Thaqafa al-Diniyya, 2006).

143. Al-Taftazani, *Ibn ʿAtaʾAllah al-Sakandari*, 163. Crucially, for Ibn ʿArabi the *zahir* and the *batin* were inextricably linked, and one looks "for what is beyond the letter ... *within* the letter itself.... just as God is at one and the same time *al-zâhir wa l-bâtin*, 'the Aparent and the Hidden.'" Michel Chodkiewicz, *An Ocean without Shore: Ibn ʿArabî, The Book, and the Law*, trans. David Streight (Albany: State University of New York Press), 22–33, quotation 24.

144. Al-Taftazani, "al-Maʿrifa al-Sufiyya (1)"; compare ʿAbd al-Halim Mahmud's emphasis on the exoteric sciences in Ibn ʿAtaʾ Allah, see Abu Rabiʿ, "Al-Azhar Sufism," 214–15.

145. Al-Taftazani, "al-Maʿrifa al-Sufiyya (1)," 551–52.

146. Ibid.; al-Taftazani, "al-Maʿrifa al-Sufiyya (2)." According to Ibn ʿArabi there were three branches of knowledge: *ʿilm al-ʿaql*, knowledge attained through reason; *ʿilm al-ahwal*, knowledge acquired through "states" of perception or inner personal experience (*dhawq*); and *ʿilm al-asrar*, knowledge of secrets, arising from the communications of the prophets and saints, and imparted by the soul to the heart. See Chittick, *Sufi Path of Knowledge*, 168–70; A. Ateş, "Ibn al-ʿArabī," in *Encyclopaedia of Islam*, 2nd ed., edited by P. Bearman, Th. Bianquis, C. E. Bosworth, E. van Donzel, and W. P. Heinrichs, Brill online, 2012, http://dx.doi.org/10.1163/1573-3912_islam_COM_0316; Chodkiewicz, introduction to Ibn al-ʿArabi, *Meccan Revelations*, vol. 2: 21.

147. Al-Taftazani, "al-Maʿrifa al-Sufiyya (2)," 576. For a related discussion of al-Ghazali's dialogical relation between the inner and outer (*batin* and *zahir*) dimensions of the human self or the way in which the exemplary conduct of the interior and exterior are refracted through each other, see Moosa, *Ghazālī*, 220–21.

148. Corbin, *Alone with the Alone*, 13, 78. Corbin controversially references esoteric hermeneutics as *taʾwil*, a term that, according to Michel Chodkiewicz, Ibn ʿArabi most often used pejoratively. "Ibn ʿArabî offers neither a *tafsîr* in the classical sense of the term, nor a *taʾwîl*, which woud be an allegorical exegesis, but rather, to use words that come up often in his writing, *ishârât*, meaning 'allusions' to certain unnoticed—and thus occasionally quite surprising—meanings." Chodkiewicz, introduction to Ibn al-ʿArabi, *Meccan Revelations*, vol. 2: 30, 53n142; see also Chodkiewicz, *An Ocean without Shore*, chap. 2; Cyrille Chodkiewicz, "The Law and the Way," in Ibn al-ʿArabi, *Meccan Revelations*, vol. 2: 80, 101n53.

149. It is "the only means of saying something that cannot be apprehended in any other way; a symbol is never 'explained' once and for all, but must be deciphered over and over again"; Corbin, *Alone with the Alone*, 14.

150. Ibid., 78. The *ẓāhir* is what is "apparent, literal, external, exoteric," and the *bāṭin* "something hidden, spiritual, internal, esoteric," ibid.

151. Chittick, *Sufi Path of Knowledge*, 168–70.

152. Al-Taftazani, "al-Maʿrifa al-Sufiyya (2)," 578; al-Taftazani, "al-Maʿrifa al-Sufiyya (1)," 554. Mahmud Amin al-ʿAlim similarly critiqued logical positivism, particularly for its inability to account for religious, ethical, and artistic phenomena, "Ma waraʾ ʿal-Mudrik al-Hissi,'" *Majallat ʿIlm al-Nafs* 5, no. 3 (1950): 361–76.

153. L. Gardet, "Kashf," *Encyclopaedia of Islam*, 2nd ed., edited by P. Bearman, Th. Bianquis, C. E. Bosworth, E. van Donzel, and W. P. Heinrichs, Brill online, 2012, http://referenceworks.brillonline.com/entries/encyclopaedia-of-islam-2/kashf-COM_0458.

154. As cited by al-Taftazani, "al-Maʿrifa al-Sufiyya (1)," 554.

155. Al-Taftazani, "al-Maʿrifa al-Sufiyya (2)," 578.

156. Al-Taftazani, "al-Idrak al-Mubashir," 370; cf. al-Taftazani, "al-Ma'rifa al-Sufiyya (1)," 554. See also al-Taftazani's discussion of Ibn Sab'in, gnosis, and intuition, "Ibn Sab'in," in *History of Islamic Philosophy*, 346–49.

157. Al-Taftazani, "al-Ma'rifa al-Sufiyya (1)," 553.

158. Ibid. It was best described, if one were to use psychological language, states al-Taftazani, as "*al-istibtun al-dhati*" or personal introspection.

159. Al-Taftazani, "al-Ma'rifa al-Sufiyya (1)," 552. On the significance of the heart to Sufi imaginaries, see Corbin, *Alone with the Alone*, 216–45, quotations, 221–22.

160. Corbin, *Alone with the Alone*, 223–24.

161. Kakar, *The Analyst and the Mystic*, 19, 22–29.

162. The notions of vision and taste within the Sufi tradition have particular resonances. Al-Ghazali, who is often recalled for his combination of a painstaking rationalism and a propensity toward mysticism, formulated his notion of "taste" after his second and near fatal existential crisis, in which he was "cured only when God Himself 'cast a light' into his heart." In *Deliverance from Error*, al-Ghazali noted, "to comprehend the 'stage beyond the intellect' there must open within a man 'another eye by which he sees the invisible and what will occur in the future.'" Prophecy, and to a lesser extent, dreams, for al-Ghazali, were possible modalities for the opening of the inner eye. Ormsby, "Poor Man's Prophecy," 144, 145, 150.

163. Al-Taftazani was careful to distinguish between the intuitive sciences and *kashf* or mystical intuition and the experience of *dhawq*. This was the result of a semantic dispute with the director of literary research at al-Azhar regarding the translation of the concept of Sufi intuition. See Mahmud al-Khudari, "Kayfa Nutarjam al-Istilah-Intuition," *Majallat 'Ilm al-Nafs* 1, no. 3 (1946): 377–82. Al-Khudari referred to intuition as *al-istilah*, but in the case of Sufis as *dhawq* or *erlebnis*. Al-Taftazani responded in "al-Idrak al-Mubashir," 369. This intellectual exchange is indicative of how closely al-Taftazani followed debates in *Majallat 'Ilm al-Nafs*.

164. Al-Taftazani, "al-Idrak al-Mubashir," 371–72.

165. Al-Taftazani, "al-Idrak al-Mubashir," 372; cf. "al-Ma'rifa al-Sufiyya (2)," 576; al-Taftazani is citing Ibn 'Arabi's *Divine Governance* (*al-Tadbirat al-Ilahiyya*), 18.

166. Al-Taftazani, "al-Idrak al-Mubashir," 372.

167. Ibn al-'Arabi, *Meccan Revelations*, vol. 1: 49.

168. On *dhawq* in al-Ghazali, see Moosa, *Ghazālī*, 234–36. Significantly, the term was translated into other contexts. Amin al-Khuli, a professor of Arabic literature at Fu'ad I University and a Qur'anic scholar, discussed the utility of psychology to the study of literature, and in particular to the comingled aesthetic experiences of religion and literature. Using the language of the miraculous (*'ijaz*) and taste or *dhawq*—al-Khuli discussed the appreciation of a Qur'anic verse, and, for example, its effects on human psychology. Amin al-Khuli, "'Ilm al-Nafs al-Adabi," *Majallat 'Ilm al-Nafs* 1, no. 1 (1945): 36–51. On al-Khuli, see Goldschmidt, *Biographical Dictionary of Modern Egypt*, 105–6.

169. Freud continues, "One could venture to explain in this way the myths of paradise and the fall of man, of God, of good and evil, of immortality ... and to transform *metaphysics* into *metapsychology*"; Freud, *The Psychopathology of Everyday Life*, SE 6: 258–59; or for Lacan, "That the symbolic is the support of that which was made into God, is beyond doubt"; "God and the *Jouissance* of Woman," 154.

170. Pandolfo, "Soul Choking," 80; Reinhard, "Freud, My Neighbor," 182. Lacan states, "*das Ding* has to be posited as exterior, as the prehistoric Other that it is impossible to forget ... something strange to me, although it is at the heart of me"; *Ethics of Psychoanalysis*, 71.

171. Costello, "Real of Religion," 80–81.

172. "Seventy Thousand Veils separate Allah, the One Reality, from the world of matter and of sense. And every soul passes before his birth through these seventy thousand. The inner half of these veils are light: the outer half, veils of darkness. For every one of the veils of light passed through, in this journey towards birth, the soul puts off a divine quality: and for every one of the dark veils, it puts *on* an earthly quality. Thus the child is born *weeping*, for the soul knows its separation from Allah, the One Reality. And when the child cries in its sleep, it is because the soul remembers something of what it has lost. Otherwise, the passage through the veils has brought with it forgetfulness (*nisyan*): and for this reason man is called *insan*.... He is now, as it were, in prison in his body, separated by these thick curtains from Allah.

But the whole purpose of Sufism, the Way of the dervish, is to give him an escape from this prison, an apocalypse of the Seventy Thousand Veils, a recovery of the original unity with The One, *while still in his body*. The body is not to be put off; it is to be refined (*talattaf*) and made spiritual—a help and not a hindrance to the spirit. It is like a metal that has to be refined by fire and transmuted. And the sheikh tells the aspirant that he has the secret of this transmutation. 'We shall throw you into the fire of Spiritual Passion (*'ushq*)' he says, 'and you will emerge refined.'" Canon W.H.T. Gairdner, *Theories, Practices, and Training Systems of a Sufi School* (London: Society for Sufi Studies, 1980), 14–15.

173. Corbin, *Alone with the Alone*, 215.

174. Asad, *Formations of the Secular*, 245. The term "conscience" is entirely inadequate to a Sufi conception of ethics. As Asad has pointed out, this conception of morality as a "domain of individual sovereignty in accordance with inner freedoms (conscience)" is decidedly secular, ibid., 239. It thus stood in contrast, say, to ecclesiastical authority or the passions once so crucial to a Christian ethical sensibility (ibid., 35–37, 106–7, 245–48). The difference, then, between the Kantian conception of inwardness and the Sufi concept of the inner secret, *sirr*, lay in the perceived sovereignty of the moral subject.

175. James DiCenso, "Kant, Freud, and the Ethical Critique of Religion," *International Journal for Philosophy of Religion* 61, no. 3 (2007): 161–79, quotation 162. For a sophisticated discussion of the paradoxical relationship between notions of the unconscious, tracing the concept from Fichte to Schelling, and the autonomous self-fashioned individual, see Matt Ffytche, *The Foundation of the Unconscious: Schelling, Freud and the Birth of the Modern Psyche* (Cambridge: Cambridge University Press, 2012).

176. Reinhard, "Freud, My Neighbor," 166.

Chapter Three: The Psychosexual Subject

1. Al-Ghazālī, *On Disciplining the Soul, Kitāb riyādat al-nafs, and On Breaking the Two Desires, Kitāb kasr al-shahwatayn: Books XXII and XXIII of the Revival of the Religious Sciences, Iḥyā' 'ulūm al-dīn*, trans. T. J. Winter (Cambridge: Islamic Texts Society, 1995).

2. Dror Ze'evi, *Producing Desire: Changing Sexual Discourse in the Ottoman Middle East, 1500–1900* (Berkeley: University of California Press, 2006), 167.

3. Ze'evi, *Producing Desire*, 15.

4. Ibid., 170. According to Ze'evi, many of the earlier sexual scripts disappeared in the late nineteenth century, as "sexual discourse moved out of the textual sphere and into the arena of intimate male and female circles, while a curtain of silence descended on the sexual stage" (165). A number of factors, he argues, contributed to this: the suppression of Sufi devotional erotica; the criticism of sexual morality by European travelers to the Middle East and by Middle Easterners to the West; and the availability of the printing press, which made the easy accessibility of erotica for the masses less desirable, ibid., 163–71.

5. Michel Foucault, *The History of Sexuality*, vol. 1, *An Introduction*, trans. Robert Hurley (New York: Vintage/Random House, 1990), 154; Ze'evi, *Producing Desire*, 171.

6. See Ze'evi, *Producing Desire*, 45–47; Liat Kozma, "'We, the Sexologists ...': Arabic Medical Writing on Sexuality, 1879–1943," *Journal of the History of Sexuality* 22, no. 3 (2013): 426–45, quotation 428.

7. Foucault, *History of Sexuality*; Howard Chiang, "Epistemic Modernity and the Emergence of Homosexuality in China," *Gender and History* 22, no. 3 (2010): 629–57. See also Arnold Davidson, *The Emergence of Sexuality: Historical Epistemology and the Formation of Concepts* (Cambridge, MA: Harvard University Press, 2004).

8. On the "woman question" in twentieth-century Egypt, see Omnia Shakry, "Schooled Mothers and Structured Play: Child Rearing in Turn-of-the-Century Egypt," in *Remaking Women: Feminism and Modernity in the Middle East*, ed. Lila Abu-Lughod (Princeton, NJ: Princeton University Press, 1998), 126–70; Lila Abu-Lughod, "Feminist Longings and Postcolonial Conditions," in *Remaking Women*, 3–32; Marilyn Booth, "Woman in Islam: Men and the 'Women's Press' in Turn-of-the-20th-Century Egypt," *International Journal of Middle East Studies* 33, no. 2 (2001): 171–201; Beth Baron, *The Women's Awakening in Egypt: Culture, Society, and the Press* (New Haven, CT: Yale University Press, 1997); Baron, *Egypt as a Woman: Nationalism, Gender, and Politics* (Berkeley: University of California Press, 2005). On the problematization of men and masculinity, see Hanan Kholoussy, "Monitoring and Medicalising Male Sexuality in Semi-Colonial Egypt," *Gender and History* 22, no. 3 (2010): 677–91; Kholoussy, *For Better, For Worse: The Marriage Crisis That Made Modern Egypt* (Stanford, CA: Stanford University Press, 2010); Wilson Jacob, *Working Out Egypt: Effendi Masculinity and Subject Formation in Colonial Modernity, 1870–1940* (Durham, NC: Duke University Press, 2011); Kozma, "We, the Sexologists."

9. Dean, *Self and Its Pleasures*, 58.

10. Murad, "Bab al-Ta'rifat: Niwa li-Qamus 'Ilm al-Nafs," 104–5.

11. See, for example, Wehr, *Dictionary of Modern Written Arabic*, 669; Rohi Ba'albaki, *al-Mawrid: Qamus 'Arabi-Inklizi* (Beirut: Dar al-'Ilm li-l-Malayyin, 2004), 798; Fakhir 'Aqil, *Mu 'jam 'Ilm al-Nafs: Inklizi-Frinsi-'Arabi* (Beirut: Dar al-'Ilm li-l-Malayyin, 1985), 52, 58; Taha, *Mawsuw'at 'Ilm al-Nafs*, 564–67.

12. Murad, "Bab al-Ta'rifat: Niwa li-Qamus 'Ilm al-Nafs," 101. Murad cited Freud's *An Autobiographical Study*, *SE* 20, extensively regarding the importance of terminology in psychoanalysis.

13. Other key terms translated in discussions of sexuality were: libido: *shahwa*; sexual drive: *al-mil al-jinsi*; genital: *tanasuli*; deviance: *inhiraf, shudhudh*; homosexuality: *al-jinsiyya al-mithliyya*; heterosexuality: *al-jinsiyya al-ghayriyya*; normal, sound: *sawi*. See, for example, Yusuf Murad, "Bab al-Ta'rifat," and Murad, "Nimu al-Tifl al-'Aqli wa-Takwin Shakhsiyyatu," *Majallat 'Ilm al-Nafs* 2, no. 1 (1946): 3–24. Murad used *tanasuli* as the translation for Freud's "genital," and although the term retains a residual denotation of regeneration, I would argue that its actual usage was polysemic and contextually specific, at times reflecting a theoretical divorce from regenerative principles. See also Najmabadi's discussion in "Genus of Sex," of the Persian "*shahvat tanasuli*," which, she argues, ties desire to heterosexual distinction, for example in marriage advice literature.

14. Jean Laplanche, *Freud and the Sexual: Essays 2000–2006*, ed. John Fletcher; trans. J. Fletcher, J. House, and N. Ray (New York: International Psychoanalytic Books, 2011), 11.

15. Jari Kaukua and Taneli Kukkonen, "Sense-Perception and Self-Awareness: Before and after Avicenna, in *Consciousness: From Perception to Reflection in the History of Philosophy*, ed. Sara Heinämaa, Vili Lähteenmäki, and Paulina Remes (Dordrecht: Springer, 2007), 95–119, 102.

16. Al-Ghazālī, *On Disciplining the Soul*, 26, 27–28. For a discussion of al-Ghazali's usage of *ghariza* as an "intrinsic feature," see Alexander Treiger, *Inspired Knowledge in Islamic Thought: Al-Ghazālī's Theory of Mystical Cognition and Its Avicennian Foundation* (London: Routledge, 2011), 125n21, n28. For other premodern usages see A. M. Goichon, *Introduction à Avicenne, son épitre des définitions* (Paris: Desclée de Brouwer 1933), 93; Goichon, *Lexique de la langue philosophique d'Ibn Sina* (Paris: Desclée de Brouwer, 1938), 263–64, nn479–80.

17. Najmabadi, "Genus of Sex," 213–14.

18. Massad, *Desiring Arabs*, 171–72.

19. Najmabadi, "Genus of Sex," 219.

20. Murad, "Nimu al-Tifl al-'Aqli." As will become clear, Murad drew heavily on Sigmund Freud, *Three Essays on the Theory of Sexuality* (1905), *SE* 7: 123–243.

21. Murad, "Nimu al-Tifl al-'Aqli," 19–23.

22. Laplanche, *Freud and the Sexual*, 19.

23. Nicholas Ray, "Forming New Knots: Jean Laplanche, 1924–2012," *Radical Philosophy* 174 (2012): 53–56, quotation 55.

24. Murad, "Nimu al-Tifl al-'Aqli," 13; Ray, "Forming New Knots."

25. Wallon, "Role of the Other in the Consciousness of the Ego," 101.

26. Laplanche, *Freud and the Sexual*, 22.

27. Murad, "Nimu al-Tifl al-'Aqli," 14–16. On the distinction between the self and the not-self in infant life, see also Suttie, *Origins of Love and Hate*, 26–37.

28. Laplanche, *Freud and the Sexual*, 9, 22.

29. Carlson, "Editor's Introduction."

30. Mahfouz, *Mirage*.

31. Murad, "Nimu al-Tifl al-'Aqli," 17. Laplanche argued that infantile Oedipus was always bipolar, "positive and negative attitudes are present in *every* identification." Further, identifications were always replacements for love relationships. In other words, "identification with the object and *not with the rival* is indispensable for any understanding of homosexuality and of heterosexuality." Laplanche, *Freud and the Sexual*, 23.

32. Murad, "Nimu al-Tifl al-'Aqli," 16–18.

33. Ibid.

34. Ibid., 18.

35. Khaled El-Rouayheb, *Before Homosexuality in the Arab-Islamic World, 1500–1800* (Chicago: University of Chicago Press, 2009), 6.

36. Murad, "Nimu al-Tifl al-'Aqli," 11.

37. Yusuf Murad, *Shifa' al-Nafs*, 36.

38. Lenn E. Goodman, "al-Rāzī," in *Encyclopaedia of Islam*, 2nd ed., edited by P. Bearman, Th. Bianquis, C. E. Bosworth, E. van Donzel, and W. P. Heinrichs. Brill online, 2012. http://dx.doi.org/10.1163/1573-3912_islam_SIM_6267.

39. Epicurus, as cited by Martha Nussbaum, *The Therapy of Desire: Theory and Practice in Hellenistic Ethics* (Princeton, NJ: Princeton University Press, 1994), 13, 102. He would have also agreed with the statement attributed to Ferenczi; "It is the physician's love which heals the patient."

40. Goodman, "al-Rāzī."

41. Abu Bakr Muhammad ibn Zakariyya al-Razi, *The Spiritual Physick of Rhazes*, trans. Arthur Arberry (London: Butler and Tanner, 1950). Among those afflicted are those "who make pleasure their sole interest and seek only for worldly gratification" (38). See also Goodman, "al-Razi"; Nussbaum, *Therapy of Desire*.

42. Al-Razi, *Spiritual Physick*, 39, "there cannot in fact be any pleasure except in proportion to prior pain."

43. Jonathan Yahalom, "Freud and Epicurean Philosophy: Revisiting Drive Theory," *Contemporary Psychoanalysis* 50, no. 3 (2014): 395–417; Nussbaum, *Therapy of Desire*, chap. 4.

44. Yahalom, "Freud and Epicurean Philosophy," 404.

45. Ibid., 404, 413.

46. Lear, *Freud*, 12, 155. Lear, much like Murad, attempts to synthesize Aristotelian virtue ethics with Freudian metapsychology, placing an emphasis on ethical life as a precondition for psychic integration and, therefore, *eudaimonia*. By his reading, the psychoanalytic emphasis on truthfulness is foundational for virtue ethics. Lear, *Freud*, chap. 1.

47. Nussbaum, *Therapy of Desire*, 137–39.

48. Murad, *Shifa' al-Nafs*.

49. Murad, "Min al-Istibtan ila al-Tahlil al-Nafsi (2)," 30.

50. My discussion of techniques of the self is reminiscent of Michel Foucault's concept of technologies of the self, concerned with the specific modalities by which individual subjectivities and dispositions are constituted by techniques of self-management "so as to transform themselves in order to attain a certain state of happiness, purity, wisdom, perfection, or immortality." See "Technologies of the Self," in *Technologies of the Self: A Seminar with Michel Foucault*, ed. L. Martin, H. Gutman, and P. Hutton (Amherst: University of Massachusetts Press, 1988), 16–49, quotation 18.

51. Murad, *Shifa' al-Nafs*, 101.

52. On catharsis as a "homeopathic hygiene for the soul," see Barbara Cassin, Jacqueline Lichtenstein, and Elisabete Thamer, "Catharsis" in *Dictionary of Untranslatables: A Philosophical Lexicon*, ed. Barbara Cassin, Emily Apter, Jacques Lezra, and Michael Wood (Princeton, NJ: Princeton University Press, 2014), 126–29. Jonathan Lear, *Love and Its Place in Nature: A Philosophical Interpretation of Freudian Psychoanalysis* (New Haven, CT: Yale University Press, 1998), chap. 2; Lear, *Open Minded*, chap. 9.

53. Murad, *Shifa' al-Nafs*, 104.

54. Ibid., 107. As Lear points out, within an Aristotelian approach ethical life based on virtues entails "a turning *towards* reality," *Freud*, 154.

55. Murad, *Shifa' al-Nafs*, 108–9.

56. On the ethical attunement of the self, see Aristotle, *The Nicomachean Ethics*, trans. Martin Ostwald (Indianapolis: Bobbs-Merrill, 1962). See also Saba Mahmood, *Politics of Piety: The Islamic Revival and the Feminist Subject* (Princeton, NJ: Princeton University Press, 2005); Charles Hirschkind, *The Ethical Soundscape: Cassette Sermons and Islamic Counter-Publics* (New York: Columbia University Press, 2006).

57. Murad, *Sikulujiyyat al-Jins*, 71.

58. Murad, "Nimu al-Tifl al-'Aqli," 15.

59. See al-Imam Abu Hamid Muhammad al-Ghazali, "Kitab Riyadat al-Nafs wa-Tahdhib al-Akhlaq wa-Mu'alajat Amrad al-Qalb," *'Ihya 'Ulum al-Din* (Cairo: Dar al-Sha'ab, n.d.) 2: 1425–81; Moosa, *Ghazālī*, 214–21; Frank Griffel, "Al-Ghazali," *Stanford Encyclopedia of Philosophy* (summer 2016 edition), Edward N. Zalta, ed., http://plato .stanford.edu/archives/sum2016/entries/al-ghazali/. For a highly relevant discussion of the psychological underpinnings of al-Ghazali's ethics, see Taneli Kukkonen, "Al-Ghazālī on the Emotions," *Islam and Rationality: The Impact of al-Ghazālī*, vol. 1, ed. Georges Tamer (Leiden: Brill, 2015), 138–64.

60. See al-Ghazali, "Bayan al-Tariq fi Riyadat al-Subyan fi Awwal Nushu'ihim wa-Wajh Ta'dibihim wa-Tahsin Akhlaqihim," *'Ihya 'Ulum al-Din* 2: 1468–72.

61. See Ḥujjat al-Islām Abū Hāmid Muḥammad Ghazzālī Ṭūsī, *Al-Ghazzali on Disciplining the Self from the Alchemy of Happiness* (*Kimiya al-saadat*), trans. Muhammad Nur Abdus Salam (Chicago: Great Books of the Islamic World, 2002), 33–34; cf. Haj, *Reconfiguring Islamic Tradition*, 86–90.

62. Murad, *Shifa' al-Nafs*, 35–36.

63. Ibid., 31–44.

64. Ibid., 63–71. This analysis occurs in the context of a discussion of hysteria, which Murad viewed as an illness equally applicable to both genders and characterized by rationalization and supplication; the hysterical conversion symptom represented a repressed wish or an imaginary solution to an actual problem.

65. Segments of the remainder of this chapter, although substantially revised and recontextualized, are based on El Shakry, "Youth as Peril and Promise: The Emergence of Adolescent Psychology in Postwar Egypt," *International Journal of Middle East Studies* 43, no. 4 (2011): 591–610.

66. On earlier Arabic writings on sexuality, see Kozma, "We, the Sexologists"; Joseph Massad, *Desiring Arabs*.

67. Kholoussy, "Monitoring and Medicalising Male Sexuality"; Kholoussy, *For Better, For Worse*; see also Wilson Chacko Jacob, "Overcoming 'Simply Being': Straight Sex, Masculinity, and Physical Culture in Modern Egypt," *Gender and History* 22, no. 3 (2010): 658–76. For a wider British empire perspective, see Philippa Levine, *Prostitution, Race, and Politics: Policing Venereal Disease in the British Empire* (New York: Routledge, 2003); Levine, "Sexuality and Empire," in *At Home with the Empire: Metropolitan Culture and the Imperial World*, ed. Catherine Hall and Sonya Rose (Cambridge: Cambridge University Press, 2006), 122–42.

68. For a discussion of how actual social practices diverged from medicalizing and moralizing discourses on prostitution, see Hanan Hammad, "Between Egyptian 'National Purity' and 'Local Flexibility': Prostitution in al-Mahalla al-Kubra in the First Half of the 20th Century," *Journal of Social History* 44, no. 3 (2011): 751–83, and Hammad, *Industrial Sexuality* (Austin: University of Texas Press, 2016). On the importance of marriage in the regulation of sexuality and the dangers of prolonged bachelorhood, see the extensive three-part article in *al-Risala* by 'Ali al-Tantawi, "al-Mathal al-'Ala li-l-Shab al-Muslim," *al-Risala* 6, no. 240 (February 7, 1938): 218–21; "al-Mathal al-'Ala li-l-Shab al-Muslim," *al-Risala* 6, no. 241 (February 14, 1938): 252–54; "al-Mathal al-'Ala li-l-Shab al-Muslim," *al-Risala* 6, no. 242 (February 21, 1938): 296–98.

69. Wilson C. Jacob, review of *Desiring Arabs*, by Joseph Massad, *H-Levant*, H-Net Reviews (September 2009), http://www.h-net.org/reviews/showrev.php?id=25004. Complex historical genealogies of gender and sexuality in the Middle Eastern context are much needed, as in Afsaneh Najmabadi's *Professing Selves: Transsexuality and Same-Sex Desire in Contemporary Iran* (Durham, NC: Duke University Press, 2013). See also Najmabadi, "Transing and Transpassing across Sex-Gender Walls in Iran," *WSQ: Women's Studies Quarterly* 36, nos. 3–4 (2008): 23–42. For a fascinating discussion of how the Western category of "homosexuality" was introduced into Chinese discourses, and the concomitant "epistemological rearrangement in the social significance of same-sex desire in modern China," see Chiang, "Epistemic Modernity." For insightful discussions of transformations of discourses of gender and sexuality spanning fin-de-siècle Muslim reformers in colonial India and later in postpartition Pakistan, see Kamran Asdar Ali, " 'Pulp Fictions': Reading Pakistani Domesticity," *Social Text* 22, no. 1 (2004): 123–45; Ali, "Progressives and 'Perverts': Partition Stories and Pakistan's Future," *Social Text* 29, no. 3 108 (2011): 1–29.

70. Laura Bier, *Revolutionary Womanhood: Feminisms, Modernity, and the State in Nasser's Egypt* (Stanford, CA: Stanford University Press, 2011), 2–3; Mervat Hatem, "The Paradoxes of State Feminism in Egypt," in *Women and Politics Worldwide*, ed. Barbara Nelson and Najwa Chadhury (New Haven, CT: Yale University Press, 1994), 226–42. For a relevant discussion of the relation between representations of women in Iraq and the Hashemite state, see Orit Bashkin, "Representations of Women in the Writings of the In-

telligentsia in Hashemite Iraq, 1921–1958," *Journal of Middle East Women's Studies* 4, no. 1 (2008): 53–82.

71. Murad presented his audience with multiple views of gender difference, there were those who argued: that gender differences were innate and constitutional; that females were incomplete males; or that males and females had the same biological beginnings but developed into distinct genders due to physical, physiological, and psychological factors. Murad, *Sikulujiyyat al-Jins*, 45–47.

72. Murad, *Sikulujiyyat al-Jins*, 41–46. Karen Horney discussed Georg Simmel's notion of masculine civilization and its repercussions on feminine psychology in "The Flight from Womanhood: The Masculinity Complex in Women as Viewed by Men and by Women," in *Feminine Psychology*, ed. Harold Kelman (New York: W. W. Norton, 1967), 54–70; Horney, "Inhibited Femininity: Psychoanalytical Contribution to the Problem of Frigidity," in *Feminine Psychology*, 71–83.

73. Murad, *Sikulujiyyat al-Jins*, 44–45; cf. Horney, "The Distrust between the Sexes," 107–18; "Problems of Marriage," 119–32, in *Feminine Psychology*.

74. Murad, *Sikulujiyyat al-Jins*, 48; see also Sigmund Freud, "Some Psychical Consequences of the Anatomical Distinction between the Sexes" (1925) *SE* 19: 241–58; "Female Sexuality" (1931), *SE* 21: 221–43; "Femininity" (1933), *SE* 22: 112–35.

75. Murad, *Sikulujiyyat al-Jins*, 49–66.

76. Murad, "Nimu al-Tifl al-'Aqli," 16–17; Murad, *Sikulujiyyat al-Jins*, 50–51.

77. Horney, "Inhibited Femininity," 74. Murad appears to be heavily indebted to Horney's work, particularly the following other essays: "The Flight from Womanhood"; "The Distrust between the Sexes"; "Problems of Marriage."

78. Murad, "Nimu al-Tifl al-'Aqli," 17.

79. Murad, *Sikulujiyyat al-Jins*, 12–43.

80. Ibid., 50–51.

81. Ibid., 51.

82. Ibid., 38–43.

83. Ibid., 99ff.

84. Ibid., 89–94.

85. Juliet Mitchell, "Introduction I," in Lacan, *Feminine Sexuality*, 1–26, quotation 7; Mitchell, *Psychoanalysis and Feminism: Freud, Reich, Laing, and Women* (New York: Vintage, 1975). For a discussion of the distinction between a historicist/deconstructionist and Lacanian perspective on sexual difference, see Copjec, *Read My Desire*, chap. 8.

86. Jacqueline Rose, "Introduction II," in Lacan, *Feminine Sexuality*, 27–57, quotation 28.

87. Ibid., 28.

88. Mitchell, "Introduction I," 14.

89. Neo-psychoanalytic approaches, such as those of Karen Horney, drew key elements from Freudian psychoanalysis but diverged from orthodox positions in a variety of ways. They include such schools as object relations theory, ego psychology, and neo-Freudianism.

90. For his critiques of Freud see Murad, *Shifa' al-Nafs*, 90–101; Murad, "al-Usus al-Nafsiyya li-l-Takamul al-Ijtima'i," *Majallat 'Ilm al-Nafs* 2, no. 3 (1947): 425–41.

91. Murad, "al-Usus al-Nafsiyya."

92. Rose, "Introduction II," 28.

93. Mitchell, "Introduction I," 3. This is diametrically opposed to a Lacanian view.

94. Murad, "Nimu al-Tifl al-'Aqli," 20; Suttie, *Origins of Love and Hate*, chap. 8. Suttie's interpretation is based on a careful reading of Freud's arguments in *Group Psychology*, *SE* 18: 65–143.

95. Suttie, *Origins of Love and Hate*, 71, 219.

96. Shakry, "Schooled Mothers and Structured Play"; Kholoussy, *For Better, For Worse*; Kenneth M. Cuno, *Modernizing Marriage: Family, Ideology, and Law in Nineteenth- and Early Twentieth-Century Egypt* (Syracuse, NY: Syracuse University Press, 2015). On the wider significance of family history to an understanding of the Middle East, gender, and modernity, see Beshara Doumani, *Family History in the Middle East: Household, Property, and Gender* (Albany: State University of New York Press, 2012).

97. Murad, *Sikulujiyyat al-Jins*, 65.

98. Ibid., 54, cf. 65.

99. Ibid., 68–73.

100. Murad's analysis bears a resemblance to Jonathan Lear's discussion of love in *Love and Its Place in Nature*, chap. 6.

101. For a case study of an adult male that likewise focuses on the dissociation between the tender and sensual component of love, but with reference to an unresolved Oedipus complex, see Mostapha Ziwer, in collaboration with M. Naim, "Aggression and Intercostal Neuralgia: A Psychosomatic Study," *Majallat ʿIlm al-Nafs* 1, no. 2 (1945): 264–70.

102. Lear, *Love and Its Place in Nature*, chaps. 5–6, quotation 153.

103. Murad referred to love as a union and oneness *"ittihad wa-tawhid"*; Murad, *Sikulujiyyat al-Jins*, 78. Jonathan Lear emphasizes Freud's understanding of love as completely consonant with "the all-inclusive and all-preserving Eros of Plato's *Symposium*," and indeed, Freud himself states, "In its origin, function, and relation to sexual love, the 'Eros' of the philosopher Plato coincides exactly with the love-force, the libido of psychoanalysis" (Freud, "Resistances to Psychoanalysis," *SE* 19: 218; Freud, *Group Psychology, SE* 18: 91; Lear, *Love and Its Place in Nature*, 140–55). In contrast to this interpretation, Lacanians argue that love "belongs to the *Lust-Ich* or pleasure ego," that is to say, love functions "as the ultimate form of self-recognition," and indeed the analyst must guard against the patient's fantasy of self-completion through another; Rose, "Introduction II," 47, 36.

104. Murad, *Sikulujiyyat al-Jins*, 87–88.

105. Ibid., 91. Horney discussed the influence of infantile and childhood experiences on later relationships in "Problems of Marriage."

106. Murad, *Sikulujiyyat al-Jins*, 92.

107. Najmabadi, "Genus of Sex," 218.

108. Murad, *Sikulujiyyat al-Jins*, 89–94.

109. Ibid., 92–94.

110. "Asiʾlat al-Qurraʾ," *Majallat ʿIlm al-Nafs* 4, no. 1 (1948): 131–34.

111. The term *shudhudh* or deviance was rarely used in this context. Joseph Massad notes that *"al-shudhudh al-jinsi"* (sexual deviance) was the most commonly used term to refer to the Western concept of homosexuality, with the exception of translators of Freud, *Desiring Arabs*, 171–72. He also cites the use of *"jinsiyyah"* (as sexuality) as having been coined in the 1950s, but its usage appears earlier in *Majallat ʿIlm al-Nafs*.

112. Interestingly, Avicenna argued that *ʿubna* ("passive" male homosexuality) was a disease of desire (*shahwa wahmiyya*, an imaginative desire), unlike al-Razi for whom it was a biological or genetic defect. See Franz Rosenthal, "Ar-Râzî on the Hidden Illness," *Bulletin of the History of Medicine* 52, no. 1 (1978): 45–60; Zeʾevi, *Producing Desire*, 37–39.

113. Crucially, many argue that such a normative and prescriptive bias toward heterosexuality and gendered being is *not* to be found in Freud himself. Henry Abelove discusses the complexity of Freud's thinking on homosexuality, his lack of moralism, and his refusal to treat it as a disease, as well as the diametrically opposed position taken up by American psychoanalysis. Abelove, "Freud, Male Homosexuality, and the Americans," in *The Lesbian and Gay Studies Reader*, ed. Henry Abelove, Michèle Aina Barale, and David Halperin (London: Routledge, 1993), 381–93.

114. Murad, *Sikulujiyyat al-Jins*, 98–99.

115. Compare Karen Horney on femininity: "Psychoanalytic insights, however, have shown that many conditions must be fulfilled in order to guarantee such normal development and that there are just as many possibilities for blockages or disturbances in the development." In "Inhibited Femininity," 78.

116. I elaborate on the significance of the question of youth and adolescence in mid-twentieth-century Egypt in "Youth as Peril and Promise." As Afsaneh Najmabadi has noted in the Iranian context, the "so-called youth crisis" often condensed questions surrounding the proper role of sexuality, marriage, romance, and youth in society. Najmabadi, "The Morning After: Travail of Sexuality and Love in Modern Iran," *International Journal of Middle East Studies* 36 (2004): 367–85.

117. Yusuf Murad, "Tamhid li-Dirasat Nafsiyyat al-Murahiq fi Misr wa-l-Aqtar al-ʿArabiyya," *Majallat ʿIlm al-Nafs* 1, no. 2 (1945): 172–82. Other types of studies focused on more empirical evaluations of adolescents. See, for example, Mahir Kamal, "Evaluations of Adolescent Personality by Adolescents and Adults," *Majallat ʿIlm al-Nafs* 3, no. 1 (1947): 152–47; Abdu Mikhail Rizk, "Smoking among Adolescents: An Objective Study," *Majallat ʿIlm al-Nafs* 3, no. 1 (1947): 144–46; Zaki Saleh, "A Questionnaire Study of the Problem Adolescent Girl in Secondary Schools," *Majallat ʿIlm al-Nafs* 7, no. 3 (1952): 410–16.

118. A test of the questionnaire on a small group of secondary school students was administered by master's students in philosophy from Fuʾad I University, with the idea of distribution to all secondary schools and scholarly institutes in Egypt and the Arab world. Murad, "Tamhid li-Dirasat Nafsiyyat al-Murahiq," 179–82.

119. Ian Hacking, *Historical Ontology* (Cambridge, MA: Harvard University Press, 2004), 99–114. On the connection between childhood and interiority, see Carolyn Steedman, *Strange Dislocations: Childhood and the Idea of Human Interiority* (Cambridge, MA: Harvard University Press, 1995).

120. Maurice Debesse, *Comment étudier les adolescents: Examen critique des confidences juvéniles* (Paris: F. Alcan, 1937); Irena Wojnar, "Maurice Debesse (1903–1998)," *Prospects: The Quarterly Review of Comparative Education* 33, no. 3 (2003): 1–19.

121. ʿAbd-al-Minʿam al-Miliji, "Nafsiyyat al-Murahiq min Mudhakkiratu," *Majallat ʿIlm al-Nafs* 5, no. 3 (1950): 351–60.

122. Al-Miliji, "Nafsiyyat al-Murahiq," 351–52.

123. Ibid., 352–53, 357.

124. Ibid., 357–58.

125. ʿAbd-al-Minʿam ʿAbd al-ʿAziz al-Miliji, "al-Shuʿur al-Dini ʿind al-Murahiq," *Majallat ʿIlm al-Nafs* 3, no. 2 (1947): 193–206, 197–98.

126. Ibid., 198.

127. Ibid., 201–2.

128. See the discussion of *jihad al-nafs* in chapter 2; al-Taftazani, "Sikulujiyat al-Tasawwuf (1)"; "Sikulujiyat al-Tasawwuf (2)."

129. Rose, "Introduction II," 52; Lacan, "God and the *Jouissance* of Woman," 147.

130. Dipesh Chakrabarty, *Provincializing Europe: Postcolonial Thought and Historical Difference* (Princeton, NJ: Princeton University Press, 2000), 35.

131. Asad *Formations of the Secular*, 225. On the fallacy of autobiography as a peculiarly Western cultural construct and the mistaken assumption of the rarity of autobiography as an Arabic literary genre, see Dwight Reynolds, *Interpreting the Self: Autobiography in the Arabic Literary Tradition* (Berkeley: University of California Press, 2001), 1–35. On Arabic autobiography see also the special issue "The Language of the Self: Autobiographies and Testimonies" in *Alif: Journal of Comparative Poetics* 22 (2002).

132. cf. Massad, *Desiring Arabs*, 100, 158.

Chapter Four: Psychoanalysis before the Law

1. *Bab al-Hadid* (Cairo Station), directed by Youssef Chahine (1958; Cairo: Typecast Releasing, 2009), DVD.

2. On Chahine's oeuvre, see Ibrahim Fawal, *Youssef Chahine* (London: British Film Institute, 2001).

3. For an excellent discussion of the "legal status of the irrational" and its relationship to psychoanalysis in France, see Dean, *The Self and Its Pleasures*, chap. 1; on the relationship between psychoanalysis and criminology in Mexico, see Gallo, *Freud's Mexico*, chap. 6; for a discussion of criminal science and its relation to state formation in Iran, see Cyrus Schayegh, "Serial Murder in Tehran: Crime, Science, and the Formation of Modern State and Society in Interwar Iran," *Comparative Studies in Society and History* 47, no. 4 (2005): 836–62.

4. As Stefania Pandolfo notes, for Lacan madness lay at the heart of human life and subjectivity and was thus not, strictly speaking, a juridical problem. The juridical approach, with its view of "absolute moral freedom and individual human responsibility," would be the hallmark of a bourgeois psychology, or a "sanitary penology"; see Pandolfo, *Knot of the Soul*; Dean, *The Self and Its Pleasures*, 52–57.

5. Muhammad Fathi, "al-Ijram 'ala daw' al-Nazariyya al-Tahliliyya li-l-Amrad al-'Asabiyya," *Majallat 'Ilm al-Nafs* 4, no. 2 (1948): 259–69. For a discussion of crime and sociology, see Dr. 'Abd al-Aziz 'Izzat, "al-Jarima wa-'Ilm al-Ijtim'a," *Majallat 'Ilm al-Nafs* 8, no. 1 (1952): 49–67.

6. Prior to teaching, Fathi was employed as a counselor for the court of appeals. For biographical information and on Fathi's significance to Egyptian criminology, see Saied Ewies, "Egypt," in *International Handbook of Contemporary Developments in Criminology: Europe, Africa, the Middle East, and Asia*, ed. Elmer Johnson (Westport, CT: Greenwood Press, 1983), 185–96, 187–88. Muhammad Fathi, *'Ilm al-Nafs al-Jina'i: 'Ilman wa-'Amalan*, vols. 1–3 (Cairo: Maktabat al-Nahda al-Misriyya, 1943, 1950, 1974). I discuss al-Babli in *Great Social Laboratory*, 120–23.

7. Ewies, "Egypt," 188.

8. Fathi, "al-Ijram," 259.

9. Ibid., 259–61. He cited Freud's "The Question of Lay Analysis," *SE* 20: 177–250, in defense of this position.

10. See Muhammad Fathi, *Mushkilat al-Tahlil al-Nafsi fi Misr: Dirasatiha min al-Nawahi al-'Ilmiyya wa-l-Ijtima'iyya wa-l-Qada'iyya wa-l-Tashri'iyya* (Cairo: Matba'at Misr, 1946). This text draws heavily on Freud's "The Question of Lay Analysis," as well as his *Autobiography*, and on Theodor Reik, *From Thirty Years with Freud* (New York: Farrar and Rinehart, 1940); Oskar Pfister, *The Psychoanalytic Method*, trans. Charles Rockwell Payne (New York: Moffat, Yard, 1917); Wilhelm Stekel, *Technique of Analytical Psychotherapy*, trans. Eden Paul and Cedar Paul (New York: Liveright, 1950), in addition to the writings and opinions of members of the British Psychoanalytical Society.

11. Sigmund Freud, "Psycho-Analysis and the Establishment of the Facts in Legal Proceedings" (1906), *SE* 9: 97–114, quotation 13; Fathi, "al-Ijram," 263–64.

12. Freud, "Psycho-Analysis and the Establishment of the Facts in Legal Proceedings," 108, 111.

13. Fathi, "al-Ijram," 263–64.

14. Ibid., 265–66. Fathi referenced Wilhelm Stekel's *Technique of Analytical Psychotherapy* in which a case is unlocked through an allusion to Edgar Allan Poe's short story "The Black Cat."

15. Elliott Colla, "Anxious Advocacy: The Novel, the Law, and Extrajudicial Appeals in Egypt," *Public Culture* 17, no. 3 (2005): 417–43.

16. Ibid., 418.

17. Ibid., 440.

18. Ibid., 418.

19. Thus, Colla states, "the investigator 'reads' the clues of the crime text and, by a combination of inductive and deductive logic, recreates the 'narrative' of the crime. Indeed, the genre's ideology is distinctly modern inasmuch as it suggests that even the irrational acts of society and individuals can best be understood through reason," 434–36.

20. Fathi, "al-Ijram," 264.

21. Ibid., 261.

22. Ibid., 262. A point he elaborated in his 1939 lecture, "The Criminal and Society," presented to *Nadi al-Quda*.

23. Ibid., 263.

24. Ibid., 266–67.

25. Ibid., 267.

26. Ibid., 268. On what the French called *autopunition*, or the commission of a crime to satisfy an unconscious need for self-punishment, see Dean, *The Self and Its Pleasures*, chap. 1.

27. Sigmund Freud, "Some Character-Types Met with in Psychoanalytic Work" (1916), *SE* 14: 309–33; 332–33.

28. Ibid. Nietzsche discusses the criminal from a sense of guilt, the pale criminal, in *Thus Spoke Zarathustra: A Book for None and All*, trans. Walter Kaufmann (New York: Penguin, 1978).

29. Fathi, "al-Ijram," 268–69.

30. Samah Selim, "Fiction and Colonial Identities: Arsène Lupin in Arabic," *Middle Eastern Literatures* 13, no. 2 (2010): 191–210, quotation 192.

31. Ibid., 195.

32. Ibid.

33. See Chandak Sengoopta, *Imprint of the Raj: How Fingerprinting Was Born in Colonial India* (London: Macmillan, 2003). Victorian polymath Francis Galton (1822–1911) spoke at the Egyptian Royal Geographical Society on the development of fingerprinting and its relevance to Egypt and criminal justice, having already observed Colonel Harvey Pasha's (the commandant of police) Identification Office. Galton was much impressed with what he saw and emphasized the utility of fingerprinting for the British Empire. For vivid descriptions, see Francis Galton, Souvenirs d'Égypte," *Bulletin de la Société Khédiviale de Géographie* 5, no. 7 (1900): 375–80; and "Identification Offices in India and Egypt," *Nineteenth Century* 48 (July 1900): 118–26.

34. Selim, "Fiction and Colonial Identities"; Mitchell, *Colonising Egypt*. Khaled Fahmy has traced many of these "individuating techniques of the modernizing, centralizing state," to the Mehmed 'Ali era, which, through novel means of counting and identifying people, inaugurated the shift away from the *shari'a* system of establishing juridical identity. Fahmy, "Birth of the 'Secular' Individual: Medical and Legal Methods of Identification in Nineteenth-Century Egypt," in *Registration and Recognition: Documenting the Person in World History*, ed. Keith Breckenridge and Simon Szreter (Oxford: Oxford University Press, 2010), 335–355, quotation 354.

35. Rudolph Peters, *Crime and Punishment in Islamic Law* (Cambridge: Cambridge University Press, 2005), 133–41. Peters states: "In 1883/1889 Islamic criminal law was totally abolished in Egypt. Only the rule that death sentences must be approved by the State

Mufti provides a reminder of the role Islamic criminal law once played in the Egyptian legal system," 141; see also Armando Salvatore, "The 'Implosion' of *Shari'a* within the Emergence of Public Normativity: The Impact on Personal Responsibility and the Impersonality of Law," in *Standing Trial: Law and the Person in the Modern Middle East*, ed. Baudouin Dupret (London: I. B. Tauris, 2004), 116–39; Asad, *Formations of the Secular*, chap. 7.

36. Selim, "Fiction and Colonial Identities," 198.

37. Khaled Fahmy, "The Anatomy of Justice: Forensic Medicine and Criminal Law in Nineteenth Century Egypt," *Islamic Law and Society* 6, no. 2 (1999): 224–71; and Fahmy, "The Police and the People in Nineteenth Century Egypt," *Die Welt des Islams* 39, no. 3 (1999): 340–77.

38. Salvatore, "'Implosion' of *Shari'a*"; and Samera Esmeir, *Juridical Humanity: A Colonial History* (Stanford, CA: Stanford University Press, 2012).

39. Salavatore, "'Implosion' of *Shari'a*."

40. Peters has shown that the *shari'a* was applied side by side with *siyasi* law until the late nineteenth century, *Crime and Punishment*, "Introduction." See also Peters, "Murder on the Nile: Homicide Trials in 19th Century Egyptian Shari'a Courts," *Die Welt des Islams* 30 (1990): 95–115; "The Codification of Criminal Law in 19th Century Egypt," in *Law, Society, and National Identity in Africa*, ed. J. M. Abun-Nasr, Ulrich Spellenberg, and Ulrike Wanitzek (Hamburg: H. Buske, 1991), 211–25; "Islamic and Secular Criminal Law," *Islamic Law and Society* 4, no. 1 (1997): 80–90; "For His Correction and as a Deterrent for Others," *Islamic Law and Society* 6 (1999): 164–93.

41. Peters, "Murder on the Nile," 103; Khaled Fahmy, "Justice, Law, and Pain in Khedivial Egypt," in Dupret, *Standing Trial*, 85–115, 93–94.

42. Peters, "Murder on the Nile," 111.

43. Fahmy, "Justice, Law, and Pain in Khedivial Egypt." My thanks to Khaled Fahmy for clarifying that the coupling of *fiqh* and *siyasa* had been practiced from the very beginning of Islamic law.

44. Ibid.; see also Fahmy, "Anatomy of Justice," 236; Peters, "Islamic and Secular Criminal Law."

45. Fahmy, "Justice, Law, and Pain in Khedivial Egypt"; Fahmy, "Anatomy of Justice"; Sir Thomas Russell, *Egyptian Service, 1902–1946* (London: J. Murray, 1949), chap. 3.

46. Baudouin Dupret, "Intention in Action: A Pragmatic Approach to Criminal Characterisation in an Egyptian Context," in Dupret, *Standing Trial*, 196–230; Russell, *Egyptian Service*, chap. 3.

47. Thus Baudouin Dupret, referring to the contemporary legal apparatus, states, "Generally speaking, the accused is thus in the situation of having to show that he or she did not have an intention to do something, that he or she did not have the inclination to carry out what the normal typification negatively evaluates or that his intention could be explained so as to excuse him or herself"; "Intention in Action," 220–21.

48. Colla, "Anxious Advocacy." See also Esmeir, *Juridical Humanity*, who narrates the transformation from Ottoman to colonial law while contesting the view that it brought order to where there was disorder.

49. Selim, "Fiction and Colonial Identities," 197–98.

50. Ibid., 202.

51. Wilson Jacob, "Eventful Transformations: al-Futuwwa between History and the Everyday," *Comparative Studies in Society and History* 49, no. 3 (2007): 689–712, quotation 689.

52. Ibid., 692.

53. Lopez analyzes the case as a testament to the emergence of a mass culture in Egypt, in which debate centered on female depravity, moral virtue, and the national loss thereof,

in a time of European influence and anticolonial nationalism. Shaun T. Lopez, "Madams, Murders, and the Media: *Akhbar al-Hawadith* and the emergence of a mass culture in 1920s Egypt," in *Re-Envisioning Egypt, 1919–1952*, ed. Arthur Goldshmidt, Amy Johnson, and Barak Salmoni (Cairo: American University in Cairo Press, 2005), 371–97. See also Lopez, "The Dangers of Dancing: The Media and Morality in 1930s Egypt," *Comparative Studies of South Asia, Africa, and the Middle East* 24, no. 1 (2004): 97–105.

54. Fathi, *Mushkilat al-Tahlil al-Nafsi*.

55. Ibid., 18–19.

56. Ibid., 19–21.

57. Ibid., 23–27.

58. Published in September 1942 by 'Abd al-Rahman al-Tawir, Booklet no. 210, ibid., 27–28.

59. Ibid., 29.

60. Ibid., 30–31.

61. For an interesting and relevant discussion of Egyptian case law with respect to the practice of medicine and bodily integrity, see Baudouin Dupret, "The Person and His Body: Medical Ethics and Egyptian Law," in Dupret, *Standing Trial*, 294–317.

62. Fathi, *Mushkilat al-Tahlil al-Nafsi*, 33–36.

63. Ibid., 37–43.

64. Ibid., 43–44, 51–53.

65. Ibid., 49–51.

66. Ibid., 51–53.

67. Ibid., 54–55.

68. Ibid., 71–74. Fathi suggested that this could be done under the rubric of the Ministry of Health or the Ministry of Social Affairs.

69. Fahmy, "Justice, Law, and Pain in Khedivial Egypt"; Fahmy, "Anatomy of Justice."

70. Fahmy, "Anatomy of Justice," asserts that any resistances to the introduction of autopsy had less to do with any allegedly Islamic resistance than with the fears of the Ottoman Turkish aristocracy and the 'ulama that their prominent role as mediators between the people and the state would be displaced by the new medical profession. Fahmy thereby dispels any teleological notion of the modernization of the courts at the hands of Europeans.

71. Ibid., 231–34.

72. Sabri Jirjis, "Bab al-Kutub al-Jadida: *Mushkilat al-Tahlil al-Nafsi fi Misr*, ta'lif Muhammad Fathi," *Majallat 'Ilm al-Nafs* 2, no. 3 (1947): 551–55. He appears to bear no relation to Shukri Jirjis. Sabri Jirjis would eventually repudiate Freud outright, much later in 1970, see Massad, "Psychoanalysis, Islam, and the Other of Liberalism," 66–67n68.

73. Franz Alexander, *The Medical Value of Psychoanalysis* (New York: International Universities Press, 1984); Franz Alexander and Hugo Staub, *The Criminal, the Judge, and the Public: A Psychological Analysis*, trans. Gregory Zilboorg (New York: Macmillan, 1931). Jirjis's assertion is, in fact, incorrect. Fathi had cited both Alexander and Jones in his *al-Tahlil al-Nafsi fi Misr*.

74. Oussama Arabi, "The Regimentation of the Subject: Madness in Islamic and Modern Arab Civil Laws," in Dupret, *Standing Trial*, 264–93, 272.

75. Ibid., 271.

76. Ibid., 266–69. For the canonical text on the status of "madness" in the medieval period, see Michael Dols, *Majnun: The Madman in Medieval Islamic Society*, ed. Diana Immisch (Oxford: Clarendon Press, 1992); on the contemporary period, see Ahmed Ragab, "Madman Walking: The Image of the Mad in the Egyptian Press," *Egypte-Monde Arabe*, troisième série, no. 4 (2007): 227–46. For a genealogy of colonial perceptions of madness

in North Africa, as well as of institutional psychiatry, see Richard C. Keller, *Colonial Madness: Psychiatry in French North Africa* (Chicago: University of Chicago Press, 2007).

77. Eugene Rogan, "Madness and Marginality: The Advent of the Psychiatric Asylum in Egypt and Lebanon," in *Outside In: On the Margins of the Modern Middle East*, ed. Eugene Rogan (London: I. B. Tauris, 2002), 104–25, 110–11; Arabi "Regimentation of the Subject," 270. Both hospitals were controlled by the mental health division of the Ministry of Public Health.

78. Arabi, "Regimentation of the Subject," 270.

79. Abou-Hatab, "Egypt," 115–16.

80. Ahmed, "Psychology in Egypt."

81. Mahmud al-Rawi, "'Uqdat Udib wa-Athariha fi al-Ijram: Hawl Maqal fi Jaridat al-Misri," *Majallat 'Ilm al-Nafs* 3, no. 1 (1947): 97–106. Fathi had published six articles from January to February 1947 for the newspaper *al-Misri*.

82. For more on *al-Riyada al-Badaniyya*, see Jacob, *Working Out Egypt*, chap. 6.

83. Freud, "Expert Opinion in the Halsmann Case" (1931), *SE* 21: 251–53, quotation 252. In the second half of the quote, Freud is citing *The Brothers Karamazov*, "But profound as psychology is, it's a knife that cuts both ways." Fyodor Dostoevsky, *The Brothers Karamazov*, ed. Ralph E. Matlaw, trans. Constance Garnett (New York: W.W. Norton and Company, 1976), 690; translated into Arabic as *al-Ikhwa Karamazuf*, trans. Sami al-Durubi (Beirut: al-Markaz al-Thaqafi al-'Arabi, 2010). See also, Freud, "Dostoevsky and Parricide" (1928), *SE* 21: 173–96.

84. Gallo, *Freud's Mexico*, 214. Gallo notes that while Freud highlights similarities between the judge and the analyst; he notes that the judge must remain confined "within the bounds of conscious thought," whereas psychoanalysts "can glimpse into the unconscious and gain a deeper understanding of the criminal psyche," 213–14.

85. Al-Rawi, "'Uqdat Udib," 98. For a discussion of the significance of Jung and the need for Arabic translations, see Najib Yusuf Badawi, "Sikubathulujiyyat al-Sihr wa-l-Tatyir," *Majallat 'Ilm al-Nafs* 7, no. 1 (1951): 35–60.

86. Al-Rawi, "'Uqdat Udib," 98–99; on *adab* see Salvatore, "'Implosion' of *Shari'a*."

87. Al-Rawi, "'Uqdat Udib." Even if one were to follow Freud's insights to their conclusion, al-Rawi noted, anthropological evidence indicated the presence of something beyond the superego, hence the widespread prevalence of taboo acts (cannibalism, incest, patricide, matricide). Further, he argued that a superego could emerge even without the resolution of the Oedipus complex. If it did not emerge then the child would be a criminal from childhood and crime would be directed toward society, as in psychopathy.

88. Salvatore, "'Implosion' of *Shari'a*," 122.

89. Al-Rawi cited Rank, *The Trauma of Birth*; Malinowski, *Father in Primitive Psychology*; Burrow, *Biology of Human Conflict*; Deutsch, *Psychology of Women*; al-Rawi, "'Uqdat Udib," 99–100.

90. Al-Rawi, "'Uqdat Udib," 99–101. Even Anna Freud, he noted, had contested the omni-explanatory nature of the Oedipus complex; ibid., 103.

91. Ibid., 102.

92. Ibid., 103.

93. Ibid., 104–5.

94. Ibid., 105.

95. Ibid., 105.

96. Ibid., 106. This is a different example from M. J., discussed above.

97. Mustafa Isma'il Suwayf, "al-Usus al-Dinamiyya li-l-Suluk al-Ijrami," *Majallat 'Ilm al-Nafs* 4, no. 3 (1949): 329–54.

98. Ibid. Suwayf argued that criminal behavior could not be thought of as a subvariety of these two types, tending to neither psychosis nor neurosis.

99. Ibid., 338–42.

100. Fredric Wertham, "Psychoauthoritarianism and the Law," *University of Chicago Law Review* 22, no. 2 (1955): 336–38, quotation 338.

101. Bruno Solby, "Review of *Dark Legend: A Study in Murder* by Fredric Wertham," *Sociometry* 4, no. 4 (1941), 423–26.

102. D. V. Hubble, "Matricide: Review of *Dark Legend: A Study in Murder* by Fredric Wertham," *British Medical Journal* 1, no. 4553 (1948): 692.

103. Suwayf's discussion of Wertham is in "al-Usus al-Dinamiyya," 348–52.

104. Wertham, as cited by Solby, "Dark Legend," 423.

105. Ibid., 423, see also Suwayf, "al-Usus al-Dinamiyya," 348–52.

106. Suwayf, "al-Usus al-Dinamiyya," 351.

107. Wertham, as cited by Solby, "Dark Legend," 424–25.

108. Suwyaf, "al-Usus al-Dinamiyya," 351–52.

109. Yusuf Murad, "Ba'd Nawahi 'Ilm al-Nafs al-Jina'i," *Majallat 'Ilm al-Nafs* 4, no. 2 (1948): 271–82. Indeed, Mustafa Isma'il Suwayf almost echoed these views in his article in the same issue, "al-Jarima wa-l-Takamul al-Ijtima'i," *Majallat 'Ilm al-Nafs* 4, no. 2 (1948): 209–20. Critiquing Lombroso's view of innate criminality, Suwayf put forth the view that the criminal was someone whose societal circumstances led him to crime, and thus criminal responsibility did not fall on him alone, but on society as well.

110. Murad, "Ba'd Nawahi 'Ilm al-Nafs al-Jina'i," 272—this is a direct quote from Kimball Young, *Personality and Problems of Adjustment* (London: Kegan Paul, Trench, Trubner, 1947).

111. Murad, "Ba'd Nawahi 'Ilm al-Nafs al-Jina'i," 272–73.

112. Ibid., 275–76.

113. Ibid., 276–77.

114. Ibid., 278. In this it was no different from the study of human behavior, requiring description, interpretation, and analysis.

115. Ibid., 279–80.

116. Murad cited the example of pioneering sociologist Dr. Hasan al-Sa'ati, "Ma'had Brostol li-l- Shabab al-Kharij 'ala al-Qanun," *Majallat 'Ilm al-Nafs* 4, no. 2 (1948): 179–84.

117. Murad, "Ba'd Nawahi 'Ilm al-Nafs al-Jina'i," 282.

118. See Abu Madyan al-Shafa'i, "al-Fa'l al-Iradi fi al-Ijram," *Majallat 'Ilm al-Nafs* 4, no. 2 (1948): 201–8, who addressed the complicated question of determining voluntarism in the criminal act, and who pushed for a study of criminals that would help ascertain criminal responsibility, a question, he noted, that needed to be studied cooperatively by psychologists and legal scholars. See also Mustafa Suwayf, "al-Jarima wa-l-Takamul al-Ijtima'i."

119. El Shakry, *Great Social Laboratory*.

120. Ewies, "Egypt."

121. Mahmud al-Rawi, "al-Qatl al-Siyasi," *Majallat 'Ilm al-Nafs* 3, no. 2 (1947): 207–14.

122. Ibid., 207–10. Countering this view, he noted that even under conditions of the primitive horde, what was at stake was never merely sexual jealousy of the father, but rather the denial of the father's privileges from the horde.

123. Ibid., 210.

124. Ibid., 210–12. He noted Jung's perspective on the proximity of collective psychology to the collective unconscious.

125. Ibid., 213.

126. Ibid., 213–14.

127. Donald M. Reid, "Political Assassination in Egypt, 1910–1954," *International Journal of African Historical Studies* 15, no. 4 (1982): 625–51.

128. Ibid., 633.

129. Ibid., 633–34.

130. Ibid., 632–36.

131. Fanon, *Wretched of the Earth*.

132. Frantz Fanon, *Black Skin, White Masks*, trans. Charles Lam Markmann (1952; New York: Grove Press, 1967).

133. Fanon, *Wretched of the Earth*, 30.

134. Fanon described this transmutation as one in which the electrified atmosphere of violence, the violence rippling underneath the skin, sedimented in muscles, and sublimated in dreams, metamorphosed into the actuality of violence as praxis. "The colonized subject discovers reality and transforms it through his praxis, his deployment of violence and his agenda for liberation"; ibid., 21.

135. Al-Rawi, drawing on Carl Jung and Gustave Le Bon, advanced a notion of political psychology as a rubric for understanding group political behavior such as strikes and revolutions. Refuting Freud's conceptualization of group psychology in terms of a primal revolt against the father, he argued that revolt as a form of self-individuation occurred as a revolt against the privileges accorded to the leader. Aggressive impulses were part of what Jung called the collective unconscious. But no action was ever merely the expression of unconscious impulses. Rather, strikes and revolts were equally expressions of a present conflict—namely, discontent against the present order and a desire to preserve the self. Revolutions were caused primarily by a "revolutionary self-awareness of the people" that their rights had been stolen. Al-Rawi outlined a framework for the "cure" of the insurrectionary spirit that prominently featured persuasion through the press and print mechanisms, enlightenment and freedom of expression, guarantees of employment, rethinking the efficacy of draconian punishment, a better understanding of political behavior on the part of the ruling elite, and the use of psychologists as experts for understanding the psyche of the individual and the group. See Mahmud al-Rawi, "Sikulujiyyat al-Idrab," *Majallat 'Ilm al-Nafs* 3, no. 3 (1948): 417–31; al-Rawi, "Sikulujiyyat al-Idrab (2)," *Majallat 'Ilm al-Nafs* 4, no. 1 (1948): 29–52.

136. Sabri Jirjis, *Mushkilat al-Suluk al-Sikubati: Bahth fi 'Ilm al-Nafs al-Tibbi al-Ijtima'i*, 1st ed. (Cairo: Dar al-Ma'arif, 1946).

137. The Egyptian Ministry of Education instituted a section specializing in mental and nervous diseases, under the administration of the School of Health directed by Sabri Jirjis. Jirjis began work at the clinic at the Ministry of Education in November 1947. See the introduction to the second edition of *Mushkilat al-Suluk al-Sikubati* (Cairo: Dar al-Ma'arif, 1949).

138. Lauren Berlant, "On the Case," *Critical Inquiry* 33, no. 4 (2007): 663–72.

139. Sabry Guergues, "An Investigation into Psychopathic Personality: Being an Attempt at Evaluating the Problem of Psychopathy in the Light of the Integrative Method," *Majallat 'Ilm al-Nafs* 1, no. 3 (1946): 391–410, quotation 410.

140. Ibid., 409–10.

141. Ibid., 408–9.

142. Ibid., 401.

143. Jirjis, *Mushkilat al-Suluk al-Sikubati*; Guergues, "Investigation into Psychopathic Personality."

144. Sabri Jirjis, *Mushkilat al-Suluk al-Sikubati: Bahth fi 'Ilm al-Nafs al-Tibbi al-Ijtima'i*, 3rd ed. (Cairo: Dar al-Ma'arif, 1958), Case Study no. 3, 46–53. Hereafter I refer to the 3rd edition, which contained the most comprehensive number of case studies.

145. Ibid., Case Study no. 2, 37–45. These cases provided interesting insights into midcentury perceptions of the disintegration of the nuclear family. In the case of M., his parents had divorced at age six, his father remarried one year later, and his mother remarried when he was twelve. Jirjis painted a portrait of a lack of familial stability and love, a successful father engrossed in work, and with a somewhat harsh and punitive disposition.

146. Ibid., Case Study no. 1, 27–37. Compare also Case Study no. 5, 59–68. W. was a case of unequalled psychopathy, he had exhibited early aberrations, such as early sexual activity, and the relentless pursuit of pleasure, and had no friendships. Such cases were characterized by what Jirjis referred to as moral turpitude, or *"naqs khalqi."*

147. Ibid., 170–99.

148. Ibid., 190–92.

149. On the malleability of emotions, particularly nationalist ones of love and hatred, see Sara Ahmed, *The Cultural Politics of Emotion* (New York: Routledge, 2004), chap. 2.

150. Fanon, *Wretched of the Earth*, 219–33.

151. Jirjis, *Mushkilat al-Suluk al-Sikubati*, 193–95.

152. Ibid., 196–97.

153. Ibid., 198–99.

154. Sabri Jirjis, "al-Jarima al-Sikubatiyya: Bayn al-Tibb al-'Aqli wa-l-Qanun," *Majallat 'Ilm al-Nafs* 4, no. 2 (1948): 161–78; M. Soueif, "The Problem of Psychopathic Behavior by S. Guerguess," *Majallat 'Ilm al-Nafs* 8, no. 1 (1952): 113–16.

155. Jirjis, *Mushkilat al-Suluk al-Sikubati*. He was not alone in this, see Dr. Muhammad 'Abd al-Hakim, a director at 'Abbasiyya Mental Hospital, "al-Tashkhis al-Muqarin li-l-Halat al-Sikubatiyya," "Discussion on the Differential Diagnosis of Psychopathic States," *Majallat 'Ilm al-Nafs* 4, no. 3 (1949): 321–28. Originally delivered as a lecture in English to the Clinical Association of Doctors of Mental Diseases, al-Khanka Mental Hospital, November 1948.

156. Dr. Walim al-Khuli, a medical doctor at al-Khanka Mental Hospital, "al-Marad al-'Aqli wa-l-Jarima," *Majallat 'Ilm al-Nafs* 4, no. 2 (1948): 225–34.

157. Soueif, "The Problem of Psychopathic Behavior by S. Guerguess"; Mahmud Hilmi, "al-Khidma al-Ijtima'iyya fi Midan al-Marad al-'Aqli," *Majallat 'Ilm al-Nafs* 3, no. 1 (1947): 113–27.

Epilogue

1. Julia Kristeva, "Conference on Rafah Nashed: Speech Delivered to the Women's Forum Organized by *Lacan Quotidien* and the *École de la cause freudienne*, October 9, 2011," trans. J. Todd Dean, *DIVISION/Review* 4 (2012): 4–6, quotation 4.

2. Ibid., 4.

3. Kristeva, *This Incredible Need to Believe*, 29. Kristeva addresses what she terms an incredible "prereligious 'need to believe'" as a mode of confronting "not only religions' past and present fundamentalist off-course drift but also the dead-ends of secularized societies," 11–12. For an earlier meditation on the relationship between religion and psychoanalysis, see Kristeva, *In the Beginning Was Love*, trans. Arthur Goldhammer (New York: Columbia University Press, 1987).

4. Kristeva, "Conference on Rafah Nashed," 4.

5. Ibid., 5.

6. Ibid.

7. Ibid.

8. Ibid. See Rafah Nached, "Tâsîn de la préexistence et de l'ambiguïté: Moi et toi, trahison ou amour?," *Psychanalyse* 21 (2011): 53–59. http://www.cairn.info/revue-psychanalyse -2011-2-page-53.htm.

9. Pandolfo, "Soul Choking," 74.

10. Kristeva, *This Incredible Need to Believe*, 68. She continues, "the fundamentalist stagnation of Islam raises a more general question about the very structure of *homo religiosis*. The latter can move beyond the *hatelove* that keeps him going only by taking a step to the side: by taking himself as an object of thought. By developing his theo-logy, by forcing it to confront the plural interpretations of his need to believe, the multiple variants of his need to believe," 70. Islam, thus postulated, lacks the *logos*. For a critique of Kristeva's Orientalist representations of Islam, see Ian Almond, *The New Orientalists: Postmodern Representations of Islam from Foucault to Baudrillard* (London: I. B. Tauris, 2007), chap. 7.

11. Kristeva, *This Incredible Need to Believe*, 42, 60, 66; Freud, *Moses and Monotheism*, *SE* 23: 92–93.

12. Benslama, *Psychoanalysis and the Challenge of Islam*, 24.

13. Massad, "Psychoanalysis, Islam, and the Other of Liberalism," 59. Stefania Pandolfo has engaged with the conceptual terms of Benslama's work and has critiqued his vision of radical Islamism as part and parcel of an annihilatory logic and a psychotic unfolding of time. See Pandolfo, "Soul Choking," 75–76.

14. Such political movements, "reinstitute forms of sociality within which a novel circulation of desire may become possible, with the emergence of a *parole* that may 'interrupt' the tyranny of the state, and not just re-inscribe the subjugation of being." Pandolfo, "Soul Choking," 75.

15. On the Iranian revolution and how a people could sacralise the roots of its identity, see Moustapha Safouan, *Speech or Death? Language as Social Order; A Psychoanalytic Study*, trans. Martin Thom (New York: Palgrave Macmillan, 2003), xi, xv.

16. Ibid., 26.

17. Ibid., 70.

18. Ibid., 49.

19. Safouan, "Interview with Colin MacCabe." Safouan elaborates: "But the idea of the necessity of the transcendental goes back to Lichtenberg's aphorism: 'there exists a species of transcendental ventriloquism by means of which men can be made to believe that something said on Earth comes from heaven.' You have to go to heaven, to have an authority, to which everybody can submit. It can't be you and me, it has to come from outside, I mean, heaven is the third. All this idea about a necessity of transcendental is from Lichtenberg's aphorism. And, of course, psychoanalysis has its share because the efficiency of law as such, is invisible; you have to give law a shape and a person and make it transcendental."

20. Thus Ebrahim Moosa notes to "comprehend the ethical subject is to grasp how the integrated soul/self becomes the addressee of divine discourse"; Moosa, *Ghazālī*, 229. See also Pandolfo, "Soul Choking," 78.

21. Pandolfo, "The Burning," 330.

22. Safouan, *Why Are the Arabs Not Free?*, 90.

23. Ibid., 91; Pandolfo, "The Burning," 330.

24. To clarify, Safouan is arguing that modern Arabic is characterized by a strict divide between two systems, one the spoken language of everyday life (a vernacular or demotic Arabic) and Modern Standard Arabic—the language of the press, high culture, and politics, and derived and modernized from the Classical Arabic of the Qur'an.

25. Safouan, *Why Are the Arabs Not Free?*, 76. In the archaic state the sovereign draws his power "from religion inasmuch as it organises ... the 'natural' belief in the order of the sacred," establishes "the indivisibility of power," is marked by "the absence of all real control of the sovereign's authority," and focuses on stability as a primary political goal (ibid., 61–62).

26. Ibid., 43.

27. Ibid., 88–89.

28. Ibid., 94.

29. Colin MacCabe, foreword to *Why Are the Arabs Not Free?*, xvii.

30. Ibid.

31. Husayn ʿAbd al-Qadir, "Safahat li-l-Nafs fi al-Turath al-ʿArabi bayn Basaʾir al-Salaf wa-Ibdaʿ al-Khalaf (wa-Taʾthur al-Muʿasirin)," in *ʿAmal al-Muʾtamir al-Awwal li-l-Muhallilin al-Nafsiyyin al-ʿArab: Fikrit al-Nafs ʿind al-ʿArab wa-Mawqaʿiha fi al-Tahlil al-Nafsi, 20–22 May 2004* (Beirut: Dar al-Farabi, 2005), 37–72. He uses the term *turath* for heritage or tradition, a heavily charged term that he feels compelled to distinguish from "chauvinistic" claims, 39–40.

32. Ibid., 41–43.

33. Ibid., 44–54. ʿAbd al-Qadir equates *al-nafs al-ammara bi-l-suʾ* with the id, *al-nafs al-mutmaʾinna* with the ego, and *al-nafs al-lawwama* with the superego. Curiously, he mentions al-Ghazali but does not cite the Qurʾan as the original source for these concepts. For more on the Qurʾan conception of the self, see my discussion in chapter 2.

34. On the lure of the "I" and the collective ends of man, see also ʿAbd al-Qadir on Mustafa Safwan, ibid., 67–68.

35. "If there is a responsibility of psychoanalysis at this time in history," Stefania Pandolfo notes, "it is that of political critique, and of the exigency of a particular stance, which Lacan named ethical." Such an ethical stance, however, must encounter itself at a limit, subjecting itself to radical critique through "an angle of visibility [that] can be attained from the living contemplation of one's own disappearance." Pandolfo, "Soul Choking," 75.

36. Henry Corbin, "Apophatic Theology as an Antidote to Nihilism," *Umbr(a)*: Semblance (2007): 59–84, 61; Corbin, "De la théologie apophatique comme antidote du nihilisme," in *Le paradoxe du monothéisme* (Paris: L'Herne, 1981), 211–58, 217. In this intensely suggestive piece, Corbin locates the origin of modern nihilism in the loss and mutilation of spiritual individuality. The disappearance of the spiritual, transcendent, angelic function of the person and the celestial pole that provides the human with his integral nature, leaves the terrestrial pole reduced to vagabondage and perdition.

adab—Social comportment, etiquette; belles-lettres

al-akhir—The other

al-akhir al-khafi—The internal other

'alam al-amr—World of Divine command

al-ana—The ego

al-ana al-a'la—The superego

après coup—*Nachträglichkeit*; afterwardness, in Freud

'aql—Reason, rationality, intellect, mind

al-'aql al-batin—The inner mind, the unconscious

bahr al-nafs—The ocean of the soul

baltagi (pl. *baltagiyya*)—Thug, mobster, or nefarious villain

baqa'—Subsistence; in Sufi thought, abiding in God, perpetuation of the "enlightened" self in the world

barzakh—Isthmus, intermediate realm; in Ibn 'Arabi, an intermediate world of the Divine imagination (between spirit and matter)

basar—Eyesight; in Sufi thought, the distinction between mere eyesight and spiritual insight

basira—Spiritual insight; in Sufi thought, the distinction between mere eyesight and spiritual insight

batin—Inner, hidden, nonmanifest, or spiritual; cf. *zahir*

batin al-zawahir—The interiority of exterior signs

dabt al-nafs—Self-control, adjustment, and rectification

al-dafi' al-gharizi—Drive; *trieb*

al-dafi' al-hayawi—Life force; libido, in Jung

dalil wa-burhan—Evidence and proof; here of the Sufis' divine secrets

damir—Conscience or censor

dhat—Self, subject, *le moi*; essence, or, in Sufi thought, Essence of God

dhawq—Taste; in Sufi thought, intimate tasting or direct personal experience, the ecstatic state of the direct experience of God

dhikr—In Sufi practice, remembrance and invocation of God through rhythmic repetition

effendi (pl. *effendiyya*)—Middle-class professional

fana'—Annihilation; in Sufi thought, the annihilation of the self or of the self in the world

fiqh—Islamic jurisprudence

firasa—Insight, perspicacity, *einsicht*; the science of judging internal meanings from external forms; natural *firasa* or physiognomy and divine *firasa* granted by God to mystics

al-firasa al-dhawqiyya—Mystical insight, judgement of spiritual essence, as opposed to natural insight, such as physiognomy

futuwwa (pl. *futuwat*)—A noble public figure who provided protection for weaker social elements, after the 1930s increasingly connoting thug, mobster, or a nefarious villain

ghariza—Instinct, impulse, urge, or nature; in classical texts, disposition or faculty

ghayr mashu'ur—Unconscious, or that which is not available to consciousness

hadith—Prophetic saying or tradition; the narration of the words or deeds of the Prophet Muhammad *hadrat al-khayal*—The imaginal world; in Ibn ʿArabi, "Presence of Imagination," a domain woven out of images

hads—conjecture or intuition

hal (pl. *ahwal*)—spiritual state, in Sufism

al-halat al-wijdaniyya al-khassa—psychic or affective states, such as annihilation of the self or mystical union with God

haraka lawlabiyya—Yusuf Murad's spiral or corkscrew-like conception of the temporal movement of human personality or society, involving partial regressions in the course of maturation

hayʾat al-maknun—"Guise of the Hidden," referring to knowledge which none knows but those who have knowledge of God

hasr—Anguish, angst, anxiety

hiss—Sensate data

idrak—Perception

ʿilm al-batin **or** *ʿilm al-haqiqa*—Knowledge or science of inner, hidden, or spiritual meanings; esoteric knowledge, relating to the heart and encapsulated in the idea of witness; cf. *ʿilm al-zahir*

ʿilm al-nafs—Psychology; the science of the soul, self, psyche

ʿilm al-nafs al-takamuli—Integrative psychology

ʿilm al-zahir—Knowledge or science of literal and apparent forms; exoteric knowledge, specifically relating to the forms of knowledge and practice laid down in the *shariʿa* and encapsulated by worship; cf. *ʿilm al-batin*

iltizam—Commitment, *engagement*, in existentialism

inhiraf—Deviance; abnormal developments

ʿirfan—Mystical knowledge; a path of knowledge leading directly to God; gnosis

ʿishq—Passionate love, passion

isqat—Projection, referring to the psychological defense mechanism

istibtun—Introspection

istinbat—Deduction or analogical reasoning

jihad—Struggle. In the Islamic tradition, there are two struggles: the inner, or greater *jihad* is the self-struggle; and the outer or lesser *jihad*, is the interpersonal and physical struggle for the maintenance of the faith.

jihad al-nafs—Inner or self-struggle, struggle of the soul, battleground of the self

jins—Sex/genus

al-jinsiyya al-mithliyya—Same-sex sexuality; homosexuality

kashf—Unveiling; in Sufi thought, mystical intuition, spiritual unveiling of that which comes between man and the extraphenomenal world

laduni—Noetic; knowledge imparted directly by God through mystical intuition

al-la-shuʿur—The unconscious

al-la-shuʿur al-mushtariq—The collective unconscious, in Jung

majhul—Hidden, unknown; obscured from immediate understanding

majnun—Insane, mad

al-manhaj al-batini—Esoteric method or program

manhaj al-istibtun—Introspective method or program

maqam (pl. *maqamat*)—Spiritual station or level, in Sufism

maʿrifa—Knowledge, cognition; in Sufism, gnosis, mystical knowledge or an illuminative cognition of the Divine

maʿrifat al-nafs—Self-knowledge

al-maʿrifa bi-Llah—Knowledge or cognition of God; gnosis, illuminative cognition of the Divine *al-maslaha al-ʿamma*—The public interest; the common good

al-mil al-gharizi—Drive; *trieb*

min haythu la-yadri—From a place he knows not

murahiq—Adolescent

murid—Disciple or novice in the Sufi relationship, learning from a master (*murshid, shaykh*)

murshid—Spiritual master in the Sufi relationship, instructing a disciple (*murid*)

mushahada—Contemplation, seeing, witnessing; in Sufi thought, contemplation of God

nafas—Breath, wind; the primordial "Divine Breath"

Nafas Rahmani—"Breath of Divine Compassion"

nafs—Soul, spirit, psyche, self; *âme*; in Sufi thought, the lower self

al-nafs al-ammara bi-l-suʾ—The commanding self, controlled by passions and impulses, that commands evil, mentioned in the Qurʾan

al-nafs al-lawwama—The rueful or reproachful self, torn between good and evil, mentioned in the Qurʾan

al-nafs al-mutmaʾinna—The tranquil self, mentioned in the Qurʾan

nahda—Renaissance, rebirth, cultural revival; refers to the late nineteenth- and early twentieth-century period of Arab intellectual and cultural efflorescence

nahdawi—Describing a thinker of the *nahda* period who forged an Arab cultural modernity

al-nahnu—The "we," the associate; the other as a unit of society or community

al-niyaba—The Parquet; the government prosecution department of the Ministry of Justice following the institution of the Napoleonic Code in Egypt in the 1880s

qalb—Heart; in Sufi thought, the intuitive organ and the center of mystical knowledge of God

qanun al-iʿada—The law of recapitulation

al-quwwa al-wahmiyya—Avicenna's "estimative faculty"

raqib—Conscience or censor

riyada—Discipline

riyadat al-nafs—Disciplining the soul; self-discipline

ruh—Spirit. According to many Sufis, the soul (*nafs*) represented the ego-affirming self, the spirit (*ruh*) affirmed the Other (God), and the two could be merged in the heart (*qalb*).

sawi—Normal

shariʿa—The religious path, sacred law and principles in Islam; cf. *siyasa* or state law

shaykh—A religious leader; in Sufism, a spiritual master in the master-disciple relationship

shudhudh—Abnormality

shuhud—Contemplation, witnessing; in Sufism, bearing witness to God's majesty

shuʿur batini—Inner affects or emotions

sirat—The straight path; the narrow and precarious bridge of the hereafter

sirr—Inner secret, divine mystery, in Sufi thought

siyasa—State law; discretionary justice exercised by the head of state and executive officials; not limited to the rules of the *shariʿa*

siyasi—Referring to or having to do with "secular" state law, as in types of evidence such as autopsy and forensic evidence

siyasat al-badan—Processes of governing the body

tabdil al-akhlaq—The "exchange of virtues," the transformation of the self from blameworthy to tranquil

tabib sharʿi—Medical examiner

tadbir al-nafs—Self-management, self-attunement

ta'dib—Discipline or correction; for al-Ghazali, this process involved the cultivation of the virtues and the elaboration of the faculty of discernment.

tadrib—Training in a general sense, for example, toilet training or ethical training

tahdhib—Attunement; disciplining, training, as of a child

tahdhib al-akhlaq—Ethical attunement; refinement of morals

tahdhib al-nafs—Self-attunement; disciplining of the soul

takamuli—Integrative; theory of psychology developed by Yusuf Murad

tamyiz—Discernment

tarbiya—Education or upbringing, as of a child; *paideia*

tariqa—Path; in Sufism, the mystical experience of the Divine can come only after an initiate follows a particular path in their spiritual training.

al-tasawwuf al-sunni—Orthodox mysticism

tawhid—Unity; in Islamic thought, refers to divine unity

ta'wid—Habituation

ta'wil—Symbolic or allegorical understanding; esoteric hermeneutics

al-tibb al-'aqli—Psychiatric medicine

'ulum al-adhwaq—Sciences of tastings; forms of knowledge that cannot be expressed, see *dhawq*

al-'ulum al-laduniyya—The intuitive sciences; knowledge from God, referring to *laduni*

al-'uqda al-udibiyya—The Oedipus complex

wataniyya—Nationalism

wahda—Unity or holism

wahdat al-nafs—Unity of the self or soul

wahdat 'ilm al-nafs—Unity of psychology

wijdan—Feeling, affect

wujud li-l-akhirin—Being or existence for others

wujud li-l-dhat—Being or existence for the self

wujud li-l-ghayr—Being or existence for the other

zahir—Outer, external, manifest, literal or apparent; cf. *batin*

REFERENCES

ʿAbd al-Hakim, Muhammad. "Al-Tashkhis al-Muqarin li-l-Halat al-Sikubatiyya." *Majallat ʿIlm al-Nafs* 4, no. 3 (1949): 321–28.

ʿAbd al-Qadir, Husayn. "Safahat li-l-Nafs fi al-Turath al-ʿArabi bayn Basaʾir al-Salaf wa-Ibdaʿ al-Khalaf (wa-Taʾthur al-Muʿasirin)." In *ʿAmal al-Muʾtamir al-Awwal li-l-Muhallilin al-Nafsiyyin al-ʿArab: Fikrit al-Nafs ʿind al-ʿArab wa-Mawqaʿiha fi al-Tahlil al-Nafsi, 20–22 May 2004* (Beirut: Dar al-Farabi, 2005), 37–72.

Abdel Kader (ʿAbd al-Qadir), Hussein. "La psychanalyse en Égypte entre un passé ambitieux et un futur incertain." *La célibataire—La psychanalyse et le monde arabe* 8 (2004): 61–73.

Abdel-Malek, Anouar ed. *Contemporary Arab Political Thought*. Translated by Michael Pallis. London: Zed Books, 1983.

Abelove, Henry. "Freud, Male Homosexuality, and the Americans." In *The Lesbian and Gay Studies Reader*, edited by Henry Abelove, Michèle Aina Barale, and David M. Halperin, 381–93. London: Routledge, 1993.

Abenante, Paola. "Inner and Outer Ways: Sufism and Subjectivity in Egypt and Beyond." *Ethnos: A Journal of Anthropology* 78, no. 4 (2013): 490–514.

Abou-El-Haj, Rifaʿat. "The Ottoman Dervish Orders as Acculturating Institutions." Unpublished manuscript.

Abou-Hatab, Fouad. "Egypt." In *International Psychology: Views from around the World*, edited by Virginia Sexton and John Hogan, 111–28. Lincoln: University of Nebraska Press, 1992.

Aboul-Ela, Hosam. "The World Republic of Theories." Unpublished manuscript.

Abu Ghurra, Ibrahim. "Fi al-Tasawwuf wa-ʿIlm al-Nafs: Ibn al-Farid wa-l-Hubb al-Ilahi li-l-Duktur Mustafa Muhammad Hilmi." *Majallat ʿIlm al-Nafs* 1, no. 2 (1945): 220–22.

Abu-Lughod, Lila. "Feminist Longings and Postcolonial Conditions." In *Remaking Women: Feminism and Modernity in the Middle East*, edited by Lila Abu-Lughod, 3–32. Princeton, NJ: Princeton University Press, 1998.

Abu Rabiʿ, Ibrahim. "Al-Azhar and Islamic Rationalism in Modern Egypt: The Philosophical Contributions of Muṣṭafā ʿAbd āl-Raziq and ʿAbd al-Ḥalim Maḥmūd." *Islamic Studies* 27, no. 2 (1988): 129–50.

——. "Al-Azhar Sufism in Modern Egypt: The Sufi Thought." *Islamic Quarterly* 32, no. 4 (1989): 208–35.

——. *Contemporary Arab Thought: Studies in Post-1967 Arab Intellectual History*. London: Pluto Press, 2004.

Adham, ʿAli. "Freud wa-l-Harb." *Al-Thaqafa* 3, no. 153 (December 2, 1941): 1564–69.

Affifi, A. E. *The Mystical Philosophy of Muḥyid dín-Ibnul ʿArabí*. Cambridge: Cambridge University Press, 1939.

Ahmed, Ramadan A. "Psychology in Egypt." In *Handbook of International Psychology*, edited by Michael J. Stevens and Danny Wedding, 387–403. New York: Brunner-Routledge, 2004.

Ahmed, Sara. *The Cultural Politics of Emotion*. New York: Routledge, 2004.

Akhtar, Salman. "Where Is India in My Psychoanalytic Work?" *Psychoanalytic Review*, special issue: *Psychoanalysis and India* 102, no. 6 (2015): 873–911.

Alexander, Franz. *The Medical Value of Psychoanalysis*. New York: International Universities Press, 1984.

Alexander, Franz, and Hugo Staub. *The Criminal, the Judge, and the Public: A Psychological Analysis*. Translated by Gregory Zilboorg. New York: Macmillan, 1931.

Ali, Kamran Asdar. "Progressives and 'Perverts': Partition Stories and Pakistan's Future."
Social Text 29, no. 3 108 (2011): 1–29.

——. "'Pulp Fictions': Reading Pakistani Domesticity." *Social Text* 22, no. 1 (2004):
123–45.

al-'Alim, Mahmud Amin. *Al-Fikr al-'Arabi bayn al-Khususiyya wa-l-Kawniyya*. Cairo:
Dar al-Mustaqbal al-'Arabi, 1996.

——. "Ma wara' 'al-Mudrik al-Hissi.'" *Majallat 'Ilm al-Nafs* 5, no. 3 (1950): 361–76.

——. "Quli Lahum ini Ahabuhum Jami'an." *Al-Musawwar*, no. 2190 (September 30,
1966): 32–33.

Almond, Ian. *The New Orientalists: Postmodern Representations of Islam from Foucault
to Baudrillard*. London: I. B. Tauris, 2007.

Anderson, Warwick, Deborah Jenson, and Richard Keller, eds. *Unconscious Dominions:
Psychoanalysis, Colonial Trauma, and Global Sovereignties*. Durham, NC: Duke University Press, 2011.

Andler, Daniel. "Cognitive Science." In *The Columbia History of Twentieth Century French
Thought*, edited by Lawrence D. Kritzman, Brian J. Reilly, and M. B. DeBevois, 175–
81. New York: Columbia University Press, 2007.

Arnaldez, R. "Ma'rifa." *Encyclopaedia of Islam*. 2nd ed., edited by P. Bearman, Th. Bianquis, C. E. Bosworth, E. van Donzel, and W. P. Heinrichs. Brill online, 2012. http://
referenceworks.brillonline.com/entries/encyclopaedia-of-islam-2/marifa-COM
_0686.

'Aqil, Fakhir. *Mu'jam 'Ilm al-Nafs: Inklizi-Frinsi-'Arabi*. Beirut: Dar al-'Ilm li-l-Malayyin,
1985.

al-'Aqqad, 'Abbas Mahmud. *Abu Nuwas al-Hasan ibn Hani', Dirasa fi al-Tahlil al-Nafsani
wa-l-Naqd al-Tarihki*. Cairo: Dar al-Hilal, 1960.

Arabi, Oussama. "The Regimentation of the Subject: Madness in Islamic and Modern
Arab Civil Laws." In Dupret, *Standing Trial*, 264–93.

Aristotle. *The Nicomachean Ethics*. Translated by Martin Ostwald. Indianapolis: Bobbs-
Merrill, 1962.

Asad, Muhammad. *The Message of the Qur'an*. Translated and Explained by Muhammad
Asad. Gibraltar: Dar al-Andalus, 1980.

Asad, Talal. *Formations of the Secular: Christianity, Islam, Modernity*. Stanford, CA:
Stanford University Press, 2003.

——. "The Idea of an Anthropology of Islam." *Occasional Papers, Center for Contemporary Arab Studies*. Washington, DC: Georgetown University, 1986.

Ash, Mitchell. *Gestalt Psychology in German Culture, 1890–1967: Holism and the Quest for
Objectivity*. Cambridge: Cambridge University Press, 1998.

"Asi'lat al-Qurra'." *Majallat 'Ilm al-Nafs* 4, no.1 (1948): 131–34.

Assmann, Jan. *Moses the Egyptian: The Memory of Egypt in Western Monotheism*. Cambridge, MA: Harvard University Press, 1998.

Ateş, A. "Ibn al-'Arabī." In *Encyclopaedia of Islam*. 2nd. ed., edited by P. Bearman, Th. Bianquis, C. E. Bosworth, E. van Donzel, and W. P. Heinrichs. Brill online, 2012. http://
dx.doi.org/10.1163/1573-3912_islam_COM_0316.

Azouri, Chawki, and Elisabeth Roudinesco, eds. *La psychanalyse dans le monde arabe et
islamique*. Beirut: Presses de l'Université Saint-Joseph, 2005.

Ba'albaki, Rohi. *Al-Mawrid: Qamus 'Arabi-Inklizi*. Beirut: Dar al-'Ilm li-l-Malayyin, 2004.

Bab al-Hadid. Directed by Youssef Chahine. DVD. 1958; Cairo: Typecast Releasing, 2009.

Badawi, Najib Yusuf. "Sikubathulujiyyat al-Sihr wa-l-Tatyir." *Majallat 'Ilm al-Nafs* 7, no.1 (1951): 35–60.

Bakan, David. *Sigmund Freud and the Jewish Mystical Tradition.* New York: Schocken Books, 1965.

Baladi, Najib. "Al-Huriyya wa-l-Madi." *Majallat 'Ilm al-Nafs* 4, no. 3 (1949): 393–406.

Bardawil, Fadi A. "When All This Revolution Melts into Air: The Disenchantment of Levantine Marxist Intellectuals." PhD diss., Columbia University, 2010.

Baring, Edward. *The Young Derrida and French Philosophy, 1945–1968.* Cambridge: Cambridge University Press, 2011.

Baron, Beth. *Egypt as a Woman: Nationalism, Gender, and Politics.* Berkeley: University of California Press, 2005.

——. *The Women's Awakening in Egypt: Culture, Society, and the Press.* New Haven, CT: Yale University Press, 1997.

Bashkin, Orit. "Representations of Women in the Writings of the Intelligentsia in Hashemite Iraq, 1921–1958." *Journal of Middle East Women's Studies* 4, no. 1 (2008): 53–82.

Behrouzan, Orkideh. *Prozak Diaries: Psychiatry and Generational Memory in Iran.* Stanford, CA: Stanford University Press, 2016.

Ben Slama, Raja. "La psychanalyse en Égypte: Un problème de non-advenue." *Topique* 110 (2010/11): 83–96.

——. "The Tree That Reveals the Forest: Arabic Translations of Freudian Terminology." *Transeuropéennes.* November 5, 2009. http://www.transeuropeennes.eu/en/articles /106/The_Tree_that_Reveals_the_Forest.

Benslama, Fethi. "Dying for Justice." Translated by Roland Végsö. *Umbr(a): A Journal of the Unconscious.* Islam (2009): 13–23.

——. "Islam and Psychoanalysis: A Tale of Mutual Ignorance." Interview by Gabriela M. Keller. Qantara.de, 2006. http://en.qantara.de/content/islam-and-psychoanalysis-a -tale-of-mutual-ignorance.

——. "Of a Renunciation of the Father." Translated by Roland Végsö. *Umbr(a): A Journal of the Unconscious.* Islam (2009): 25–33.

——. *Psychoanalysis and the Challenge of Islam.* Translated by Robert Bononno. Minneapolis: University of Minnesota Press, 2009.

Benslama, Fethi, and Jean-Luc Nancy. "Translations of Monotheisms." Translated by Ed Pluth. In special issue on "Islam and Psychoanalysis," *S, Journal of the Jan van Eyck Circle for Lacanian Ideology Critique* 2, edited by Sigi Jöttkandt and Joan Copjec (2009): 74–89.

Bergson, Henri. *Al-Dahik: Bahth fi Dallalat al-Mudhik (Le rire: Essai sur la signification du comique).* Translated by Sami al-Durubi. Cairo: Dar al-Katib al-Misri, 1947.

——. *Laughter: An Essay on the Meaning of the Comic.* Translated by Cloudsley Brereton and Fred Rothwell. Los Angeles: Green Integer, 1999.

——. *Mind-Energy.* Translated by H. Wildon Carr. London: Macmillan, 1920.

——. *Al-Taqa al-Ruhiyya (L'energie spirituelle).* Translated by Sami al-Durubi. Cairo: Dar al-Fikr al-'Arabi, 1946.

——. *Time and Free Will: An Essay on the Immediate Data of Consciousness.* Translated by F. L. Pogson. New York: Harper Torchbooks, 1960.

Berlant, Lauren. "On the Case." *Critical Inquiry* 33, no. 4 (2007): 663–72.

Bernstein, Richard J. *Freud and the Legacy of Moses.* Cambridge: Cambridge University Press, 1998.

Bettelheim, Bruno. *Freud and Man's Soul: An Important Re-Interpretation of Freudian Theory.* London: Flamingo, 1985.

Bier, Laura. *Revolutionary Womanhood: Feminisms, Modernity, and the State in Nasser's Egypt*. Stanford, CA: Stanford University Press, 2011.

Blowers, Geoffrey H., and Serena Yang Hsueh Chi. "Freud's *Deshi*: The Coming of Psychoanalysis to Japan." *Journal of the History of the Behavioral Sciences* 33, no. 2 (1997): 115–26.

Booth, Marilyn. "Woman in Islam: Men and the 'Women's Press' in Turn-of-the-20th-Century Egypt." *International Journal of Middle East Studies* 33, no. 2 (2001): 171–201.

Borossa, Julia. "The Extensibility of Psychoanalysis in Ahmed Alaidy's *Being Abbas el Abd* and Bahaa Taher's *Love in Exile*." *Journal of Postcolonial Writing* 47, no. 4 (2011): 404–15.

Brickman, Celia. "Primitivity, Race, and Religion in Psychoanalysis." *Journal of Religion* 82, no. 1 (2002): 53–74.

Brooks, John I., III. *The Eclectic Legacy: Academic Philosophy and the Human Sciences in Nineteenth-Century France*. Newark: University of Delaware Press, 1998.

Buqtur, Zakariyya Ibrahim. "Al-Dallala al-Siykulujiyya li-l-Nazra." *Majallat 'Ilm al-Nafs* 6, no. 2 (1950–51): 225–32.

———. "Mushkilat al-Shu'ur." *Majallat 'Ilm al-Nafs* 3, no. 2 (1947): 259–62.

———. "Sikulujiyyat al-Ghiyab." *Majallat 'Ilm al-Nafs* 6, no. 1 (1950): 3–12.

Burrow, Trigant. *The Biology of Human Conflict*. New York: Macmillan, 1937.

Bush, J. Andrew. "How 'God Becomes a Lover': Sufi Poetry and the Finitude of Desire in Kurdistan." *Journal of Middle East Women's Studies* 12, no. 1 (2016): 68–87.

Calverley, E. E., and I. R. Netton. "Nafs." In *Encyclopaedia of Islam*. 2nd ed., edited by P. Bearman, Th. Bianquis, C. E. Bosworth, E. van Donzel, and W. P. Heinrichs. Brill online, 2012. http://dx.doi.org/10.1163/1573-3912_islam_COM_0833.

Capps, Donald, ed. *Freud and Freudians on Religion: A Reader*. New Haven, CT: Yale University Press, 2001.

Carlson, Marvin. "Editor's Introduction." In Carlson, *Arab Oedipus*, 1–13.

Carlson, Marvin, ed. *The Arab Oedipus: Four Plays from Egypt and Syria*. New York: Martin E. Segal Theatre Center Publications, 2005.

Carroy, Jacqueline, and Regine Plas. "How Pierre Janet Used Pathological Psychology to Save the Philosophical Self." *Journal of the History of the Behavioral Sciences* 36, no. 3 (2000): 231–40.

Cassin, Barbara, Jacqueline Lichtenstein, and Elisabete Thamer. "Catharsis." In *Dictionary of Untranslatables: A Philosophical Lexicon*, edited by Barbara Cassin, Emily Apter, Jacques Lezra, and Michael Wood, 126–29. Princeton, NJ: Princeton University Press, 2014.

Cassullo, Gabriele. "Back to the Roots: The Influence of Ian D. Suttie on British Psychoanalysis." Translated by Francesco Capello. *American Imago* 67, no. 1 (2010): 5–22.

Certeau, Michel de. *The Mystic Fable*. Vol. 1, *The Sixteenth and Seventeenth Centuries*. Translated by Michael B. Smith. Chicago: University of Chicago Press, 1992.

Chakrabarty, Dipesh. *Provincializing Europe: Postcolonial Thought and Historical Difference*. Princeton, NJ: Princeton University Press, 2000.

Chiang, Howard. "Epistemic Modernity and the Emergence of Homosexuality in China." *Gender and History* 22, no. 3 (2010): 629–57.

Chittick, William C. "Divine Names and Theophanies." In Ibn al-'Arabi, *The Meccan Revelations*. Vol. 1, *Selected Texts of al-Futûhât al-Makkiya*, 27–64.

———. "On Sufi Psychology: A Debate between the Soul and the Spirit." In *Consciousness and Reality: Studies in Memory of Toshihiko Izutsu*, edited by Sayyid Jalal al-Din

Ashtiyani, Hideichi Matsubara, Takashi Iwami, and Akiro Matsumoto, 341–66. Leiden: Brill, 2000.

———. *The Self-Disclosure of God: Principles of Ibn al-'Arabi's Cosmology*. Albany: State University of New York Press, 1998.

———. *The Sufi Path of Knowledge: Ibn al-'Arabi's Metaphysics of Imagination*. Albany: State University of New York Press, 1989.

———. "Taṣawwuf, 2. Ibn al-'Arabī and after in the Arabic and Persian Lands and Beyond." In *Encyclopaedia of Islam*. 2nd ed., edited by P. Bearman, Th. Bianquis, C. E. Bosworth, E. van Donzel, and W. P. Heinrichs. http://dx.doi.org/10.1163/1573-3912_islam _COM_1188.

———. "Towards Sainthood: Saints and Stations." In Ibn al-'Arabi, *The Meccan Revelations*. Vol. 1, *Selected Texts of al-Futûhât al-Makkiya*, 125–97.

———. "Waḥdat al-S̲h̲uhūd." In *Encyclopaedia of Islam*. 2nd ed., edited by P. Bearman, Th. Bianquis, C. E. Bosworth, E. van Donzel, and W. P. Heinrichs. http://dx.doi.org /10.1163/1573-3912_islam_SIM_7819.

Chodkiewicz, Cyrille. "The Law and the Way." In Ibn al-'Arabi, *The Meccan Revelations*. Vol. 2, *Selected Texts of al-Futûhât al-Makkiya*, 57–104.

Chodkiewicz, Michel. Introduction to *The Meccan Revelations*. Vol 2, *Selected Texts of al-Futûhât al-Makkiya*, by Ibn al-'Arabi, 3–55.

———. *An Ocean without Shore: Ibn 'Arabî, the Book, and the Law*. Translated by David Streight. Albany: State University of New York Press.

Christmann, Andreas. "Reclaiming Mysticism: Anti-Orientalism and 'Islamic Mysticism' in Postcolonial Egypt." In *Religion, Language, and Power*, edited by Nile Green and Mary Searle-Chatterjee, 57–79. New York: Routledge 2008.

———. "Reconciling Sufism with Theology: Abū l-Wafā al-Taftāzānī and the Construct of 'al-Taṣawwuf al-Islāmī' in Modern Egypt." In *Sufism and Theology*, edited by Ayman Shihadeh, 177–98. Edinburgh: Edinburgh University Press, 2007.

Colla, Elliott. "Anxious Advocacy: The Novel, the Law, and Extrajudicial Appeals in Egypt." *Public Culture* 17, no. 3 (2005): 417–43.

Cooper, Frederick. "Conflict and Connection: Rethinking Colonial African History." *American Historical Review* 99, no. 5 (1994): 1516–45.

Copjec, Joan. "Introduction: Islam and the Exotic Science." *Umbr(a): A Journal of the Unconscious*. Islam (2009): 5–11.

———. *Read My Desire: Lacan against the Historicists*. London: Verso, 2015.

Corbin, Henry. *Alone with the Alone: Creative Imagination in the Sufism of Ibn 'Arabi*. Princeton, NJ: Princeton University Press, 1998.

———. "Apophatic Theology as an Antidote to Nihilism." *Umbr(a): A Journal of the Unconscious*. Semblance (2007): 59–84.

———. "De la théologie apophatique comme antidote du nihilism." In *Le paradoxe du monothéisme*, 211–58. Paris: L'Herne, 1981.

Costello, Stephen J. "The Real of Religion and Its Relation to Truth as Cause." *Letter* 13 (Summer 1998): 69–81.

Crockett, Clayton. "On Sublimation: The Significance of Psychoanalysis for the Study of Religion." *Journal of the American Academy of Religion* 68, no. 4 (2000): 837–55.

Cuno, Kenneth M. *Modernizing Marriage: Family, Ideology, and Law in Nineteenth- and Early Twentieth-Century Egypt*. Syracuse, NY: Syracuse University Press, 2015.

Danner, Victor. Introduction to *The Book of Wisdom, Ibn 'Ata'illah and Intimate Conversations, Kwaja Abdullah Ansari*, 5–43. Translated by Victor Danner and Wheeler M. Thackston. New York: Paulist Press, 1978.

Davidson, Arnold. *The Emergence of Sexuality: Historical Epistemology and the Formation of Concepts*. Cambridge, MA: Harvard University Press, 2004.

Dean, Carolyn. *The Self and Its Pleasures: Bataille, Lacan, and the History of the Decentered Subject*. Ithaca, NY: Cornell University Press, 1992.

Debesse, Maurice. *Comment étudier les adolescents: Examen critique des confidences juvéniles*. Paris: F. Alcan, 1937.

Deleuze, Gilles. *Bergsonism*. Translated by Hugh Tomlinson and Barbara Habberjam. New York: Zone Books, 1991.

Derrida, Jacques. "Geopsychoanalysis: '... and the Rest of the World.'" *American Imago* 48, no. 2 (1991): 199–231.

——. *Margins of Philosophy*. Translated by Alan Bass. Chicago: University of Chicago Press, 1985.

Deutsch, Helene. *The Psychology of Women: A Psychoanalytic Interpretation*, vols. 1 and 2. New York: Grune and Stratton, 1944–45.

Diagne, Souleymane Bachir. *Bergson postcolonial: L'élan vital dans la pensée de Léopold Sédar Senghor et de Mohamed Iqbal*. Paris: CNRS Editions, 2011.

Di-Capua, Yoav. "Arab Existentialism: An Invisible Chapter in the Intellectual History of Decolonization." *American Historical Review* 117, no. 4 (2012): 1061–91.

——. "The Intellectual Revolt of the 1950s and the 'Fall of the Udabā.'" In *Reflections on/of the Political in Arabic Literature since the 1940s*, edited by Friederike Pannewick, Georges Khalil, and Yvonne Albers, 89–104. Wiesbaden: Ludwig Reichert Verlag, 2015.

——. *No Exit: Arab Existentialism, Jean-Paul Sartre, and Decolonization*. Chicago: University of Chicago Press, 2018.

DiCenso, James J. "Kant, Freud, and the Ethical Critique of Religion." *International Journal for Philosophy of Religion* 61, no. 3 (2007): 161–79.

——. *The Other Freud: Religion, Culture, and Psychoanalysis*. New York: Routledge, 1999.

——. "Symbolism and Subjectivity: A Lacanian Approach to Religion." *Journal of Religion* 74, no. 1 (1994): 45–64.

Dols, Michael. *Majnun: The Madman in Medieval Islamic Society*. Edited by Diana Immisch. Oxford: Clarendon Press, 1992.

Dostoevsky, Fyodor. *The Brothers Karamazov*. Edited by Ralph E. Matlaw. Translated by Constance Garnett. New York: W. W. Norton, 1976.

——. *Al-Ikhwa Karamazuf*. Translated by Sami al-Durubi. Beirut: al-Markaz al-Thaqafi al-'Arabi, 2010.

Doumani, Beshara, ed. *Family History in the Middle East: Household, Property, and Gender*. Albany: State University of New York Press, 2012.

Dupret, Baudouin. "Intention in Action: A Pragmatic Approach to Criminal Characterisation in an Egyptian Context." In Dupret, *Standing Trial*, 196–230.

——. "The Person and His Body: Medical Ethics and Egyptian Law." In Dupret, *Standing Trial*, 294–317.

Dupret, Baudouin, ed. *Standing Trial: Law and the Person in the Modern Middle East*. London: I. B. Tauris, 2004.

Dusuqi, Kamal. "Bab al-Kutub al-Jadida: Nisha' al-Fikr fi al-Tifl." Review of Henri Wallon, *Les origines de la pensée chez l'enfant* (1945). *Majallat 'Ilm al-Nafs* 2, no. 1 (1946): 178–80.

El-Rouayheb, Khaled. *Before Homosexuality in the Arab-Islamic World, 1500–1800*. Chicago: University of Chicago Press, 2009.

El Shakry, Omnia. "The Arabic Freud: The Unconscious and the Modern Subject." *Modern Intellectual History* 11, no. 1 (2014): 89–118.

———. *The Great Social Laboratory: Subjects of Knowledge in Colonial and Postcolonial Egypt*. Stanford, CA: Stanford University Press, 2007.

———. "'History without Documents': The Vexed Archives of Decolonization in the Middle East." *American Historical Review* 120, no. 3 (2015): 920–34.

———. "Schooled Mothers and Structured Play: Child Rearing in Turn-of-the-Century Egypt." In *Remaking Women: Feminism and Modernity in the Middle East*, edited by Lila Abu-Lughod, 126–70. Princeton, NJ: Princeton University Press, 1998.

———. "Youth as Peril and Promise: The Emergence of Adolescent Psychology in Postwar Egypt." *International Journal of Middle East Studies* 43, no. 4 (2011): 591–610.

Elshakry, Marwa. "Knowledge in Motion: The Cultural Politics of Modern Science Translations in Arabic." *Isis* 99, no. 4 (2008): 701–30.

———. *Reading Darwin in Arabic, 1860–1950*. Chicago: University of Chicago Press, 2013.

Ernst, Carl W. *Words of Ecstasy in Sufism*. Albany: State University of New York, 1985.

Esmeir, Samera. *Juridical Humanity: A Colonial History*. Stanford, CA: Stanford University Press, 2012.

Etkind, Alexander. *Eros of the Impossible: The History of Psychoanalysis in Russia*. Translated by Noah and Maria Rubins. Boulder, CO: Westview Press, 1997.

Ewies ('Uways), Saied. "Egypt." In *International Handbook of Contemporary Developments in Criminology: Europe, Africa, The Middle East, and Asia*, edited by Elmer Johnson, 185–96. Westport, CT: Greenwood Press, 1983.

Ewing, Katherine Pratt. *Arguing Sainthood: Modernity, Psychoanalysis, and Islam*. Durham, NC: Duke University Press, 1997.

Fahmy, Khaled. "The Anatomy of Justice: Forensic Medicine and Criminal Law in Nineteenth Century Egypt." *Islamic Law and Society* 6, no. 2 (1999): 224–71.

———. "Birth of the 'Secular' Individual: Medical and Legal Methods of Identification in Nineteenth-Century Egypt." In *Registration and Recognition: Documenting the Person in World History*, edited by Keith Breckenridge and Simon Szreter, 335–55. Oxford: Oxford University Press, 2010.

———. "Justice, Law, and Pain in Khedivial Egypt." In Dupret, *Standing Trial*, 85–115.

———. "The Police and the People in Nineteenth Century Egypt." *Die Welt des Islams* 39, no. 3 (1999): 340–77.

Fanon, Frantz. *Black Skin, White Masks*. Translated by Charles Lam Markmann. New York: Grove Press, 1967.

———. *Mu'adhdhabu al-Ard (Les damnés de la terre)*. Translated by Sami al-Durubi and Jamal al-Atasi. Damascus: al-Matba'a al-Ta'awuniyya, 1968.

———. *The Wretched of the Earth*. Translated by Richard Philcox. New York: Grove Press, 2004.

Farag, S. E. "Egypt." In *International Handbook of Psychology*, edited by A. R. Gilgen and C. K. Gilgen, 174–83. New York: Greenwood Press, 1987.

Fathi, Muhammad. "Al-Ijram 'ala daw' al-Nazariyya al-Tahliliyya li-l-Amrad al-'Asabiyya." *Majallat 'Ilm al-Nafs* 4, no. 2 (1948): 259–69.

———. *'Ilm al-Nafs al-Jina'i: 'Ilman wa-'Amalan*, vols. 1–3. Cairo: Maktabat al-Nahda al-Misriyya, 1943, 1950, 1974.

———. *Mushkilat al-Tahlil al-Nafsi fi Misr: Dirasatiha min al-Nawahi al-'Ilmiyya wa-l-Ijtima'iyya wa-l-Qada'iyya wa-l-Tashri'iyya*. Cairo: Matba'at Misr, 1946.

Fawal, Ibrahim. *Youssef Chahine*. London: British Film Institute, 2001.

Fayek, Ahmed. "Islam and Its Effect on my Practice of Psychoanalysis." *Psychoanalytic Psychology* 21, no. 3 (2004): 452–57.

Fenton, Paul B. "Judaism and Sufism." In *History of Islamic Philosophy*, edited by Seyyed Hossein Nasr and Oliver Leaman, 755–68. Abingdon, UK: Routledge, 2007.

Ffytche, Matt. *The Foundation of the Unconscious: Schelling, Freud, and the Birth of the Modern Psyche.* Cambridge: Cambridge University Press, 2012.

Fink, Bruce. *The Lacanian Subject: Between Language and Jouissance.* Princeton, NJ: Princeton University Press, 1995.

Foucault, Michel. *The History of Sexuality.* Vol. 1, *An Introduction.* Translated by Robert Hurley. New York: Vintage/Random House, 1990.

———. "Technologies of the Self." In *Technologies of the Self: A Seminar with Michel Foucault,* edited by Luther Martin, Huck Gutman, and Patrick Hutton, 16–49. Amherst: University of Massachusetts Press, 1988.

Frangie, Samer. "Theorizing from the Periphery: The Intellectual Project of Mahdi ʿAmil." *International Journal of Middle East Studies* 44, no. 3 (2012): 465–82.

Freud, Sigmund. *The Standard Edition of the Complete Psychological Works of Sigmund Freud,* vols. 1–24. Translated and edited by James Strachey, in collaboration with Anna Freud, assisted by Alix Strachey and Alan Tyson. London: Hogarth Press, 1981.

———. *Tafsir al-Ahlam.* Translated by Mustafa Safwan and reviewed by Mustafa Ziywar. Cairo: Dar al-Maʿarif, 2004.

Frishkopf, Michael. "Shaykh Yasin al-Tuhami: A Typical Layla Performance." *Garland Encyclopedia of World Music,* vol. 6 (2002).

———. "Thus Spake the Reed Flute." *Al-Ahram Weekly* 864 (September 27–October 3, 2007). http://weekly.ahram.org.eg/Archive/2007/864/profile.htm.

Frosh, Stephen. "Hauntings: Psychoanalysis and Ghostly Transmission." *American Imago* 69, no. 2 (2012): 241–64.

Gairdner, W.H.T. Canon. *Theories, Practices, and Training Systems of a Sufi School.* London: Society for Sufi Studies, 1980.

Gallo, Rubén. *Freud's Mexico: Into the Wilds of Psychoanalysis.* Cambridge, MA: MIT Press, 2010.

Galton, Francis. "Identification Offices in India and Egypt." *Nineteenth Century* 48 (July 1900): 118–26.

———. "Souvenirs d'Égypte." *Bulletin de la Société Khédiviale de Géographie* 5, no. 7 (1900): 375–80.

Gardet, L. "Kashf." *Encyclopaedia of Islam.* 2nd ed., edited by P. Bearman, Th. Bianquis, C. E. Bosworth, E. van Donzel, and W. P. Heinrichs. Brill online, 2012. http://referenceworks.brillonline.com/entries/encyclopaedia-of-islam-2/kashf-COM_0458.

Gay, Peter. *A Godless Jew: Freud, Atheism, and the Making of Psychoanalysis.* New Haven, CT: Yale University Press, 1989.

Gershoni, Israel. "The Demise of the 'Liberal Age'?: ʿAbbas Mahmud al-ʿAqqad and Egyptian Responses to Fascism during World War II." In Hanssen and Weiss, *Arabic Thought beyond the Liberal Age: Towards an Intellectual History of the Nahda,* 298–322.

al-Ghazali (al-Ghazālī), Abu Hamid Muhammad. *Al-Ghazali's Path to Sufism and His Deliverance from Error (al-Munqidh min al-Dalal).* Translated by R. J. McCarthy. Louisville, KY: Fons Vitae, 2000.

———. *Al-Ghazzali on Disciplining the Self from the Alchemy of Happiness (Kimiya al-saadat).* Translated by Muhammad Nur Abdus Salam. Chicago: Great Books of the Islamic World, 2002.

———. *Ihya' Ulum al-Din.* Vols. 1–4. Cairo: Dar al-Shaʿab, n.d.

———. *The Marvels of the Heart, Kitāb sharḥ ʿajāʾib al-qalb, Book 21 of The Revival of the Religious Sciences, Iḥyāʾ ʿulūm al-dīn.* Translated with an introduction and notes by Walter James Skellie. Louisville, KY: Fons Vitae, 2010.

———. *The Niche of Lights: A Parallel English-Arabic Text.* Translated, introduced, and annotated by David Buchman. Provo, UT: Brigham Young University Press, 1998.

——. *On Disciplining the Soul, Kitāb riyādat al-nafs, and On Breaking the Two Desires, Kitāb kasr al-shahwatayn, Books XXII and XXIII of the Revival of the Religious Sciences, Iḥyā' 'ulūm al-dīn*. Translated with an introduction and notes by T. J. Winter. Cambridge: Islamic Texts Society, 1995.

Ginsburg, Ruth, and Ilana Pardes, eds. *New Perspectives on Freud's Moses and Monotheism*. Berlin: Walter de Gruyter, 2006.

Glejzer, Richard R. "Lacan with Scholasticism: Agencies of the Letter." *American Imago* 54, no. 2 (1997): 105–22.

Goichon, A. M. *Introduction à Avicenne, son épitre des définitions*. Paris: Desclée de Brouwer, 1933.

——. *Lexique de la langue philosophique d'Ibn Sina*. Paris: Desclée de Brouwer, 1938.

Goldschmidt, Arthur, Jr. *Biographical Dictionary of Modern Egypt*. Cairo: American University in Cairo Press, 2000.

Goldstein, Jan. "The Advent of Psychological Modernism in France: An Alternate Narrative." In *Modernist Impulses in the Human Sciences*, edited by Dorothy Ross, 190–209. Baltimore: Johns Hopkins University Press, 1994.

——. "Foucault and the Post-Revolutionary Self: The Uses of Cousinian Pedagogy in Nineteenth-Century France." In *Foucault and the Writing of History*, edited by Jan Goldstein, 99–115. London: Wiley-Blackwell, 1994.

——. *The Post-Revolutionary Self: Politics and Psyche in France, 1750–1850*. Cambridge, MA: Harvard University Press, 2005.

Goodman, L. E. "Al-Rāzī." In *Encyclopaedia of Islam*. 2nd ed., edited by P. Bearman, Th. Bianquis, C. E. Bosworth, E. van Donzel, and W. P. Heinrichs. Brill online, 2012. http://dx.doi.org/10.1163/1573-3912_islam_SIM_6267.

Gorelick, Nathan. "Fethi Benslama and the Translation of the Impossible in Islam and Psychoanalysis." *Umbr(a): A Journal of the Unconscious*. Islam (2009): 188–92.

——. "Translating the Islamicate Symptom: A Review Essay of *Doing Psychoanalysis in Tehran* and *Lacan and Religion*." *SCTIW Review: Journal of the Society for Contemporary Thought and the Islamicate World*, June 9, 2015.

Griffel, Frank. "Al-Ghazali." *Stanford Encyclopedia of Philosophy*. Summer 2016 edition. Edited by Edward N. Zalta. http://plato.stanford.edu/archives/sum2016/entries/al -ghazali/.

Gril, Denis. "The Science of Letters." In Ibn al-'Arabi, *The Meccan Revelations*. Vol. 2, *Selected Texts of al-Futûhât al-Makkiya*, 105–219.

Guergues (Jirjis), Sabry. "An Investigation into Psychopathic Personality: Being an Attempt at Evaluating the Problem of Psychopathy in the Light of the Integrative Method." *Majallat 'Ilm al-Nafs* 1, no. 3 (1946): 391–410.

Guerlac, Suzanne. *Thinking in Time: An Introduction to Henri Bergson*. Ithaca, NY: Cornell University Press, 2006.

Hacking, Ian. *Historical Ontology*. Cambridge, MA: Harvard University Press, 2004.

Haj, Samira. *Reconfiguring Islamic Tradition: Reform, Rationality, and Modernity*. Stanford, CA: Stanford University Press, 2009.

al-Hakim, Tawfiq. "Introduction to King Oedipus." In Carlson, *Arab Oedipus*, 16–40.

——. *King Oedipus*. In Carlson, *Arab Oedipus*, 41–119.

Halim, Insi. "Bab al-Kutub al-Jadida: Dirasat fi Ilm al-Nafs al-Tatbiqi." Review of vol. 1, *La psychologie différentielle* (1949), of Henri Piéron's *Traité de psychologie appliquée*. *Majallat 'Ilm al-Nafs* 5, no. 2 (1949–50): 315–18.

Hammad, Hanan. "Between Egyptian 'National Purity' and 'Local Flexibility': Prostitution in al-Mahalla al-Kubra in the First Half of the 20th Century." *Journal of Social History* 44, no. 3 (2011): 751–83.

———. *Industrial Sexuality: Gender, Urbanization, and Social Transformation in Egypt*. Austin: University of Texas Press, 2016.

Hanssen, Jens, and Max Weiss. *Arabic Thought beyond the Liberal Age: Towards an Intellectual History of the Nahda*. Cambridge: Cambridge University Press, 2016.

Harding, Christopher. "The Therapeutic Method of Kosawa Heisaku: 'Religion' and the 'Psy Disciplines.'" In *Japanese Contributions to Psychoanalysis*. Vol. 4, edited by Toyoaki Ogawa, 151–68. Tokyo: Japan Psychoanalytic Society, 2014.

Hartnack, Christiane. "Colonial Dominions and the Psychoanalytic Couch: Synergies of Freudian Theory with Bengali Hindu Thought and Practices in British India." In Anderson, Jenson, and Keller, *Unconscious Dominions*, 97–111.

al-Hasani, Keith. "The Qur'an and the Name-of-the-Father." In special issue on "Islam and Psychoanalysis," *S, Journal of the Jan van Eyck Circle for Lacanian Ideology Critique* 2, edited by Sigi Jöttkandt and Joan Copjec (2009): 90–95.

Hatem, Mervat. "The Paradoxes of State Feminism in Egypt." In *Women and Politics Worldwide*, edited by Barbara Nelson and Najwa Chadhury, 226–42. New Haven, CT: Yale University Press, 1994.

Hegel, Georg Wilhelm Friedrich. *Phenomenology of Spirit*. Translated by A. V. Miller. Oxford: Oxford University Press, 1977.

Herzog, Dagmar. *Cold War Freud: Psychoanalysis in an Age of Catastrophes*. Cambridge: Cambridge University Press, 2017.

Hilmi, Mahmud. "Al-Khidma al-Ijtima'iyya fi Midan al-Marad al-'Aqli." *Majallat 'Ilm al-Nafs* 3, no. 1 (1947): 113–27.

Hilmi, Muhammad Mustafa. *Al-Haya al-Ruhiyya fi al-Islam*. Cairo: Dar Ihya' al-Kutub al-'Arabiyya, 1945.

———. *Ibn al-Farid wa-l-Hubb al-Ilahi*. 2nd ed. Cairo: Dar al-Ma'arif, 1985.

———. "Al-Khasa'is al-Nafsiyya li-l-Riyadat wa-l-Adhwaq al-Sufiyya." *Majallat 'Ilm al-Nafs* 6, no. 3 (1951): 329–45.

Hirschkind, Charles. *The Ethical Soundscape: Cassette Sermons and Islamic Counter-Publics*. New York: Columbia University Press, 2006.

Hirt, Jean-Michel. "To Believe or to Interpret." Translated by Kristina Valendinova. In special issue on "Islam and Psychoanalysis," *S, Journal of the Jan van Eyck Circle for Lacanian Ideology Critique* 2 (2009): 10–13.

Hodgson, Marshall. *The Venture of Islam: Conscience and History in a World Civilization*. Vol. 1, *The Classical Age of Islam*. Chicago: University of Chicago Press, 1974.

Homayounpour, Gohar. *Doing Psychoanalysis in Tehran*. Cambridge, MA: MIT Press, 2012.

Horney, Karen. "The Distrust between the Sexes." In *Feminine Psychology*, 107–18.

———. *Feminine Psychology*. Edited and with an introduction by Harold Kelman. New York: W. W. Norton, 1967.

———. "The Flight from Womanhood: The Masculinity Complex in Women as Viewed by Men and by Women." In *Feminine Psychology*, 54–70.

———. "Inhibited Femininity: Psychoanalytical Contribution to the Problem of Frigidity." In *Feminine Psychology*, 71–83.

———. *New Ways in Psychoanalysis*. New York: Norton, 1939.

———. "Problems of Marriage." In *Feminine Psychology*, 119–32.

Hubble, D. V. "Matricide: Review of *Dark Legend: A Study in Murder* by Fredric Wertham." *British Medical Journal* 1, no. 4553 (1948): 692.

Hutchins, William M. *Tawfiq al-Hakim: A Reader's Guide*. Boulder, CO: Lynne Rienner, 2003.

Ian, Marcia. "Freud, Lacan, and Imaginary Secularity." *American Imago* 54, no. 2 (1997): 123–47.

Ibn al-'Arabi (Ibn 'Arabi). *The Bezels of Wisdom*. Translated by R.W.J. Austin. New York: Paulist Press, 1980.

———. *Divine Governance of the Human Kingdom. At-Tadbirat al-ilahiyyah fi islah al-mamlakat al-insaniyyah*. Interpreted by Shaikh Tosun Bayrak al-Jerrahi al-Halveti. Louisville, KY: Fons Vitae, 1997.

———. *Kitab al-ahadiyyah: The One Alone*. In *Divine Governance of the Human Kingdom*, 231–53.

———. *The Meccan Revelations*. Vol. 1, *Selected Texts of al-Futûhât al-Makkiya*. Edited by Michel Chodkiewicz. Translated by William C. Chittick and James W. Morris. New York: Pir Press, 2002.

———. *The Meccan Revelations*. Vol. 2, *Selected Texts of al-Futûhât al-Makkiya*. Edited by Michel Chodkiewicz. Translated by Cyrille Chodkiewicz and Denis Gril. New York: Pir Press, 2004.

al-'Iraqi, Muhammad 'Atif, ed. *Al-Duktur Abu al-Wafa al-Ghunaymi al-Taftazani: Ustad-han li-l-Tasawwuf wa-Mufakkiran Islamiyyan, 1930–1994*. Cairo: Dar al-Hidaya li-l-Tiba'a wa-l-Nashr wa-l-Tawzi', 1995.

al-Iskandari (al-Sakandari), Ibn 'Ata' Allah. *The Book of Illumination. Kitab al-Tanwir fi Isqat al-Tadbir*. Translated by Scott Alan Kugle. Louisville, KY: Fons Vitae, 2005.

———. *The Book of Wisdom. Ibn 'Ata'illah and Intimate Conversations, Kwaja Abdullah Ansari*. Translated by Victor Danner and Wheeler M. Thackston. New York: Paulist Press, 1978.

———. *The Key to Salvation: A Sufi Manual of Invocation*. Translated by Mary Ann Koury Danner. Cambridge: Islamic Texts Society, 1996.

———. *The Subtle Blessings in the Saintly Lives of Abū al-'Abbās al-Mursī and His Master Abū al-Ḥasan al-Shādhilī, The Founders of the Shādhilī Order*. Translated by Nancy Roberts. Louisville, KY: Fons Vitae, 2005.

Izutsu, Toshihiko. *Sufism and Taoism: A Comparative Study of Key Philosophical Concepts*. Berkeley: University of California Press, 1983.

'Izzat, 'Abd al-Aziz. "Al-Jarima wa-'Ilm al-Ijtim'a." *Majallat 'Ilm al-Nafs* 8, no. 1 (1952): 49–67.

Jackson, Sherman. *Sufism for Non-Sufis? Ibn 'Aṭa'Allāh al-Sakandarī's Taj al-'Arūs*. Oxford: Oxford University Press, 2012.

Jacob, Wilson Chacko. "Eventful Transformations: *Al-Futuwwa* between History and the Everyday." *Comparative Studies in Society and History* 49, no. 3 (2007): 689–712.

———. "Overcoming 'Simply Being': Straight Sex, Masculinity, and Physical Culture in Modern Egypt." *Gender and History* 22, no. 3 (2010): 658–76.

———. "Review of *Desiring Arabs*, by Joseph Massad." *H-Levant*, H-Net Reviews. September 2009. http://www.h-net.org/reviews/showrev.php?id=25004.

———. *Working Out Egypt: Effendi Masculinity and Subject Formation in Colonial Modernity, 1870–1940*. Durham, NC: Duke University Press, 2011.

Ja'far, Muhammad. "Naqd Maqal 'Ma'na al-Takamul al-Ijtima'i 'ind Birjsun.'" *Majallat 'Ilm al-Nafs* 5, no. 3 (1950): 454–56.

Jambet, Christian. "Four Discourses on Authority in Islam." Translated by Sigi Jöttkandt. In special issue on "Islam and Psychoanalysis," *S, Journal of the Jan van Eyck Circle for Lacanian Ideology Critique* 2 (2009): 44–61.

———. "The Stranger and Theophany." Translated by Roland Végsö. *Umbr(a): A Journal of the Unconscious*. The Dark God (2005): 27–41.

James, William. *The Varieties of Religious Experience: A Study in Human Nature*. New York: Penguin Books, 1982.

Jay, Martin. *Downcast Eyes: The Denigration of Vision in Twentieth Century French Thought*. Berkeley: University of California Press, 1993.

Jirjis, Sabri. "Bab al-Kutub al-Jadida: *Mushkilat al-Tahlil al-Nafsi fi Misr*, ta'lif Muhammad Fathi." *Majallat 'Ilm al-Nafs* 2, no. 3 (1947): 551–55.

———. "Al-Jarima al-Sikubatiyya: Bayn al-Tibb al-'Aqli wa-l-Qanun." *Majallat 'Ilm al-Nafs* 4, no. 2 (1948): 161–78.

———. *Mushkilat al-Suluk al-Sikubati: Bahth fi 'Ilm al-Nafs al-Tibbi al-Ijtima'i*. Cairo: Dar al-Ma'arif, 1946. Revised and expanded third edition, Cairo: Dar al-Ma'arif, 1958.

Johansen, Julian. *Sufism and Islamic Reform in Modern Egypt: The Battle for Islamic Tradition*. Oxford: Clarendon Press, 1996.

Johnston, Adrian. "Jacques Lacan." In *The Stanford Encyclopedia of Philosophy*. Summer 2014 edition. Edited by Edward N. Zalta. http://plato.stanford.edu/archives/sum2014/entries/lacan/.

Jones, James W. *Contemporary Psychoanalysis and Religion: Transference and Transcendence*. New Haven, CT: Yale University Press, 1993.

Jong, Frederick de. "Opposition to Sufism in Twentieth Century Egypt (1900–1970): A Preliminary Survey." In *Islamic Mysticism Contested: Thirteen Centuries of Controversies and Polemics*, edited by Frederick de Jong and Bernd Radtke, 310–23. Leiden: Brill, 1999.

Joseph, Suad. "Learning Desire: Relational Pedagogies and the Desiring Female Subject in Lebanon." *Journal of Middle East Women's Studies* 1, no. 1 (2005): 79–109.

———. "Thinking Intentionality: Arab Women's Subjectivity and Its Discontents." *Journal of Middle East Women's Studies* 8, no. 2 (2012): 1–25.

Joseph, Suad, ed. *Intimate Selving in Arab Families: Gender, Self, and Identity*. Syracuse, NY: Syracuse University Press, 1999.

Jöttkandt, Sigi, and Joan Copjec. "Editorial." In special issue on "Islam and Psychoanalysis," *S, Journal of the Jan van Eyck Circle for Lacanian Ideology Critique* 2 (2009): 2–4.

al-Jurjani, 'Ali Ibn Muhammad. *Al-Ta'rifat*. Beirut: 'Alam al-Kutub, 1987.

Kakar, Sudhir. *The Analyst and the Mystic: Psychoanalytic Reflections on Religion and Mysticism*. New Delhi: Penguin, 2007.

Kamal, Mahir. "Evaluations of Adolescent Personality by Adolescents and Adults." *Majallat 'Ilm al-Nafs* 3, no. 1 (1947): 152–47.

Kapila, Shruti. "The 'Godless' Freud and His Indian Friends: An Indian Agenda for Psychoanalysis." In *Psychiatry and Empire*, edited by Sloan Mahone and Megan Vaughan, 124–52. Basingstoke, UK: Palgrave Macmillan, 2007.

Kaplan, Gregory, and William B. Parsons, eds. *Disciplining Freud on Religion: Perspectives from the Humanities and Social Sciences*. Lanham, MD: Lexington Books, 2010.

Kassab, Elizabeth Suzanne. *Contemporary Arab Thought: Cultural Critique in Comparative Perspective*. New York: Columbia University Press, 2010.

Kaukua, Jari. "I in the Eye of God: Ibn 'Arabī on the Divine Human Self." *Journal of the Muhyiddin Ibn 'Arabi Society* 47 (2010): 1–22.

Kaukua, Jari, and Taneli Kukkonen. "Sense-Perception and Self-Awareness: Before and after Avicenna. In *Consciousness: From Perception to Reflection in the History of Philosophy*, edited by Sara Heinämaa, Vili Lähteenmäki, and Paulina Remes, 95–119. Dordrecht: Springer, 2007.

Keller, Richard C. *Colonial Madness: Psychiatry in French North Africa*. Chicago: University of Chicago Press, 2007.

Kesel, Marc De. *Eros and Ethics: Reading Jacques Lacan's Seminar VII*. Translated by Sigi Jöttkandt. Albany: State University of New York Press, 2009.

Khan, Naveeda. *Muslim Becoming: Aspiration and Skepticism in Pakistan*. Durham, NC: Duke University Press, 2012.

Khanna, Ranjana. *Algeria Cuts: Women and Representation, 1830 to the Present*. Stanford, CA: Stanford University Press, 2008.

——. *Dark Continents: Psychoanalysis and Colonialism*. Durham, NC: Duke University Press, 2003.

Khatibi, Abdelkebir. "Frontiers: Between Psychoanalysis and Islam." Translated by P. Burcu Yalim. *Third Text* 23, no. 6 (2009): 689–96.

Kholoussy, Hanan. *For Better, For Worse: The Marriage Crisis That Made Modern Egypt*. Stanford, CA: Stanford University Press, 2010.

——. "Monitoring and Medicalising Male Sexuality in Semi-Colonial Egypt." *Gender and History* 22, no. 3 (2010): 677–91.

al-Khudari, Mahmud. "Kayfa Nutarjam al-Istilah-Intuition." *Majallat 'Ilm al-Nafs* 1, no. 3 (1946): 377–82.

al-Khuli, Amin. "'Ilm al-Nafs al-Adabi." *Majallat 'Ilm al-Nafs* 1, no. 1 (1945): 36–51.

al-Khuli, Walim. "Al-Marad al-'Aqli wa-l-Jarima." *Majallat 'Ilm al-Nafs* 4, no. 2 (1948): 225–34.

Kojève, Alexandre. *Introduction to the Reading of Hegel*. Translated by James H. Nichols Jr. Ithaca, NY: Cornell University Press, 1980.

Kozma, Liat. "'We, the Sexologists ...': Arabic Medical Writing on Sexuality, 1879–1943." *Journal of the History of Sexuality* 22, no. 3 (2013): 426–45.

Kripal, Jeffrey J. "*The Enigma of the Oceanic Feeling: Revisioning the Psychoanalytic Theory of Mysticism* by William B. Parsons." *Journal of Religion* 80, no. 2 (2000): 372–74.

Kristeva, Julia. "Conference on Rafah Nashed: Speech Delivered to the Women's Forum Organized by *Lacan Quotidien* and the *École de la cause freudienne*, October 9, 2011." Translated by J. Todd Dean. *DIVISION/Review: A Publication of Division 39 of the American Psychological Association* (Spring 2012): 4–6.

——. *In the Beginning Was Love*. Translated by Arthur Goldhammer. New York: Columbia University Press, 1987.

——. *This Incredible Need to Believe*. Translated by Beverly Bie Brahic. New York: Columbia University Press, 2009.

Kukkonen, Taneli. "Al-Ghazālī on the Emotions." In *Islam and Rationality: The Impact of al-Ghazālī*. Vol. 1, edited by Georges Tamer, 138–64. Leiden: Brill, 2015.

——. "The Self as Enemy, the Self as Divine: A Crossroads in the Development of Islamic Anthropology." In *Ancient Philosophy of the Self*, edited by Paulina Remes and Juha Sihvola, 205–24. Dordrecht: Springer Science + Business Media BV, 2008.

Lacan, Jacques. *Feminine Sexuality: Jacques Lacan and the école freudienne*. Edited by Juliet Mitchell and Jacqueline Rose. Translated by Jacqueline Rose. New York: W. W. Norton, 1985.

——. "God and the *Jouissance* of The Woman. A Love Letter." In *Feminine Sexuality*, 137–61.

——. "The Mirror Stage as Formative of the Function of the I as Revealed in Psychoanalytic Experience." In *Écrits: A Selection*, translated by Alan Sheridan, 1–7. New York: W. W. Norton, 1977.

——. *The Seminar of Jacques Lacan, Book I: Freud's Papers on Technique, 1953–1954*. Edited by Jacques-Alain Miller. Translated by John Forrester. New York: W. W. Norton, 1991.

——. *The Seminar of Jacques Lacan, Book III: The Psychoses, 1955–1956*. Edited by Jacques-Alain Miller. Translated by Russell Grigg. New York: W. W. Norton, 1993.

——. *The Seminar of Jacques Lacan, Book VII: The Ethics of Psychoanalysis, 1959–1960*. Edited by Jacques-Alain Miller. Translated by Dennis Porter. New York: W. W. Norton, 1992.

Lalande, André. *Vocabulaire technique et critique de la philosophie*. Paris: Presses Universitaires de France, 1951.

Lane, Edward William. *An Arabic-English Lexicon in Eight Parts*. Part 8. Beirut: Librairie du Liban, 1968.

"The Language of the Self: Autobiographies and Testimonies." Special issue, *Alif: Journal of Comparative Poetics* 22 (2002).

Laplanche, Jean. *Freud and the Sexual: Essays 2000–2006*. Edited by John Fletcher. Translated by John Fletcher, Jonathan House, and Nicholas Ray. New York: International Psychoanalytic Books, 2011.

Laroui, Abdallah. *The Crisis of the Arab Intellectual: Traditionalism or Historicism?* Translated by Diarmid Cammell. Berkeley: University of California Press, 1976.

Lear, Jonathan. *Freud*. 2nd ed. London: Routledge, 2015.

——. *Love and Its Place in Nature: A Philosophical Interpretation of Freudian Psychoanalysis*. New Haven, CT: Yale University Press, 1998.

——. *Open Minded: Working Out the Logic of the Soul*. Cambridge, MA: Harvard University Press, 1999.

Leuba, James. *The Psychology of Religious Mysticism*. Abingdon, UK: Routledge, 1925.

Levine, Philippa. *Prostitution, Race, and Politics: Policing Venereal Disease in the British Empire*. New York: Routledge, 2003.

——. "Sexuality and Empire." In *At Home with the Empire: Metropolitan Culture and the Imperial World*, edited by Catherine Hall and Sonya Rose, 122–42. Cambridge: Cambridge University Press, 2006.

Lopez, Shaun T. "The Dangers of Dancing: The Media and Morality in 1930s Egypt." *Comparative Studies of South Asia, Africa, and the Middle East* 24, no. 1 (2004): 97–105.

——. "Madams, Murders, and the Media: *Akhbar al-Hawadith* and the Emergence of a Mass Culture in 1920s Egypt." In *Re-Envisioning Egypt, 1919–1952*, edited by Arthur Goldschmidt, Amy Johnson, and Barak A. Salmoni, 371–97. Cairo: American University in Cairo Press, 2005.

MacCabe, Colin. Foreword to *Why Are the Arabs Not Free? The Politics of Writing*, by Moustapha Safouan, ix–xvii. Malden, MA: Blackwell, 2007.

Mack, Michael. "The Savage Science: Sigmund Freud, Psychoanalysis, and the History of Religion." *Journal of Religious History* 30, no. 3 (2006): 331–53.

Mahfouz, Naguib. *The Mirage*. Translated by Nancy Roberts. New York: Anchor Books, 2012.

Mahmood, Saba. *Politics of Piety: The Islamic Revival and the Feminist Subject*. Princeton, NJ: Princeton University Press, 2005.

Majeed, Javed. *Muhammad Iqbal: Islam, Aesthetics, and Postcolonialism*. New York: Routledge, 2009.

Makdisi, G. "Ibn ʿAṭāʾ Allāh al-Iskandari." In *Encyclopaedia of Islam*. 2nd ed., edited by P. Bearman, Th. Bianquis, C. E. Bosworth, E. van Donzel, and W. P. Heinrichs. Brill online, 2012. http://dx.doi.org/10.1163/1573-3912_islam_SIM_3092.

Malinowski, Bronislaw. *The Father in Primitive Psychology*. Redditch, UK: Read Books, 2013.

Manjapra, Kris. *Age of Entanglement: German and Indian Intellectuals across Empire*. Cambridge, MA: Harvard University Press, 2014.

Manzalaoui, Mahmoud. "The Pseudo-Aristotelian 'Kitab Sirr al-Asrar': Facts and Problems." *Oriens* 23/24 (1974): 147–257.

Marcus, Paul. "Religion without Promises: The Philosophy of Emmanuel Levinas and Psychoanalysis." *Psychoanalytic Review* 93, no. 6 (2006): 923–51.

Massad, Joseph. *Desiring Arabs*. Chicago: University of Chicago Press, 2007.

——. "Psychoanalysis, Islam, and the Other of Liberalism." *Umbr(a): A Journal of the Unconscious*. Islam (2009): 43–68.

Maucade, Julien. "Cogito and the Subject of Arab Culture." Translated by Sigi Jöttkandt and Edward Pluth. In special issue on "Islam and Psychoanalysis," *S, Journal of the Jan van Eyck Circle for Lacanian Ideology Critique* 2 (2009): 6–9.

McLarney, Ellen Anne. *Soft Force: Women in Egypt's Islamic Awakening*. Princeton, NJ: Princeton University Press, 2015.

Meijer, Roel. *The Quest for Modernity: Secular Liberal and Left-Wing Political Thought in Egypt, 1945–1958*. London: RoutledgeCurzon, 2002.

al-Miliji, 'Abd-al-Min'am 'Abd al-'Aziz. "Nafsiyyat al-Murahiq min Mudhakkiratu." *Majallat 'Ilm al-Nafs* 5, no. 3 (1950): 351–60.

——. "Al-Shu'ur al-Dini 'ind al-Murahiq." *Majallat 'Ilm al-Nafs* 3, no. 2 (1947): 193–206.

Milner, Marion. *The Suppressed Madness of Sane Men*. London: Routledge, 1988.

Mitchell, Juliet. "Introduction I." In Lacan, *Feminine Sexuality*, 1–26.

——. *Psychoanalysis and Feminism: Freud, Reich, Laing, and Women*. New York: Vintage, 1975.

Mitchell, Timothy. *Colonising Egypt*. Cambridge: Cambridge University Press, 1988.

Mittermaier, Amira. *Dreams That Matter: An Anthropology of the Imagination in Modern Egypt*. Berkeley: University of California Press, 2011.

Mohamed, Mohamed Mosaad Abdelaziz. "Ibn 'Aṭā' Allāh al-Sakandarī: A Sufi, 'Alim and Faqīh." *Comparative Islamic Studies* 9, no. 1 (2013): 41–65.

Moosa, Ebrahim. *Ghazālī and the Poetics of Imagination*. Chapel Hill: University of North Carolina Press, 2005.

Mourad (Murad), Youssef. "La conduite de l'effort d'après Pierre Janet." *Majallat 'Ilm al-Nafs* 5, no. 3 (1950): 478–90.

——. *La physiognomonie arabe et le kitāb al-firāsa de Fakhr al-Dīn al-Rāzī*. Paris: Librairie Orientaliste Paul Geuthner, 1939.

Mura, Andrea. "Islamism Revisited: A Lacanian Discourse Critique." *European Journal of Psychoanalysis* 1 (2014): 107–26.

Murad, Yusuf. "Bab al-Kutub al-Jadida: Min al-Fa'l ila al-Fikr." Review of Henri Wallon, *De l'acte à la pensée, essays de psychologie comparée* (1942). *Majallat 'Ilm al-Nafs* 2, no. 1 (1946): 176–78.

——. "Bab al-Kutub al-Jadida: Tatawwur al-Tifl min al-Wajha al-Sikulujiyya." Review of Henri Wallon, *L'evolution psychologique de l'enfant* (1941). *Majallat 'Ilm al-Nafs* 1, no. 2 (1945): 209–10.

——. "Bab al-Ta'rifat: al-Majmu'a al-Khamisa min Mustalahat 'Ilm al-Nafs." *Majallat 'Ilm al-Nafs* 3, no. 3 (1948): 467–70.

——. "Bab al-Ta'rifat: al-Majmu'a al-Rabi'a min Mustalahat 'Ilm al-Nafs." *Majallat 'Ilm al-Nafs* 2, no. 2 (1946): 362–69.

——. "Bab al-Ta'rifat: al-Majmu'a al-Thalitha min Mustalahat 'Ilm al-Nafs." *Majallat 'Ilm al-Nafs* 1, no. 3 (1946): 382–84.

——. "Bab al-Ta'rifat: al-Majmu'a al-Thaniyya." *Majallat 'Ilm al-Nafs* 1, no. 2 (1945): 243–48.

——. "Bab al-Ta'rifat: Niwa li-Qamus 'Ilm al-Nafs." *Majallat 'Ilm al-Nafs* 1, no. 1 (1945): 100–106.

——. "Ba'd Nawahi 'Ilm al-Nafs al-Jina'i." *Majallat 'Ilm al-Nafs* 4, no. 2 (1948): 271–82.

——. *Dirasat fi al-Takamul al-Nafsi.* Cairo: Mu'assasat al-Khanji bi-l-Qahira, 1958.

——. *'Ilm al-Nafs fi al-Fann wa-l-Haya.* Cairo: Dar al-Hilal, 1966.

——. "'Ilm al-Nafs fi Khidmat al-Intaj al-Qawmi." *Majallat 'Ilm al-Nafs* 8, no. 2 (1952–53): 145–52.

——. "'Ilm al-Nafs al-Sina'i." *Majallat 'Ilm al-Nafs* 3, no. 3 (1948): 329–42.

——. *Mabadi' 'Ilm al-Nafs al-'Amm.* 7th ed. Cairo: Dar al-Ma'arif, 1978.

——. "Al-Manhaj al-Takamuli wa-Tasnif Waqa'i' al-Nafsiyya." *Majallat 'Ilm al-Nafs* 1, no. 3 (1946): 273–304.

——. "Min al-Istibtan ila al-Tahlil al-Nafsi." *Majallat 'Ilm al-Nafs* 7, no. 3 (1952): 301–10.

——. "Min al-Istibtan ila al-Tahlil al-Nafsi." In Wahba, *Yusuf Murad wa-l-Madhhab al-Takamuli,* 113–22.

——. "Min al-Istibtan ila al-Tahlil al-Nafsi (2): Manhaj al-Tahlil al-Nafsi wa-Tabiya'tu al-Takamuliyya." *Majallat 'Ilm al-Nafs* 8, no. 1 (1952): 15–32.

——. "Nimu al-Tifl al-'Aqli wa-Takwin Shakhsiyyatu." *Majallat 'Ilm al-Nafs* 2, no. 1 (1946): 3–24.

——. *Shifa' al-Nafs.* Cairo: Dar al-Ma'arif, 1943.

——. *Sikulujiyyat al-Jins.* Cairo: Dar al-Ma'arif, 1954.

——. "Tamhid li-Dirasat Nafsiyyat al-Murahiq fi Misr wa-l-Aqtar al-'Arabiyya." *Majallat 'Ilm al-Nafs* 1, no. 2 (1945): 172–82.

——. "Al-Usus al-Nafsiyya li-l-Takamul al-Ijtima'i." *Majallat 'Ilm al-Nafs* 2, no. 3 (1947): 425–42.

Murad, Yusuf, and Mustafa Ziywar. "Tasdir." *Majallat 'Ilm al-Nafs* 1, no. 1 (1945): 10–12.

Murad, Yusuf, and Mustafa Ziywar, eds. *Majallat 'Ilm al-Nafs.* Vols. 1–8. Issued by the Society of Integrative Psychology. Cairo: Dar al-Ma'arif, 1945–53.

Muruwa, Husayn. *Dirasa Naqdiyya fi daw' al-Manhaj al-Waqi'i.* Beirut: Makatabat al-Ma'arif, 1965.

Musa, Salama. *Al-'Aql al-Batin, aw Maknunat al-Nafs.* Cairo: al-Hilal, 1928.

Nached, Rafah. "Tâsîn de la préexistence et de l'ambiguïté: Moi et toi, trahison ou amour?" *Psychanalyse* 21 (2011): 53–59. https://www.cairn.info/revue-psychanalyse-2011-2-page-53.htm.

Naji, Ibrahim. "Al-Shabab al-Misri wa-l-Mushkila al-Jinsiyya." *Al-Hilal* 47 (1938): 57–60.

Najib, Mustafa. *A'lam Misr fi al-Qarn al-'Ishrin.* Qalyub, Egypt: al-Ahram, 1996.

Najmabadi, Afsaneh. "Genus of Sex: Or the Sexing of *Jins.*" *International Journal of Middle East Studies* 45, no. 2 (2013): 211–31.

——. "The Morning After: Travail of Sexuality and Love in Modern Iran." *International Journal of Middle East Studies* 36, no. 3 (2004): 367–85.

——. *Professing Selves: Transsexuality and Same-Sex Desire in Contemporary Iran.* Durham, NC: Duke University Press, 2013.

——. "Transing and Transpassing across Sex-Gender Walls in Iran." *Women's Studies Quarterly* 36, nos. 3–4 (2008): 23–42.

Nandy, Ashis. *The Savage Freud and Other Essays on Possible and Retrievable Selves.* Princeton: Princeton University Press, 1995.

Nayal, Kamal al-Din 'Abd al-Hamid. "Athar 'Alaqat al-Tifl bi-Walidayhi fi Zawajuhu." *Majallat 'Ilm al-Nafs* 7, no. 1 (1951): 25–33.

Nietzsche, Friedrich. *Thus Spoke Zarathustra: A Book for None and All.* Translated by Walter Kaufmann. New York: Penguin, 1978.

Nussbaum, Martha. *The Therapy of Desire: Theory and Practice in Hellenistic Ethics.* Princeton, NJ: Princeton University Press, 1994.

"Nusus Mukhtara fi 'Ilm al-Nafs." Translated selections of Paul Guillaume, *Psychologie* (1931), Henri Piéron, *Psychologie experimentale* (1927), Théodule-Armand Ribot, *Les maladies de la personalité* (1881). *Majallat 'Ilm al-Nafs* 1, no. 2 (1945): 233–42.

al-Nuwayhi, Muhammad. *Nafsiyyat Abi Nuwas*. Cairo: Maktabat al-Khanji, 1970.

Ormsby, Eric. "The Poor Man's Prophecy: Al-Ghazālī on Dreams." In *Dreaming across Boundaries: The Interpretation of Dreams in Islamic Lands*, edited by Louise Marlow, 142–52. Boston: Ilex Foundation, 2008.

Pandolfo, Stefania. " 'The Burning': Finitude and the Politico-Theological Imagination of Illegal Migration." *Anthropological Theory* 7, no. 3 (2007): 329–63.

———. *Impasse of the Angels: Scenes from a Moroccan Space of Memory*. Chicago: University of Chicago Press, 1997.

———. *Knot of the Soul: Madness, Psychoanalysis, Islam*. Chicago: University of Chicago Press, 2017.

———. " 'Soul Choking': Maladies of the Soul, Islam, and the Ethics of Psychoanalysis." *Umbr(a): A Journal of the Unconscious*. Islam (2009): 71–103.

———. "The Thin Line of Modernity: Some Moroccan Debates on Subjectivity." In *Questions of Modernity*, edited by Timothy Mitchell, 115–47. Minneapolis: University of Minnesota Press, 2000.

Parsons, William. *The Enigma of the Oceanic Feeling: Revisioning the Psychoanalytic Theory of Mysticism*. Oxford: Oxford University Press, 1999.

———. "The Oceanic Feeling Revisited." *Journal of Religion* 78, no. 4 (1998): 501–23.

Peters, Rudolph. "The Codification of Criminal Law in 19th Century Egypt." In *Law, Society, and National Identity in Africa*, edited by Jamil M. Abun-Nasr, Ulrich Spellenberg, and Ulrike Wanitzek, 211–25. Hamburg: H. Buske, 1991.

———. *Crime and Punishment in Islamic Law: Theory and Practice from the Sixteenth to the Twenty-First Century*. Cambridge: Cambridge University Press, 2005.

———. "For His Correction and as a Deterrent for Others." *Islamic Law and Society* 6, no. 2 (1999): 164–93.

———. "Islamic and Secular Criminal Law." *Islamic Law and Society* 4, no. 1 (1997): 80–90.

———. "Murder on the Nile: Homicide Trials in 19th Century Egyptian Shari'a Courts." *Die Welt des Islams* 30, no. 1/4 (1990): 95–115.

Pfister, Oskar. *The Psychoanalytic Method*. Translated by Charles Rockwell Payne. New York: Moffat, Yard, 1917.

Phillips, Adam. *Becoming Freud: The Making of a Psychoanalyst*. New Haven, CT: Yale University Press, 2014.

Plotkin, Mariano Ben. *Freud in the Pampas: The Emergence and Development of Psychoanalytic Culture in Argentina*. Stanford, CA: Stanford University Press, 2001.

Pound, Marcus. "Towards a Lacanian Theology of Religion." *New Blackfriars* 84, no. 993 (2003): 510–20.

Powell, Eve Troutt. *A Different Shade of Colonialism: Egypt, Great Britain, and the Mastery of the Sudan*. Berkeley: University of California Press, 2003.

Prothro, E. Terry, and H. Levon Melikian. "Psychology in the Arab Near East." *Psychological Bulletin* 52 (1955): 303–10.

"Psychoanalysis and India." Special Issue, *Psychoanalytic Review* 102, no. 6 (2015).

Pursley, Sara. "The Stage of Adolescence, Anticolonial Time, Youth Insurgency, and the Marriage Crisis in Hashimite Iraq." *History of the Present* 3, no. 2 (2013): 160–97.

al-Qushayri, Abu'l-Qasim. *Al-Qushayri's Epistle on Sufism: Al-Risalah al-qushayriyya fi 'ilm al-tasawwuf*. Translated by Alexander Knysh. Reading, UK: Garnet Publishing, 2007.

Qutb, Sayyid. *Al-Naqd al-Adabi, Usuluh wa-Manhajihu.* Beirut: Dar al-Shuruq, 1970.

Ragab, Ahmed. "Madman Walking: The Image of the Mad in the Egyptian Press." *Egypte-Monde Arabe,* troisième série, no. 4 (2007): 227–46.

Ramzi, Ishaq. *'Ilm al-Nafs al-Fardi: Usulu wa-Tatbiqu.* 2nd ed. Cairo: Dar al-Ma'arif bi-Misr, 1961.

Rank, Otto. *The Trauma of Birth.* With a new introduction by Dr. E. James Lieberman. New York: Dover Books, 1993.

al-Rawi, Mahmud. "Al-Qatl al-Siyasi." *Majallat 'Ilm al-Nafs* 3, no. 2 (1947): 207–14.

——. "Sikulujiyyat al-Idrab." *Majallat 'Ilm al-Nafs* 3, no. 3 (1948): 417–31.

——. "Sikulujiyyat al-Idrab (2)." *Majallat 'Ilm al-Nafs* 4, no. 1 (1948): 29–52.

——. "'Uqdat Udib wa-Athariha fi al-Ijram: Hawl Maqal fi Jaridat al-Misri." *Majallat 'Ilm al-Nafs* 3, no. 1 (1947): 97–106.

Ray, Nicholas. "Forming New Knots: Jean Laplanche, 1924–2012." *Radical Philosophy* 174 (2012): 53–56.

al-Razi, Abu Bakr Muhammad ibn Zakariyya. *The Spiritual Physick of Rhazes.* Translated by Arthur Arberry. London: Butler and Tanner, 1950.

Reid, Donald M. "Political Assassination in Egypt, 1910–1954." *International Journal of African Historical Studies* 15, no. 4 (1982): 625–51.

Reik, Theodor. *From Thirty Years with Freud.* New York: Farrar and Rinehart, 1940.

Reinhard, Kenneth. "Freud, My Neighbor." *American Imago* 54, no. 2 (1997): 165–95.

Reinhard, Kenneth, and Julia Reinhard Lupton. "The Subject of Religion: Lacan and the Ten Commandments." *Diacritics* 33, no. 2 (2003): 71–97.

Reynolds, Dwight. *Interpreting the Self: Autobiography in the Arabic Literary Tradition.* Berkeley: University of California Press, 2001.

Rice, Emmanuel. *Freud and Moses: The Long Journey Home.* Albany: State University of New York Press, 1990.

Ricoeur, Paul. *Freud and Philosophy: An Essay on Interpretation.* New Haven, CT: Yale University Press, 1970.

Rizk, Abdu Mikhail. "Smoking among Adolescents: An Objective Study." *Majallat 'Ilm al-Nafs* 3, no. 1 (1947): 144–46.

Rogan, Eugene. "Madness and Marginality: The Advent of the Psychiatric Asylum in Egypt and Lebanon." In *Outside In: On the Margins of the Modern Middle East,* edited by Eugene Rogan, 104–25. London: I. B. Tauris, 2002.

Rose, Jacqueline. "Introduction II." In Lacan, *Feminine Sexuality,* 27–57.

——. "Response to Edward Said." In Said, *Freud and the Non-European,* 65–79.

Rosenthal, Franz. "Ar-Râzî on the Hidden Illness." *Bulletin of the History of Medicine* 52, no. 1 (1978): 45–60.

Roudinesco, Elisabeth. *Jacques Lacan.* Translated by Barbara Bray. New York: Columbia University Press, 1997.

——. *Jacques Lacan and Co.: A History of Psychoanalysis in France, 1925–1985.* Chicago: University of Chicago Press, 1990.

——. "The Mirror Stage: An Obliterated Archive." In *The Cambridge Companion to Lacan,* edited by Jean-Michel Rabaté, 25–34. Cambridge: Cambridge University Press, 2003.

Russell, Thomas, Sir. *Egyptian Service, 1902–1946.* London: J. Murray, 1949.

al-Sa'ati, Hasan. "Ma'had Brostol li-l-Shabab al-Kharij 'ala al-Qanun." *Majallat 'Ilm al-Nafs* 4, no. 2 (1948): 179–84.

Safouan, Moustapha. "Five Years of Psychoanalysis in Cairo." Translated by Juliet Flower MacCannell. *Umbr(a): A Journal of the Unconscious.* Islam (2009): 35–42.

——. "Interview with Colin MacCabe." *Zamyn.* http://www.zamyn.org/interviews/maccabe-safouan/interview.html.

——. *Speech or Death? Language as Social Order: A Psychoanalytic Study*. Translated by Martin Thom. New York: Palgrave Macmillan, 2003.

——. *Why Are the Arabs Not Free? The Politics of Writing*. Malden, MA: Blackwell, 2007.

Said, Edward W. *Freud and the Non-European*. London: Verso, 2003.

Saleh, Zaki. "A Questionnaire Study of the Problem Adolescent Girl in Secondary Schools." *Majallat 'Ilm al-Nafs* 7, no. 3 (1952): 410–16.

Salvatore, Armando. "The 'Implosion' of *Shari'a* within the Emergence of Public Normativity: The Impact on Personal Responsibility and the Impersonality of Law." In Dupret, *Standing Trial*, 116–39.

Santner, Eric L. *On the Psychotheology of Everyday Life: Reflections on Freud and Rosenzweig*. Chicago: University of Chicago Press, 2001.

Sarton, George. "Review of Mourad, *La physiognomonie*." *Isis* 33, no. 2 (1941): 248–49.

Sartre, Jean-Paul. *Being and Nothingness: An Essay in Phenomenological Ontology*. Translated by Hazel E. Barnes. New York: Washington Square Press, 1966.

Sayyid, Bobby S. *A Fundamental Fear: Eurocentrism and the Emergence of Islamism*. London: Zed Books, 1997.

Scarfone, Dominique. *The Unpast: The Actual Unconscious*. Translated by Dorothée Bonnigal-Katz. New York: Unconscious in Translation, 2015.

Schayegh, Cyrus. "Serial Murder in Tehran: Crime, Science, and the Formation of Modern State and Society in Interwar Iran." *Comparative Studies in Society and History* 47, no. 4 (2005): 836–62.

——. "'A Sound Mind Lives in a Healthy Body': Texts and Contexts in the Iranian Modernists' Scientific Discourse of Health, 1910s–40s." *International Journal of Middle East Studies* 37, no. 2 (2005): 167–88.

——. *Who Is Knowledgeable Is Strong: Science, Class, and the Formation of Modern Iranian Society, 1900–1950*. Berkeley: University of California Press, 2009.

Seigel, Jerrold. *The Idea of the Self: Thought and Experience in Western Europe since the Seventeenth Century*. Cambridge: Cambridge University Press, 2005.

Selim, Samah. "Fiction and Colonial Identities: Arsène Lupin in Arabic." *Middle Eastern Literatures* 13, no. 2 (2010): 191–210.

——. *The Novel and the Rural Imaginary in Egypt, 1885–1985*. London: Routledge, 2004.

Sells, Michael. "Bewildered Tongue: The Semantics of Mystical Union in Islam." In *Mystical Union and Monotheistic Faith: An Ecumenical Dialogue*, edited by Moshe Idel and Bernard McGinn, 87–124. New York: Macmillan, 1989.

——. "Ibn 'Arabī's Garden among the Flames: A Reevaluation." *History of Religions* 23, no. 4 (1984): 287–315.

——. "Ibn 'Arabī's Polished Mirror: Perspective Shift and Meaning Event." *Studia Islamica* 67 (1988): 121–49.

——. "The Infinity of Desire: Love, Mystical Union, and Ethics in Sufism." In *Crossing Boundaries: Essays on the Ethical Status of Mysticism*, edited by G. William Barnard and Jeffrey J. Kripal, 184–229. New York: Seven Bridges Press, 2002.

Sengoopta, Chandak. *Imprint of the Raj: How Fingerprinting Was Born in Colonial India*. London: Macmillan, 2003.

Seshadri-Crooks, Kalpana. "The Primitive as Analyst: Postcolonial Feminism's Access to Psychoanalysis." *Cultural Critique*, no. 28 (Autumn 1994): 175–218.

al-Shafa'i, Abu Madyan. "Al-Fa'l al-Iradi fi al-Ijram." *Majallat 'Ilm al-Nafs* 4, no. 2 (1948): 201–8.

al-Sharuni, Yusuf. "Bab al-Kutub al-Jadida: *al-Taqa al-Ruhiyya*, ta'lif Henri Birjsun." Review of Arabic Translation of Henri Bergson, *L'energie spirituelle*. *Majallat 'Ilm al-Nafs* 2, no. 3 (1947): 527–30.

———. "Yusuf Murad: Ra'idan wa-Ustadhan." *Al-Majalla* 10, no. 119 (1966): 21–28.

Sheehi, Stephen. *Foundations of Modern Arab Identity*. Gainesville: University Press of Florida, 2004.

———. "Inscribing the Arab Self: Butrus al-Bustani and Paradigms of Subjective Reform." *British Journal of Middle Eastern Studies* 27, no. 1 (2000): 7–24.

Sirriyeh, Elizabeth. *Sufis and Anti-Sufis: The Defence, Rethinking, and Rejection of Sufism in the Modern World*. Richmond, UK: Curzon, 1999.

Škof, Lenart. *Breath of Proximity: Intersubjectivity, Ethics, and Peace*. Dordrecht: Springer, 2015.

Slavet, Eliza. *Racial Fever: Freud and the Jewish Question*. New York: Fordham University Press, 2009.

Solby, Bruno. "Review of *Dark Legend: A Study in Murder* by Fredric Wertham." *Sociometry* 4, no. 4 (1941): 423–26.

Soueif (Suwayf), M. I. "Bergson's Theory of Social Integration." *Majallat 'Ilm al-Nafs* 5, no. 2 (1949–50): 326–32.

———. "Review: The Problem of Psychopathic Behavior by S. Guerguess." *Majallat 'Ilm al-Nafs* 8, no. 1 (1952): 113–16.

Soueif (Suwayf), Moustafa I., and Ramadan A. Ahmed. "Psychology in the Arab World: Past, Present, and Future." *International Journal of Group Tensions* 30, no. 3 (2001): 211–40.

Stavrakakis, Yannis. "Wallon, Lacan, and the Lacanians: Citation Practices and Repression." *Theory, Culture, and Society* 24, no. 4 (2007): 131–38.

Steedman, Carolyn. *Strange Dislocations: Childhood and the Idea of Human Interiority*. Cambridge, MA: Harvard University Press, 1995.

Stekel, Wilhelm. *Technique of Analytical Psychotherapy*. Translated by Eden Paul and Cedar Paul. New York: Liveright, 1950.

Stimilli, Davide. *The Face of Immortality: Physiognomy and Criticism*. Albany: State University of New York Press, 2005.

al-Suhrawardi, Shihab al-Din. *'Awarif al-Ma'arif*. Al-Juz' al-Awwal. Edited by 'Abd al-Halim Mahmud and Mahmud Ibn Sharif. Cairo: Dar al-Ma'arif, 1993.

———. *'Awarif al-Ma'arif*. Al-Juz' al-Thani. Edited by 'Abd al-Halim Mahmud and Mahmud Ibn Sharif. Cairo: Dar al-Ma'arif, 2000.

Suttie, Ian. *Origins of Love and Hate*. London: Regan Paul, 1935.

Suwayf, Mustafa Isma'il. "Al-Jarima wa-l-Takamul al-Ijtima'i." *Majallat 'Ilm al-Nafs* 4, no. 2 (1948): 209–20.

———. "Ma'na al-Takamul al-Ijtima'i 'ind Birjsun." *Majallat 'Ilm al-Nafs* 5, no. 2 (1949–50): 203–36.

———. "Al-Tahlil al-Nafsi wa-l-Fannan," *Majallat 'Ilm al-Nafs* 2, no. 2 (1946): 282–302.

———. "Al-Usus al-Dinamiyya li-l-Suluk al-Ijrami." *Majallat 'Ilm al-Nafs* 4, no. 3 (1949): 329–54.

———. "Yusuf Murad: Ra'id al-Manhaj al-Takamuli." *Al-Fikr al-Mu'asir* 21 (1966): 62–68.

Sviri, Sara. "The Self and Its Transformation in Sufism: With Special Reference to Early Literature." In *Self and Self-Transformation in the History of Religions*, edited by David Shulman and Guy G. Stroumsa, 195–215. Oxford: Oxford University Press, 2002.

al-Taftazani, Abu al-Wafa al-Ghunaymi. *Ibn 'Ata' Allah al-Sakandari wa-Tasawwufu*. 2nd ed. Cairo: Maktabat al-Anjlu al-Misriyya, 1969.

———. *Ibn Sab'in wa-Falsafat al-Sufiyya*. Beirut: Dar al-Kitab al-Libnani, 1973.

———. "Al-Idrak al-Mubashir 'ind al-Sufiyya." *Majallat 'Ilm al-Nafs* 4, no. 3 (1949): 369–72.

———. *'Ilm al-Kalam wa-Ba'd Mushkilatih*. Cairo: Maktabat al-Qahira al-Haditha, 1966.

——. *Madhkhal ila al-Tasawwuf al-Islami*. 3rd ed. Cairo: Dar al-Thaqafa li-l-Nashr wa-l-Tawziʿ, 1979.

——. "Al-Maʿrifa al-Sufiyya: Adatuha wa-Manhajuha wa-Mawduʿiha ʿind Sufiyyat al-Muslimin (1)." *Al-Risala* 19, no. 932 (1951): 550–54.

——. "Al-Maʿrifa al-Sufiyya: Adatuha wa-Manhajuha wa-Mawduʿiha ʿind Sufiyyat al-Muslimin (2)." *Al-Risala* 19, no. 933 (1951): 576–78.

——. "Sikulujiyyat al-Tasawwuf (1)." *Majallat ʿIlm al-Nafs* 5, no. 2 (1949): 291–96.

——. "Sikulujiyyat al-Tasawwuf (2)." *Majallat ʿIlm al-Nafs* 5, no. 3 (1950): 377–84.

al-Taftazani, Abu al-Wafa al-Ghunaymi, and Oliver Leaman. "Ibn Sabʿin." In *History of Islamic Philosophy*, edited by Seyyed Hossein Nasr and Oliver Leaman, 346–49. Abingdon, UK: Routledge, 2007.

Taha, Farag ʿAbd al-Qadir. *Mawsuwʿat ʿIlm al-Nafs wa-l-Tahlil al-Nafsi*. Cairo: Dar Suʿad al-Sabbah, 1993.

al-Tantawi, ʿAli. "Al-Mathal al-ʿAla li-l-Shab al-Muslim." *Al-Risala* 6, no. 240 (February 7, 1938): 218–21.

——. "Al-Mathal al-ʿAla li-l-Shab al-Muslim." *Al-Risala* 6, no. 241 (February 14, 1938): 252–54.

——. "Al-Mathal al-ʿAla li-l-Shab al-Muslim." *Al-Risala* 6, no. 242 (February 21, 1938): 296–98.

Tarabishi, Jurj. *ʿUqdat Udib fi al-Riwaya al-ʿArabiyya*. Beirut: Dar al-Taliʿa, 1982.

Taylor, Charles. *Sources of the Self: The Making of the Modern Identity*. Cambridge, MA: Harvard University Press, 1989.

Thayer, Joseph Henry. *A Greek-English Lexicon of the New Testament: Being Grimm's Wilke's Clavis Novi Testamenti*. Translated, revised, and enlarged by Joseph Henry Thayer. New York: American Book, 1889.

Toews, John. "Historicizing Psychoanalysis: Freud in His Time and for Our Time." *Journal of Modern History* 63, no. 3 (1991): 504–45.

Toscano, Alberto. *Fanaticism: On the Uses of an Idea*. London: Verso, 2010.

Treiger, Alexander. *Inspired Knowledge in Islamic Thought: Al-Ghazālī's Theory of Mystical Cognition and Its Avicennian Foundation*. London: Routledge, 2011.

Viego, Antonio. *Dead Subjects: Towards a Politics of Loss in Latino Studies*. Durham, NC: Duke University Press, 2007.

Wahba, Murad. "Al-La-Shuʿur ʿind Birjsun." *Majallat ʿIlm al-Nafs* 8, no. 2 (1952–53): 213–22.

——. "Yusuf Murad Kama ʿAriftuhu." In Wahba, *Yusuf Murad wa-l-Madhhab al-Takamuli*, 3–9.

Wahba, Murad, ed. *Yusuf Murad Faylasufan*. Cairo: al-Hayaʾ al-Misriyya al-ʿAmma li-l-Kitab, 2012.

——. *Yusuf Murad wa-l-Madhhab al-Takamuli*. Cairo: al-Hayaʾ al-Misriyya al-ʿAmma li-l-Kitab, 1974.

Wahl, William H. "Pathologies of Desire and Duty: Freud, Ricoeur, and Castoriadis on Transforming Religious Culture." *Journal of Religion and Health* 47, no. 3 (2008): 398–414.

Wallon, Henri. "Athar ʿal-Akhir' fi Takwin al-Shuʿur bi-l-Dhat." Translated and annotated by Yusuf Murad. *Majallat ʿIlm al-Nafs* 2, no. 2 (1946): 252–67.

——. "Le role de 'l'autre' dans le conscience du 'moi.'" *Majallat ʿIlm al-Nafs* 2, no. 1 (1946): 215–26.

——. "The Role of the Other in the Consciousness of the Ego." In *The World of Henri Wallon*, edited by Gilbert Voyat, 91–103. New York: Jason Aronson, 1984.

Webb, Richard E., and Michael Sells. "Lacan and Bion: Psychoanalysis and the Mystical Language of 'Unsaying.'" *Theory and Psychology* 5, no. 2 (1995): 195–215.

Weber, Alden O. "*Gestalttheorie* and the Theory of Relations." *Journal of Philosophy* 35, no. 22 (1938): 589–606.

Wehr, Hans. *A Dictionary of Modern Written Arabic*. Edited by J. Milton Cowan. 3rd ed. Ithaca, NY: Spoken Language Services, 1976.

Weiss, Max, and Jens Hanssen, eds. *Arabic Thought against the Authoritarian Age: Towards an Intellectual History of the Present*. Cambridge: Cambridge University Press, 2017.

Wertham, Fredric. "Psychoauthoritarianism and the Law." *University of Chicago Law Review* 22, no. 2 (1955): 336–38.

West, Ranyard. *Conscience and Society*. London: Methuen, 1942.

Wojnar, Irena. "Maurice Debesse (1903–1998)." *Prospects: The Quarterly Review of Comparative Education* 33, no. 3 (2003): 1–19.

Wolfson, Elliot. *Language, Eros, Being: Kabbalistic Hermeneutics and Poetic Imagination*. New York: Fordham University Press, 2005.

Yahalom, Jonathan. "Freud and Epicurean Philosophy: Revisiting Drive Theory." *Contemporary Psychoanalysis* 50, no. 3 (2014): 395–417.

Yerushalmi, Yosef Hayim. *Freud's Moses: Judaism Terminable and Interminable*. New Haven, CT: Yale University Press, 1991.

Young, Kimball. *Personality and Problems of Adjustment*. London: Kegan Paul, Trench, Trubner, 1947.

Zarruq, Ahmad Bin Muhammad. *Qawa'id al-Tasawwuf*. Cairo: Maktabat al-Thaqafa al-Diniyya, 2006.

Ze'evi, Dror. *Producing Desire: Changing Sexual Discourse in the Ottoman Middle East, 1500–1900*. Berkeley: University of California Press, 2006.

Zhang, Li. "Bentuhua: Culturing Psychotherapy in Postsocialist China." *Culture, Medicine, and Psychiatry* 38, no. 2 (2014): 283–305.

——. "Cultivating Happiness: Psychotherapy, Spirituality, and Well-Being in a Transforming Urban China." In *Handbook of Religion and the Asian City: Aspiration and Urbanization in the Twenty-First Century*, edited by Peter van der Veer, 315–32. Oakland: University of California Press, 2015.

Ziwer (Ziywar), Mostapha, in collaboration with M. Naim. "Aggression and Intercostal Neuralgia: A Psychosomatic Study." *Majallat 'Ilm al-Nafs* 1, no. 2 (1945): 264–70.

Ziywar, Mustafa. "Bab al-Kutub al-Jadida: *'Ilm al-Nafs al-'Amali* li-l-Duktur Aziz Farid." *Majallat 'Ilm al-Nafs* 1, no. 1 (1945): 75–78.

Žižek, Slavoj. "A Glance into the Archives of Islam." *lacan.com*, 2006. http://www.lacan.com/zizarchives.htm.

Zoueïn, Josette. "Freud en arabe: Notice bibliographique." *Che vuoi?* 21 (2004): 100–104. https://www.cairn.info/revue-che-vuoi-2004-1-page-101.htm.

A NOTE ON THE TYPE

THIS BOOK has been composed in Miller, a Scotch Roman typeface designed by Matthew Carter and first released by Font Bureau in 1997. It resembles Monticello, the typeface developed for The Papers of Thomas Jefferson in the 1940s by C. H. Griffith and P. J. Conkwright and reinterpreted in digital form by Carter in 2003.

Pleasant Jefferson ("P. J.") Conkwright (1905–1986) was Typographer at Princeton University Press from 1939 to 1970. He was an acclaimed book designer and AIGA Medalist.

The ornament used throughout this book was designed by Pierre Simon Fournier (1712–1768) and was a favorite of Conkwright's, used in his design of the *Princeton University Library Chronicle*.

CPSIA information can be obtained
at www.ICGtesting.com
Printed in the USA
JSHW030144230320
4842JS00003B/7

9 780691 203102